Darling R —
Now
Wh R x

London 1984

OTHER MEN'S FLOWERS

TO MY SON

*who shares my love for poetry but thinks his
father's taste a little old-fashioned*

OTHER MEN'S FLOWERS

An Anthology of Poetry Compiled by

A. P. WAVELL

[Field-Marshal Earl Wavell
G.C.B., G.C.S.I., G.C.I.E., C.M.G., M.C.]

MEMORIAL EDITION

WITH AN INTRODUCTION BY HIS SON

*I have gathered a posie of other men's flowers
and nothing but the thread that
binds them is my own*
MONTAIGNE

JONATHAN CAPE
THIRTY BEDFORD SQUARE
LONDON

FIRST PUBLISHED 1944
REPRINTED 1944, 1946, 1948, 1950, 1951

MEMORIAL EDITION 1952
REPRINTED 1954, 1955
NEW EDITION, TYPE RESET 1958
REPRINTED 1963, 1965
REPRINTED IN THIS FORMAT 1968, 1971, 1975, 1978, 1982

JONATHAN CAPE LTD, 30 BEDFORD SQUARE
LONDON WC1

ISBN 0 224 60750 2

PRINTED AND BOUND BY BUTLER AND TANNER LTD
FROME AND LONDON

ARRANGEMENT

1. MUSIC, MYSTERY AND MAGIC

2. GOOD FIGHTING

3. LOVE AND ALL THAT

4 · THE CALL OF THE WILD

5. CONVERSATION PIECES

6. THE LIGHTER SIDE

7. HYMNS OF HATE

8. RAGBAG

9. LAST POST

OUTSIDE THE GATE

INTRODUCTION

I HAVE been asked to write an introduction for this memorial edition of *Other Men's Flowers*. It seems an intrusion to bring another mood to the joyous style of the original prefaces and the racy notes to the poems that are so characteristically my father's own. Yet some introduction must mark the publishers' happy notion for a farewell printing of this anthology, which has cheered so many people in anxious days, and in which my father unconsciously revealed some facets of his personality to the public at large in the only way his nature allowed. My excuse for not passing this privilege to some practised pen is that *Other Men's Flowers* was first to have been just a family folio. In the brief respite of six months between staving off the German assault on the Middle East in the Spring of 1941, and turning to meet the challenge of Japan at the end of the year, my father found time to list his favourite poems and explain his choice in the prefaces to each section. The family all made their suggestions, and we reminded him of poems we knew he loved, but had forgotten to include: the poems that we had heard read to us as children in the coveted hour before bedtime — that abiding part of many children's education. So it all began as an idea for a family conversation but we gradually prevailed upon him to let the world join in, and the literary members of his Staff nurtured the conspiracy with the publishers.

For other acclamations and tributes in his career he 'daffed the world aside and bid it pass', but he never tried to conceal his evident surprise and delight at the success of this book. It brought him into association with writers whose work he had long enjoyed but whom he had never expected to know as friends; it brought a continuous blush of letters from all sorts and conditions of men in many lands who might not otherwise have addressed a Field Marshal.

Indeed only the other day there came a letter to my father from a man in his sixties — so enthusiastic in his new-found pleasure in poetry from reading this book that he forgot for the moment that my father was gone. This is as it should be. 'The quick heart quickens from the heart that's dead.' Then, best of all, his book was a new sesame to the hearts of his oldest and dearest friends.

A gallant soldier who carried this anthology on active service commented on W. H. Davies's poem 'Leisure': 'The hour of meditation is essential. If it is not kept we cannot survive, we are already far advanced into the darkness.'

Here then was a refreshment of the spirit to ease the strenuous cares of the Viceroyalty and to dispel his disappointment when he was not allowed to complete his task in India.

In his unfailing way my father always answered everyone, plain man or scholar, who wrote to applaud or challenge his selection. Nevertheless I must here thank collectively, on behalf of my family, all those who brought the joy of poetic jousting to the leisure of his closing years.

The distinctive criterion of his choice of poems was that they were all at one time in his head. All these and more besides. I have heard him cap a story by reciting a dozen lines from Virgil learnt forty years ago — or open his morning newspaper and seeing Sir So-and-So cited after several other public figures in a famous scandal, lead off at once from one of Chesterton's more ribald rhymes:

> Prince, Bayard would have smashed his sword
> To see the sort of knights you dub.
> Is that the last of them — O, Lord!
> Will someone take me to a pub?

Then jogging home from one of the early morning cavalcade gallops across the plains behind New Delhi, I posed some over-earnest question about the possible revolutionary change of society in England when the war was over — and his eye twinkled as he began to reply:

> It may be we shall rise the last as Frenchmen rose the first,
> Our wrath come after Russia's wrath, and our wrath be the worst,
> It may be we were meant to mark, by our riot and our rest,
> God's scorn for all men governing. It may be Beer is best!

No wonder that with this resource of mind, he could bear with patience the rebuffs of the Council table.

Since my father gently twits me for my taste in poetry by a characteristic banter against himself for being old-fashioned, I may perhaps be excused a few words about this. The enjoyment of modern poetry is in all ages largely a matter of what idiom you have grown up with and become accustomed to. An old nobleman writing to a young friend in June 1828 says that there was no modern poetry worth the name, that tradition had gone, that sense and euphony had given place to wilful obscurities, and so on. Tom Moore in his journal confesses that he can make little or nothing of Shelley's poems. Similarly the inverted metaphor, the clipped syntax, the allusive symbolism of poetry today puzzle those ears attuned to the bountiful self-explanatory passages of the Georgian poets. But these poets had extended the development of the Romantic age in English poetry to its fulfilment, and there had to be a fresh start.

I do enjoy the poets that my generation has admired — Cecil Day Lewis, Auden, Ezra Pound (in his early lyrics), Sidney Keyes and others — while for me Gerard Manley Hopkins and T. S. Eliot belong to the company of the foremost singers in our tongue. My own selection, circumscribed by no memory test, would include more Shakespeare, Shelley, George Herbert, Beddoes, Meredith, Wilfred Owen, and Hardy. Yet the core of the poetry that I love is in this book — especially Browning and Kipling. Indeed I would ask for more Kipling still — 'The Roman Centurion's Song', 'The way through the woods', 'When earth's last picture is painted', 'Our Lady of the Sack-cloth', 'The Return of the Children' (his tenderest poem), and his poem about Shakespeare, 'The Craftsman'.

I sympathize too with my father's omissions. Wordsworth, Tennyson and Milton may have had the finest ears of all our English poets but they were lonely men without a sense of humour. The subject matter of their poetry is for the most part the Classical mythologies or medieval romances. They are prophets of the destiny of Man in Nature. But they never knew much about men. 'Tennyson was always a great child — so should I have been but for the battle of Beaumont Hamel' wrote Wilfred Owen. The flat of the matter is that you are either by temperament predominantly interested in people or in nature — Flowers, Animals, Colours, Birds. Perhaps I forget that in the fresh curiosity of childhood and in the leisurely contemplation of old age we are more fascinated by the eternal miracle of the seasons than in the thrust and scurry of our work in middle life.

Nevertheless this anthology is an anthology of poems about people, of men and women in their loves and in their sorrows, voyaging, fighting, laughing in all the human situations of the mystery of life and death. Hence its appeal, surely, to men of every estate, who may find in the rough-hewn rhyme of a poem about homely pleasures and plain virtues a response in their hearts that they did not discover before in the more mannered diction of the classical anthologies.

> There they are, my fifty men and women
> Naming me the fifty poems finished.

These opening lines of Browning's great poem to his wife may fitly fashion the farewell to the last printing of this book. My father for his 'One word more' called his favourite section of the book 'The Ragbag', from my mother's brocades that have travelled with her round the world. With great skill and determination my mother has always overcome every obstacle the War Office and Foreign Office can put in the path of adventurous wives, beginning with a journey across the North Sea, Scandinavia, and the length of Russia to Tiflis in 1916 to getting packed for Java in 1942.

To whatever part of the earth my father has gone in the path of duty — there has followed our home. Few soldiers' families can have been so much together and so happy as we have. I have heard my mother say herself that she is 'very tribal'.

Every soldier is a 'vagabond' and that is the title of my mother's choice of poem for inclusion in this book. The 'gipsy fires' of that poem may have felt a little bewildered by the two hundred Lutyens marble hearths of our last Government Residence in New Delhi — but the wings of the house became a leave camp and a warm welcome was there for all the men and women of every rank who were serving far away from their own homes.

The Ragbag was the right symbol for all this.

A soldier and the son of a soldier has no settled home and, after all the travel and turmoil are over, his body lies in the peaceful cloister garth at Winchester, played to its rest at the close of a summer's day by a Piper of his beloved Regiment.

As his body passed, amidst the surrounding affection of his friends and fellow-commanders, on its last journey from the Norman Chapel of the Tower of London — all was arranged with due fidelity. Yet his country's spontaneous recognition and gratitude lay in the silent faces of the men and women who stood on rooftops of warehouses on the banks of London's river, and in the country villages along the route.

If it be the mark of a man's nobility to attract a worthy response in others, let my father, always loyally served, be judged above all in the virtue and kindness that crystallized round his bedside in the closing passage of his life in the skill of his doctors and nurses. For fourteen days after his operation all went well. Then on a Saturday came an unexpected haemorrhage. He was expected to collapse at once. But gallant as ever in adversity he fought on for four days and nights and there was in his surgeon a man of equal courage to fight with him.

While he was holding so tenaciously these four days to life, nearly all the time fully conscious, we cannot tell what passed through his mind. For those by his bedside there was the same sturdy humour as of old. Perhaps he used 'the magic of the imagery' of the Hound of Heaven as in former times of stress 'to distract my mind from peril or disaster':

> I dimly guess what Time in mists confounds;
> Yet ever and anon the trumpet sounds
> From the hid battlements of Eternity.

Twice, during these days, there came upon me moments of fore-boding. On the Sunday morning a heavy thunderstorm burst over London and I remembered of a sudden that such a thunderstorm had broken out three hundred years ago that very day when Montrose — greatest of all Highland leaders — was walking to his execution, and it seemed that history was trying to play one of its tricks of fancy. The other moment came three nights later when in the early hours of Empire Day I took down from the shelves of the library of the Nursing Home a book of verse for solace, and came upon this poem by Francis Bret Harte:

RELIEVING GUARD

> Came the relief, 'What, sentry, ho!
> How passed the night through thy long waking?'
> 'Cold, cheerless, dark — as may befit
> The hour before the dawn is breaking.'

'No sight?' 'No sound?' 'No, nothing save
The plover from the marshes calling
And in yon Western sky, about
An hour ago, a star was falling.'

'A star? There's nothing strange in that.'
'No, nothing; but, above the thicket
Somehow it seemed to me that God
Somewhere had just relieved a picket.'

And in the morning it was goodbye.

The guard-orders of his tour of duty are in this book — in the brave, gay lines of the poets he loved.

A. J. W.

PREFACE TO REVISED EDITION

'OTHER MEN'S FLOWERS' was a war baby, conceived as a relaxation to the mind during campaigns in the East. War babies do not always thrive nor are they always popular. I am naturally gratified that this one has had some success. It shows that the British-speaking people, even in these restless days, have not yet forgotten their great heritage of poetry; and that the verse with which I stored my memory when younger has still the power to please many.

I take this opportunity to thank all those who have written to me about the anthology. I have much appreciated their kind and helpful comments. A tribute which I greatly valued came in the form of an annotated copy which a friend sent me. The annotations had been made by a soldier who read *Other Men's Flowers* during the period of his final training for D-Day in Normandy. As he read each poem he put the date on which and sometimes the circumstances in which he had read it; and added his comments of enjoyment, indifference or dislike. He had finished the volume while crossing to Normandy and had fallen in battle shortly afterwards. I often turn up that copy and read the comments, which reveal a fine, somewhat puritan, character and shrewd judgment. I am proud that my selection should have helped him in those days, and that it was on the whole to his taste. I hope that it may have helped and entertained many such others. If so, it served its purpose.

I have not made many alterations in this new edition. I have added a few old favourites which have always been in my memory, but had escaped from it temporarily; and one or two new poems which I have read since the original anthology was compiled. I have altered some of the notes in the light of fresh knowledge. But substantially this is the same selection. I hope that it may continue to give some pleasure and afford some help in these difficult days. I have a great belief in the inspiration of poetry towards courage and vision and in its driving power. And we want all the courage and vision at our command, in days of crisis when our future prosperity and greatness hang in the balance.

April 1947   W.

'I HAVE gathered a posie of other men's flowers and nothing but the thread that binds them is my own.' So wrote Montaigne; and I have borrowed his title, my memory being the binding thread.

This is a purely personal anthology. I have read much poetry; and since I had once a very retentive memory for verse much has remained in my head. I have had less opportunity to read poetry during these late years of war. When I do so, I find that I read the old favourites rather than fresh poets or poems; so that with failing memory it is unlikely that I shall acquire much more by heart. It amused me lately to set down in a notebook — mainly with a view to discussion with my son, who shares my liking for poetry — the poems I could repeat entire or in great part. I have now collected and arranged the poems I set down. I did it with no idea of publication, but my son and others have suggested that the collection might appeal to a wider circle.

I ask no one to applaud my choice. I do not always applaud it myself, but a part of me from which I cannot dissociate myself, my memory, has made this selection and I am too old to alter it. On the whole I think it is a reasonable choice from the almost inexhaustible treasure of English poetry, for a workaday man who prefers plain gold, silver or metal work to elaborate jewellery.

Browning and Kipling are the two poets whose work has stayed most in my memory, since I read them in impressionable youth. I have never regretted my choice. They have courage and humanity, and their feet are usually on the ground. G. K. Chesterton has the same qualities, with a more romantic and less practical strain; he has become my third favourite, and much of his verse is in my heart and my head; there also is much of Masefield, the poet of adventure and toil by land and sea. I have enjoyed the poetry of those who have their eyes on the stars, like Keats and Shelley, without memorizing much of it. Wordsworth's and Tennyson's verses have never registered an impression on my memory, they seem to me to belong to a limbo which is earthy without being quite human and star-gazing without being inspired. Some of the Elizabethans, and Blake and Francis Thompson, have left in my brain clear traces of their imagery; but blank verse does not seem to stay there easily, so there is little of Shakespeare, often though I read him. There is something of Macaulay and Scott, those makers of sword-and-dagger rhyme, left from my boyhood days. *Horatius*, with its arresting first stanza about Lars Porsena and his Nine Gods, was the earliest poem I got by heart, as a small boy. Admiring aunts used to give me threepence for reciting it from beginning to end; a wiser uncle gave me sixpence for a promise to do nothing of the kind. A little later, 'Morning Lines' at Winchester laid a foundation on which my memory ever since has been building and furnishing. Here is the finished house; for it is unlikely that I shall add much more.

I sometimes fear that the stream of English poetry is running dry and turning muddy; but my son, for whose judgment I have very great respect, reads both the old and the new poets and on the whole prefers the latter, so perhaps it is just that I am growing old. I hope so, since I hold true the following from one who had the vision of the poet:

CALIPH   Ah, if there shall ever arise a nation whose people have
          forgotten poetry or whose poets have forgotten the people,
          though they send their ships round Taprobane and their
          armies across the hills of Hindustan, though their city be
          greater than Babylon of old, though they mine a league into
          earth or mount to the stars on wings — what of them?
HASSAN   They will be a dark patch upon the world.

I cannot claim that I can now repeat by heart all the poems in this anthology. I think I can safely claim that I once could; and I can still repeat to myself — for repeating verse to others is seldom popular — nearly all that is printed here. My As.D.C. have to listen politely when I quote verse to them — that is a privilege of a Commander-in-Chief; my wife and daughters have quietly but firmly cured me of the habit as far as they are concerned. I would warn young men, when they find young women willing, even apparently anxious, to listen to them repeating poetry, to watch their step very carefully.

Driving a motor car alone or riding a horse alone I often declaim out loud; but not when walking, walking for me is somehow a more serious business and does not seem to loosen my memory to verse; perhaps pace is required as an incentive. I neither sing nor recite poetry in my bath. I have never piloted an aeroplane alone, but I feel

it would move me to declaim in the skies. Practically all the verse in
this collection is capable of being declaimed, it seems to me a function
of poetry that it should be so. Poetry in its origins was certainly a
declamatory art, usually post-prandial or post-proeliatory. It is one
of my charges against modern poetry that it does not easily lend itself
to memorizing or declamation. The Prime Minister, Mr Winston
Churchill, has stored in his prodigious memory much poetry which
he declaims on apt occasion; I have had the pleasure of hearing some
of the verses of this anthology repeated by him — with characteristic
gusto. Lord Allenby was another under whom I served with a great
store of poetry in his head and the ability to give it forth in season.
My experience is that one can never properly appreciate a poem until
one has got it by heart: memory stumbles over a word or a line and so
wonders why the poet wrote it so, and then savours it slowly that its
meaning and relish may stay.

Most of the poems are given in full; I have abridged one or two
long ones of which the whole has not been in my memory.

I ask indulgence for the conditions in which this anthology has
been compiled. It was not originally intended for publication; and
the prefaces to the Sections and the Notes to some poems have been
written hurriedly in the short leisures of a very busy life; they should
not be taken too seriously. The Notes are not altogether my fault,
the publisher asked for them.

New Delhi
  April 1943

ACKNOWLEDGMENTS

THE Compiler's thanks are due to the following for permission to publish certain copyright material in this Anthology: Hon. Herbert Asquith and Sidgwick & Jackson Ltd, 'The Volunteer' by Herbert Asquith; Mrs Raymond Asquith, 'In Praise of Young Girls' by Raymond Asquith; Mr Hilaire Belloc and Gerald Duckworth & Co. Ltd, poems by Hilaire Belloc; Miss Greta Briggs, 'London under Bombardment'; Sidgwick & Jackson Ltd, 'The Dead' by Rupert Brooke; the Trustees of the late Lord Tweedsmuir and Thomas Nelson & Sons, Ltd, 'Fratri Dilectissimo' from *Montrose* by John Buchan; Miss Collins and Methuen & Co. Ltd, four poems and also an extract from 'Fantasia' by G. K. Chesterton from *Collected Poems*; Miss Collins and J. M. Dent & Sons, Ltd, 'The Praise of Dust' by G. K. Chesterton from *The White Knight*; Miss Collins and Oxford University Press, an extract from 'O God of earth and altar' by G. K. Chesterton from *Enlarged Songs of Praise*; Miss Collins, three poems by G. K. Chesterton; Jonathan Cape Ltd, 'Leisure' by W. H. Davies from *Collected Poems*; Mr Walter de la Mare and Faber & Faber Ltd, poems by Walter de la Mare from *Collected Poems*; John Lane The Bodley Head Ltd, 'Cynara' by Ernest Dowson from *Collected Poems*; Martin Secker & Warburg Ltd, 'War Song of the Saracens' and 'The Old Ships' by James Elroy Flecker from *Collected Poems*; William Heinemann Ltd, extracts from *Hassan* by James Elroy Flecker; Jonathan Cape Ltd, 'Mending Wall' by Robert Frost from *Collected Poems*; William Heinemann Ltd, 'Never Get Out' and 'Courage' by John Galsworthy; The Clarendon Press, Oxford, 'The Motor Bus' by A. D. Godley from *Reliquiae*, ed. C. R. L. Fletcher; Mr Oliver St John Gogarty, 'The Boon Companion' and 'To Death'; Lady Desborough, poems by Julian Grenfell; the Trustees of the Hardy Estate and Macmillan & Co. Ltd, 'Weathers' and 'Afterwards' by Thomas Hardy from *Collected Poems*; Mr Ralph Hodgson and Macmillan & Co. Ltd, poems by Ralph Hodgson from *Poems*; Oxford University Press, extract from 'Inversnaid' by Gerard Manley Hopkins; William Heinemann Ltd, extract from 'The Teak Forest' by Laurence Hope; the Trustees of the late A. E. Housman and Jonathan Cape Ltd, poems by A. E. Housman from *Collected Poems*; John Murray, 'Tam i' the Kirk' by Violet Jacob from *Songs of Angus*; Mrs George Bambridge, Methuen & Co. Ltd and The Macmillan

Company, Toronto, nineteen poems by Rudyard Kipling from *The Seven Seas, The Five Nations, Barrack Room Ballads, The Years Between* and *Departmental Ditties*; Mrs George Bambridge and Macmillan & Co. Ltd, London, and The Macmillan Company, Toronto, ten poems by Rudyard Kipling from *Rewards and Fairies, Kim, Plain Tales from the Hills, Puck of Pook's Hill, Debits and Credits*, and *Limits and Renewals*; Mrs George Bambridge, 'Boxing' from *Rudyard Kipling's Verse: Definitive Edition*; Mr Noel F. Sharp, 'The Kye-Song of St Bride' by Fiona Macleod; the representatives of the late Andrew Lang and Messrs Longmans Green & Co. Ltd, 'The Odyssey' by Andrew Lang; Mr John Masefield, William Heinemann Ltd, and The Macmillan Company, Toronto, poems by John Masefield, from *Collected Poems*; The Ryerson Press, 299 Queen Street West, Toronto, Canada, 'In Flanders Fields' by John McCrae from *In Flanders Fields and Other Poems*; Miss Edna St V. Millay and Harper & Brothers, 'My Candle' by Edna St V. Millay from *A Few Figs from Thistles*; the Executors of the late Sir Henry Newbolt and John Murray, 'Drake's Drum' by Sir Henry Newbolt from *Poems New and Old*; Mr Siegfried Sassoon and William Heinemann Ltd, 'Good-morning; good-morning!' by Siegfried Sassoon; Miss Dorothy L. Sayers, 'The English War'; Constable & Co. Ltd, 'Rendezvous' by Alan Seeger; Bowes & Bowes Ltd, 'To R. K.' by J. K. Stephen; William Heinemann Ltd, 'The Garden of Proserpine' by Algernon Charles Swinburne; Mr Wilfrid Meynell, poems by Francis Thompson; Mr Vyvyan Holland, poems by Oscar Wilde; Mrs Yeats and Macmillan & Co. Ltd, 'When You are Old' and 'An Irish Airman Foresees his Death' by W. B. Yeats from *Collected Poems*; Mr Francis Brett Young and William Heinemann Ltd, 'Hic Jacet Arthurus' and 'Atlantic Charter' by Francis Brett Young from *The Island*.

Thanks are due also to the *Daily Telegraph* for permission to reprint 'London Under Bombardment'; to Messrs Chatto & Windus for permission to include 'Romance' and 'Requiem' by Robert Louis Stevenson.

If, through inability to trace the present copyright owners, any copyright material is included for which permission has not specifically been sought, apologies are tendered in advance to proprietors and publishers concerned.

The illustration facing p. 438 is reproduced by kind permission of the owner of the picture, Captain E. G. Spencer-Churchill, M.C.

1. MUSIC, MYSTERY AND MAGIC

POETS writing lyrics choose words for their beauty and set them to dance to a tune. So on a lower scale does the theatrical manager select his chorus. The aim of the lyrical poet, as of the stage manager, is to create glamour and illusion that will take our minds from the common circumstances of everyday life and fix them on the world as it ought to be, had men not gods designed it. The poet may protest against this comparison that it is a commercial instinct, at the highest, that guides the theatrical manager in his choice; while the poet is moved only by his vision of beauty and regards not the public taste. Yet the greatest of all poets wrote with his eye very much on the public; and no poet really despises success and a long run for his work — indeed some claim the longest possible run, immortal fame: and a few may have achieved it.

Music, mystery and magic are the essence of the highest poetry. And surely it should also have meaning. The poems in this section are those that have stayed in my head for those qualities. The first one, *The Hound of Heaven*, has had a special place in my life, as a charm in danger or trouble. Many years ago a friend gave me a copy of Francis Thompson's lyric at St Andrews, where I was playing golf. I had it by heart in a very few readings and from that day I have used the magic of its imagery in my times of stress, to distract my mind from peril or disaster. I have repeated the words of this greatest of all lyrics under fire, on a rough Channel crossing, in pain of body or mind.

Religion depends on mystery or magic and uses music to attract the faithful. So poems dealing with religion are included in this section.

There are few modern poems here — by modern I mean the betwixt-wars poets, 1919-39, years that are better forgotten in the history of our people, when the spirit grew tired and disillusioned and the body slack and soft. To my poor ear and old-fashioned understanding most modern poetry lacks dignity and has neither beauty nor tune; magic is replaced by unintelligibility; and the only mystery to me is that anyone reads much of it. It is as though a theatrical manager chose an ungainly chorus who could neither dance nor sing nor act, but could only posture and grimace to capture attention. Worse still, modern poetry seems to me to lack the essential quality of courage, of a gallant outlook on the pains and pleasures of this world through which we have to pass; where we — the rank and file — want leadership and encouragement from those gifted with power over words, not defeatism and depression. A poet is a man to whom vision is given beyond his fellows. Of what use is that vision if he expresses it in words unintelligible to all but a small circle, and doubtfully to them? The world soon begins to suspect that he has no vision, and is therefore no poet. And without vision, as the prophet said, the people perish. We might well have perished in this war without Mr Churchill.

Much of the work of T. S. Eliot has obvious dignity and beauty, and is a pleasure to read as long as one makes no effort to solve his cryptograms; but some of it seems deliberately ugly as well as cryptic. I look on him as one who has sinned against the light of poetry by wrapping his great talent in the napkin of obscurity. He has himself said, I believe, that 'If the poetical work of the last twenty years is worthy of being classified at all, it is as belonging to a period of search for a proper modern colloquial idiom'. If he is right, it certainly seems as if some of the betwixt-wars poets had left no rubbish-heap unturned, no gutter unexplored in their search. My son finds their works interesting and I bow to his younger, fresher appraisement. But I go back and warm my ageing memory at the embers of the older, braver poets whom I know.

I do not know what is being written now. At Dunkirk the true spirit of our people flashed out like a sword from its sheath; with it I hope flashed out a fresh inspiration of poetry.   *A. P. W.*

THE HOUND OF HEAVEN

Francis Thompson

I FLED Him, down the nights and down the days;
    I fled Him, down the arches of the years;
I fled Him, down the labyrinthine ways
    Of my own mind; and in the mist of tears
I hid from Him, and under running laughter.

Up vistaed hopes I sped;
And shot, precipitated,
Adown Titanic glooms of chasmèd fears,
From those strong Feet that followed, followed after.

But with unhurrying chase,
And unperturbèd pace,
Deliberate speed, majestic instancy,
They beat — and a Voice beat
More instant than the Feet —
'All things betray thee, who betrayest Me.'

I pleaded, outlaw-wise,
By many a hearted casement, curtained red,
Trellised with intertwining charities;
(For, though I knew His love Who followèd,
Yet was I sore adread
Lest, having Him, I must have naught beside).
But, if one little casement parted wide,
The gust of His approach would clash it to.
Fear wist not to evade, as Love wist to pursue.
Across the margent of the world I fled,
And troubled the gold gateways of the stars,
Smiting for shelter on their clangèd bars;
Fretted to dulcet jars
And silvern clatter the pale ports o' the moon.
I said to Dawn: Be sudden — to Eve: Be soon;
With thy young skiey blossoms heap me over
From this tremendous Lover —
Float thy vague veil about me, lest He see!
I tempted all His servitors, but to find
My own betrayal in their constancy,
In faith to Him their fickleness to me,
Their traitorous trueness, and their loyal deceit.
To all swift things for swiftness did I sue;
Clung to the whistling mane of every wind.
But whether they swept, smoothly fleet,
The long savannahs of the blue;

Or whether, Thunder-driven,
They clanged his chariot 'thwart a heaven,
Plashy with flying lightnings round the spurn o' their feet:—
Fear wist not to evade as Love wist to pursue.

Still with unhurrying chase,
And unperturbèd pace,
Deliberate speed, majestic instancy,
Came on the following Feet,
And a Voice above their beat —
'Naught shelters thee, who wilt not shelter Me.'

I sought no more that after which I strayed
In face of man or maid;
But still within the little children's eyes
Seems something, something that replies,
They at least are for me, surely for me!
I turned me to them very wistfully;
But just as their young eyes grew sudden fair
With dawning answers there,
Their angel plucked them from me by the hair.
'Come then, ye other children, Nature's — share
With me' (said I) 'your delicate fellowship;
Let me greet you lip to lip,
Let me twine with you caresses,
Wantoning
With our Lady-Mother's vagrant tresses,
Banqueting
With her in her wind-walled palace,
Underneath her azured daïs,
Quaffing, as your taintless way is,
From a chalice
Lucent-weeping out of the dayspring.'
So it was done:
I in their delicate fellowship was one —
Drew the bolt of Nature's secrecies.
I knew all the swift importings
On the wilful face of skies;

I knew how the clouds arise
  Spumèd of the wild sea-snortings;
    All that's born or dies
  Rose and drooped with; made them shapers
Of mine own moods, or wailful or divine;
    With them joyed and was bereaven.
    I was heavy with the even,
  When she lit her glimmering tapers
  Round the day's dead sanctities.
  I laughed in the morning's eyes.
I triumphed and I saddened with all weather,
  Heaven and I wept together,
And its sweet tears were salt with mortal mine;
Against the red throb of its sunset-heart
    I laid my own to beat,
    And share commingling heat;
But not by that, by that, was eased my human smart.
In vain my tears were wet on Heaven's grey cheek.
For ah! we know not what each other says,
  These things and I; in sound *I* speak —
Their sound is but their stir, they speak by silences.
Nature, poor stepdame, cannot slake my drouth;
  Let her, if she would owe me,
Drop yon blue bosom-veil of sky, and show me
  The breasts o' her tenderness:
Never did any milk of hers once bless
    My thirsting mouth.

    Nigh and nigh draws the chase,
    With unperturbèd pace,
Deliberate speed, majestic instancy;
    And past those noisèd Feet
    A voice comes yet more fleet —
'Lo! naught contents thee, who content'st not Me.'

Naked I wait Thy love's uplifted stroke!
My harness piece by piece Thou hast hewn from me,
    And smitten me to my knee;

I am defenceless utterly.
I slept, methinks, and woke,
And, slowly gazing, find me stripped in sleep.
In the rash lustihead of my young powers,
I shook the pillaring hours
And pulled my life upon me; grimed with smears,
I stand amid the dust o' the moulded years —
My mangled youth lies dead beneath the heap.
My days have crackled and gone up in smoke,
Have puffed and burst as sun-starts on a stream.
Yea, faileth now even dream
The dreamer, and the lute the lutanist;
Even the linked fantasies, in whose blossomy twist
I swung the earth a trinket at my wrist,
Are yielding; cords of all too weak account
For earth with heavy griefs so overplussed.
Ah! is Thy love indeed
A weed, albeit an amaranthine weed,
Suffering no flowers except its own to mount?
Ah! must —
Designer infinite! —
Ah! must Thou char the wood ere Thou canst limn with it?
My freshness spent its wavering shower i' the dust;
And now my heart is as a broken fount,
Wherein tear-drippings stagnate, spilt down ever
From the dank thoughts that shiver
Upon the sighful branches of my mind.
Such is; what is to be?
The pulp so bitter, how shall taste the rind?
I dimly guess what Time in mists confounds;
Yet ever and anon a trumpet sounds
From the hid battlements of Eternity;
Those shaken mists a space unsettle, then
Round the half-glimpsèd turrets slowly wash again.
But not ere him who summoneth
I first have seen, enwound
With glooming robes purpureal, cypress-crowned;
His name I know, and what his trumpet saith.

Whether man's heart or life it be which yields
    Thee harvest, must Thy harvest-fields
    Be dunged with rotten death?

      Now of that long pursuit
      Comes on at hand the bruit;
    That Voice is round me like a bursting sea:
      'And is thy earth so marred,
      Shattered in shard on shard?
    Lo, all things fly thee, for thou fliest Me!
      Strange, piteous, futile thing!
Wherefore should any set thee love apart?
Seeing none but I makes much of naught?' (He said),
'And human love needs human meriting:
      How hast thou merited —
Of all man's clotted clay the dingiest clot?
      Alack, thou knowest not
How little worthy of any love thou art!
Whom wilt thou find to love ignoble thee,
      Save Me, save only Me?
All which I took from thee I did but take,
      Not for thy harms,
But just that thou might'st seek it in My arms.
      All which thy child's mistake
Fancies as lost, I have stored for thee at home:
      Rise, clasp My hand, and come!'

      Halts by me that footfall:
      Is my gloom, after all,
Shade of His hand, outstretched caressingly?
      'Ah, fondest, blindest, weakest,
      I am He Whom thou seekest!
Thou dravest love from thee, who dravest Me.'

SWEET CONTENT

THOMAS DEKKER

ART thou poor, yet hast thou golden slumbers?
    O sweet content!
Art thou rich, yet is thy mind perplex'd?
    O punishment!
Dost thou laugh to see how fools are vex'd
To add to golden numbers golden numbers?
    O sweet content! O sweet, O sweet content!
Work apace, apace, apace, apace;
Honest labour bears a lovely face;
Then hey nonny nonny — hey nonny nonny!

Canst drink the waters of the crispèd spring?
    O sweet content!
Swim'st thou in wealth, yet sink'st in thine own tears?
    O punishment!
Then he that patiently want's burden bears,
No burden bears, but is a king, a king!
    O sweet content! O sweet, O sweet content!
Work apace, apace, apace, apace;
Honest labour bears a lovely face;
Then hey nonny nonny — hey nonny nonny!

KUBLA KHAN

SAMUEL TAYLOR COLERIDGE

IN Xanadu did Kubla Khan
  A stately pleasure-dome decree:
Where Alph, the sacred river, ran
Through caverns measureless to man
  Down to a sunless sea.
So twice five miles of fertile ground
With walls and towers were girdled round
And there were gardens bright with sinuous rills
Where blossom'd many an incense-bearing tree;

And here were forests ancient as the hills,
Enfolding sunny spots of greenery.

But O, that deep romantic chasm which slanted
Down the green hill athwart a cedarn cover!
A savage place! as holy and enchanted
As e'er beneath a waning moon was haunted
By woman wailing for her demon-lover!
And from this chasm, with ceaseless turmoil seething,
As if this earth in fast thick pants were breathing,
A mighty fountain momently was forced;
Amid whose swift half-intermitted burst
Huge fragments vaulted like rebounding hail,
Or chaffy grain beneath the thresher's flail:
And 'mid these dancing rocks at once and ever
It flung up momently the sacred river.
Five miles meandering with a mazy motion
Through wood and dale the sacred river ran,
Then reach'd the caverns measureless to man,
And sank in tumult to a lifeless ocean:
And 'mid this tumult Kubla heard from far
Ancestral voices prophesying war!

The shadow of the dome of pleasure
    Floated midway on the waves;
Where was heard the mingled measure
    From the fountain and the caves.
It was a miracle of rare device,
A sunny pleasure-dome with caves of ice!

A damsel with a dulcimer
    In a vision once I saw:
It was an Abyssinian maid,
    And on her dulcimer she play'd,
Singing of Mount Abora.
Could I revive within me,
    Her symphony and song,
To such a deep delight 'twould win me,

That with music loud and long,
I would build that dome in air,
That sunny dome! those caves of ice!
And all who heard should see them there,
And all should cry, Beware! Beware!
His flashing eyes, his floating hair!
Weave a circle round him thrice,
   And close your eyes with holy dread,
   For he on honey-dew hath fed,
And drunk the milk of Paradise.

Note

I once amused myself by drawing a sketch map of Kubla Khan's pleasaunce from the data in the text, which give, I think, sufficient guide to make a reasonable map, though there are one or two debatable problems. Of Kubla Khan it is recorded by one of his biographers that twice a year specially appointed officials brought four or five hundred carefully chosen maidens to his court. These were weeded down to thirty or so by a board of court officials and then handed over to the Ladies of the Household for a course of instruction before being presented to the King, which perhaps accounts for the otherwise somewhat sudden and perplexing appearance of the Abyssinian damsel. The ancestral voices heard by Kubla Khan presumably came from his famous grandfather Genghiz Khan, the greatest of the Mongols. Kubla Khan's own wars included two expeditions to Japan in 1274 and 1281, which were unfortunately unsuccessful.   *A. P. W.*

THE TIGER

WILLIAM BLAKE

TIGER, tiger, burning bright,
In the forests of the night,
What immortal hand or eye
Could frame thy fearful symmetry?

In what distant deeps or skies
Burnt the fire of thine eyes?
On what wings dare he aspire?
What the hand dare seize the fire?

And what shoulder and what art
Could twist the sinews of thy heart?
And, when thy heart began to beat,
What dread hand and what dread feet?

What the hammer? What the chain?
In what furnace was thy brain?
What the anvil? What dread grasp
Dare its deadly terrors clasp?

When the stars threw down their spears,
And water'd heaven with their tears,
Did He smile His work to see?
Did He who made the lamb make thee?

Tiger, tiger, burning bright
In the forests of the night,
What immortal hand or eye
Dare frame thy fearful symmetry?

DREAM-PEDLARY
Thomas Lovell Beddoes

I

If there were dreams to sell,
   What would you buy?
Some cost a passing bell;
   Some a light sigh,
That shakes from Life's fresh crown
Only a rose-leaf down.
If there were dreams to sell,
Merry and sad to tell,
And the crier rung the bell,
   What would you buy?

II

A cottage lone and still,
  With bowers nigh,
Shadowy, my woes to still,
  Until I die.
Such pearl from Life's fresh crown
Fain would I shake me down.
Were dreams to have at will,
This would best heal my ill,
  This would I buy.

III

But there were dreams to sell
  Ill didst thou buy;
Life is a dream, they tell,
  Waking, to die.
Dreaming a dream to prize,
is wishing ghosts to rise:
  And, if I had the spell
  To call the buried well,
    Which one would I?

IV

If there are ghosts to raise,
  What shall I call,
Out of hell's murky haze,
  Heaven's blue pall?
Raise my loved long-lost boy
To lead me to his joy.
  There are no ghosts to raise;
  Out of death lead no ways;
    Vain is the call.

V

Know'st thou not ghosts to sue?
  No love thou hast.
Else lie, as I will do,
  And breathe thy last.

So out of Life's fresh crown
Fall like a rose-leaf down.
    Thus are the ghosts to woo;
    Thus are all dreams made true,
        Ever to last!

Note

I love this rather mystical poem, though I am never quite certain whether I have interpreted the poet's meaning correctly. He committed suicide at an early age and went to woo his ghosts; I wonder if he found them. For the sake of this beautiful lyric I hope that his dreams were made true or that he had untroubled rest.   *A. P. W.*

ODE TO A NIGHTINGALE

John Keats

My heart aches, and a drowsy numbness pains
    My sense, as though of hemlock I had drunk,
Or emptied some dull opiate to the drains
    One minute past, and Lethe-wards had sunk:
'Tis not through envy of thy happy lot,
    But being too happy in thy happiness,
        That thou, light-wingèd Dryad of the trees,
            In some melodious plot
    Of beechen green, and shadows numberless,
        Singest of summer in full-throated ease.

O for a draught of vintage! that hath been
    Cool'd a long age in the deep-delvèd earth,
Tasting of Flora and the country-green,
    Dance, and Provençal song, and sunburnt mirth!
O for a beaker full of the warm South!
    Full of the true, the blushful Hippocrene,
        With beaded bubbles winking at the brim,
            And purple-stainèd mouth;
    That I might drink, and leave the world unseen,
        And with thee fade away into the forest dim:

Fade far away, dissolve, and quite forget
  What thou among the leaves hast never known,
The weariness, the fever, and the fret
  Here, where men sit and hear each other groan;
Where palsy shakes a few, sad, last grey hairs,
Where youth grows pale, and spectre-thin, and dies;
    Where but to think is to be full of sorrow
      And leaden-eyed despairs;
   Where beauty cannot keep her lustrous eyes,
   Or new Love pine at them beyond to-morrow.

Away! away! for I will fly to thee,
  Not charioted by Bacchus and his pards,
But on the viewless wings of Poesy,
  Though the dull brain perplexes and retards:
Already with thee! tender is the night,
  And haply the Queen-Moon is on her throne,
    Cluster'd around by all her starry Fays;
      But here there is no light,
  Save what from heaven is with the breezes blown
    Through verdurous glooms and winding mossy ways.

I cannot see what flowers are at my feet,
  Nor what soft incense hangs upon the boughs,
But, in embalmèd darkness, guess each sweet
  Wherewith the seasonable month endows
The grass, the thicket, and the fruit-tree wild;
  White hawthorn, and the pastoral eglantine;
    Fast-fading violets cover'd up in leaves;
      And mid-May's eldest child,
  The coming musk-rose, full of dewy wine,
    The murmurous haunt of flies on summer eves.

Darkling I listen; and for many a time
  I have been half in love with easeful Death,
Call'd him soft names in many a musèd rhyme,
  To take into the air my quiet breath;
Now more than ever seems it rich to die,

To cease upon the midnight with no pain,
　　While thou art pouring forth thy soul abroad
　　　　In such an ecstasy!
Still wouldst thou sing, and I have ears in vain —
　　To thy high requiem become a sod.

Thou wast not born for death, immortal Bird!
No hungry generations tread thee down;
The voice I hear this passing night was heard
In ancient days by emperor and clown:
Perhaps the self-same song that found a path
　　Through the sad heart of Ruth, when, sick for home,
　　　She stood in tears amid the alien corn;
　　　　The same that ofttimes hath
Charm'd magic casements, opening on the foam
　　Of perilous seas, in faery lands forlorn.

Forlorn! the very word is like a bell
　　To toll me back from thee to my sole self!
Adieu! the fancy cannot cheat so well
　　As she is famed to do, deceiving elf.
Adieu! adieu! thy plaintive anthem fades
　　Past the near meadows, over the still stream,
　　Up the hill-side; and now 'tis buried deep
　　　　In the next valley-glades:
Was it a vision, or a waking dream?
　　Fled is that music: — do I wake or sleep?

FROM THE NIGHT OF FOREBEING
An Ode After Easter
FRANCIS THOMPSON

In the chaos of preordination, and night of our forebeings.
SIR THOMAS BROWNE

Et lux in tenebris erat, et tenebræ eam non comprehenderunt.　　ST JOHN

[Extract]
CAST wide the folding doorways of the East,
For now is light increased!

And the wind-besomed chambers of the air,
See they be garnished fair;
And look the ways exhale some precious odours,
And set ye all about wild-breathing spice,
Most fit for Paradise!
Now is no time for sober gravity,
Season enough has Nature to be wise;
But now discinct, with raiment glittering free,
Shake she the ringing rafters of the skies
With festal footing and bold joyance sweet,
And let the earth be drunken and carouse!
For lo, into her house
Spring is come home with her world-wandering feet,
And all things are made young with young desires;
And all for her is light increased
In yellow stars and yellow daffodils,
And East to West, and West to East,
Fling answering welcome-fires,
By dawn and day-fall, on the jocund hills.
And ye, winged minstrels of her fair meinie,
Being newly coated in glad livery,
Upon her steps attend,
And round her treading dance, and without end
Reel your shrill lutany.
What popular breath her coming does out-tell
The garrulous leaves among!
What little noises stir and pass
From blade to blade along the voluble grass!
O Nature, never-done
Ungaped-at Pentecostal miracle,
We hear thee, each man in his proper tongue!
Break, elemental children, break ye loose
From the strict frosty rule
Of grey-beard Winter's school.
Vault, O young winds, vault in your tricksome courses
Upon the snowy steeds that reinless use
In cœrule pampas of the heaven to run;
Foaled of the white sea-horses,

Washed in the lambent waters of the sun.
Let even the slug-abed snail upon the thorn
Put forth a conscious horn!
Mine elemental co-mates, joy each one;
And ah, my foster-brethren, seem not sad —
No, seem not sad,
That my strange heart and I should be so little glad.
Suffer me at your leafy feast
To sit apart, a somewhat alien guest,
And watch your mirth,
Unsharing in the liberal laugh of earth;
Yet with a sympathy
Begot of wholly sad and half-sweet memory —
The little sweetness making grief complete;
Faint wind of wings from hours that distant beat,
When I, I too,
Was once, O wild companions, as are you, —
Ran with such wilful feet;
Wraith of a recent day and dead,
Risen wanly overhead,
Frail, strengthless as a noon-belated moon,
Or as the glazing eyes of watery heaven,
When the sick night sinks into deathly swoon.

A higher and a solemn voice
I heard through your gay-hearted noise;
A solemn meaning and a stiller voice
Sounds to me from far days when I too shall rejoice,
Nor more be with your jollity at strife.
O prophecy
Of things that are, and are not, and shall be!
The great-vanned Angel March
Hath trumpeted
His clangorous 'Sleep no more' to all the dead —
Beat his strong vans o'er earth, and air, and sea.
And they have heard;
Hark to the *Jubilate* of the bird
For them that found the dying way to life!

And they have heard,
And quicken to the great precursive word;
Green spray showers lightly down the cascade of the larch;
The graves are riven,
And the Sun comes with power amid the clouds of heaven!
Before his way
Went forth the trumpet of the March;
Before his way, before his way
Dances the pennon of the May!
O Earth, unchilded, widowed Earth, so long
Lifting in patient pine and ivy-tree
Mournful belief and steadfast prophecy,
Behold how all things are made true!
Behold your bridegroom cometh in to you,
Exceeding glad and strong.
Raise up your eyes, O raise your eyes abroad!
No more shall you sit sole and vidual,
Searching, in servile pall,
Upon the hieratic night the star-sealed sense of all.
Rejoice, O barren, and look forth abroad!
Your children gathered back to your embrace
See with a mother's face.
Look up, O mortals, and the portent heed;
In very deed,
Washed with new fire to their irradiant birth,
Reintegrated are the heavens and earth!
From sky to sod,
The world's unfolded blossom smells of God.

Note

There is a lot more of this poem, but it becomes metaphysical
and does not please me as much as this first lovely part. *A. P. W.*

THE RIME OF THE ANCIENT MARINER

SAMUEL TAYLOR COLERIDGE

[Extracts]

Part I

An ancient Mariner meeteth three gallants bidden to a wedding feast, and detaineth one.

IT is an ancient Mariner,
And he stoppeth one of three.
'By thy long grey beard and glittering eye,
Now wherefore stopp'st thou me?

The Bridegroom's doors are open'd wide,
And I am next of kin;
The guests are met, the feast is set:
May'st hear the merry din.'

He holds him with his skinny hand,
'There was a ship,' quoth he.
'Hold off! unhand me, grey-beard loon!'
Eftsoons his hand dropt he.

The Wedding-Guest is spellbound by the eye of the old seafaring man, and constrained to hear his tale.

He holds him with his glittering eye –
The Wedding-Guest stood still,
And listens like a three years' child:
The Mariner hath his will.

The Wedding-Guest sat on a stone:
He cannot choose but hear;
And thus spake on that ancient man,
The bright-eyed Mariner.

'The ship was cheer'd, the harbour clear'd,
Merrily did we drop
Below the kirk, below the hill,
Below the lighthouse top.

The Sun came up upon the left,
Out of the sea came he!
And he shone bright, and on the right
Went down into the sea.

The Mariner tells how the ship sailed southward with a good wind and fair weather, till it reached the Line.

Higher and higher every day,
Till over the mast at noon — '
The Wedding-Guest here beat his breast,
For he heard the loud bassoon.

The bride hath paced into the hall,
Red as a rose is she;
Nodding their heads before her goes
The merry minstrelsy.

The Wedding-Guest heareth the bridal music; but the Mariner continueth his tale.

The Wedding-Guest he beat his breast,
Yet he cannot choose but hear;
And thus spake on that ancient man,
The bright-eyed Mariner.

'And now the Storm-blast came, and he
Was tyrannous and strong:
He struck with his o'ertaking wings,
And chased us south along.

The ship drawn by a storm toward the South Pole.

With sloping masts and dipping prow,
As who pursued with yell and blow
Still treads the shadow of his foe,
And forward bends his head,
The ship drove fast, loud roar'd the blast,
And southward aye we fled.

And now there came both mist and snow,
And it grew wondrous cold:
And ice, mast-high, came floating by,
As green as emerald.

And through the drifts the snowy clifts
Did send a dismal sheen:
Nor shapes of men nor beasts we ken —
The ice was all between.

The land of ice, and of fearful sounds, where no living thing was to be seen.

The ice was here, the ice was there,
The ice was all around:
It crack'd and growl'd, and roar'd and howl'd,
Like noises in a swound!

Till a great sea-bird, called the Albatross, came through the snow-fog, and was received with great joy and hospitality.
At length did cross an Albatross,
Thorough the fog it came;
As if it had been a Christian soul,
We hail'd it in God's name.

It ate the food it ne'er had eat,
And round and round it flew.
The ice did split with a thunder-fit;
The helmsman steer'd us through!

And lo! the Albatross proveth a bird of good omen, and followeth the ship as it returned northward through fog and floating ice.
And a good south wind sprung up behind;
The Albatross did follow,
And every day, for food or play,
Came to the mariners' hollo!

In mist or cloud, on mast or shroud,
It perch'd for vespers nine;
Whiles all the night, through fog-smoke white,
Glimmer'd the white moonshine.'

The ancient Mariner inhospitably killeth the pious bird of good omen.
'God save thee, ancient Mariner,
From the fiends, that plague thee thus! —
Why look'st thou so?' — 'With my crossbow
I shot the Albatross.

. . . . .

Part III

The western wave was all aflame,
The day was wellnigh done!
Almost upon the western wave
Rested the broad, bright Sun;
When that strange shape drove suddenly
Betwixt us and the Sun.

And straight the Sun was fleck'd with bars
(Heaven's Mother send us grace!),
As if through a dungeon-grate he peer'd
With broad and burning face.

It seemeth him but the skeleton of a ship.

Alas! (thought I, and my heart beat loud)
How fast she nears and nears!
Are those her sails that glance in the Sun,
Like restless gossameres?

Are those her ribs through which the Sun
Did peer, as through a grate?
And is that Woman all her crew?
Is that a Death? and are there two?
Is Death that Woman's mate?

And its ribs are seen as bars on the face of the setting Sun. The Spectre-Woman and her Death-mate, and no other, on board the skeleton ship. Like vessel, like crew!

Her lips were red, her looks were free,
Her locks were yellow as gold:
Her skin was as white as leprosy,
The Nightmare Life-in-Death was she,
Who thicks man's blood with cold.

The naked hulk alongside came,
And the twain were casting dice;
"The game is done! I've won! I've won!"
Quoth she, and whistles thrice.

Death and Life-in-Death have diced for the ship's crew, and she (the latter) winneth the ancient Mariner.

The Sun's rim dips; the stars rush out:
At one stride comes the dark;
With far-heard whisper, o'er the sea,
Off shot the spectre-bark.

No twilight within the courts of the Sun.

We listen'd and look'd sideways up!
Fear at my heart, as at a cup,
My life-blood seem'd to sip!
The stars were dim, and thick the night,
The steersman's face by his lamp gleam'd white;

At the rising of the Moon.

From the sails the dew did drip —
Till clomb above the eastern bar
The hornèd Moon, with one bright star
Within the nether tip.

One after another.

One after one, by the star-dogg'd Moon,
Too quick for groan or sigh,
Each turn'd his face with a ghastly pang,
And cursed me with his eye.

His shipmates drop down dead.

Four times fifty living men
(And I heard nor sigh nor groan),
With heavy thump, a lifeless lump,
They dropp'd down one by one.

But Life-in-Death begins her work on the ancient Mariner.

The souls did from their bodies fly —
They fled to bliss or woe!
And every soul, it pass'd me by
Like the whizz of my crossbow!'

Part IV

The Wedding-Guest feareth that a spirit is talking to him.

'I fear thee, ancient Mariner!
I fear thy skinny hand!
And thou art long, and lank, and brown,
As is the ribb'd sea-sand.

I fear thee and thy glittering eye,
And thy skinny hand so brown.' —
'Fear not, fear not, thou Wedding-Guest!
This body dropt not down.

But the ancient Mariner assureth him of his bodily life, and proceedeth to relate his horrible penance.

Alone, alone, all, all alone,
Alone on a wide, wide sea!
And never a saint took pity on
My soul in agony.

He despiseth the creatures of the calm.

The many men, so beautiful!
And they all dead did lie:
And a thousand thousand slimy things
Lived on; and so did I.

I look'd upon the rotting sea,
And drew my eyes away;
I look'd upon the rotting deck,
And there the dead men lay.

And envieth that they should live, and so many lie dead.

I look'd to heaven, and tried to pray;
But or ever a prayer had gusht,
A wicked whisper came, and made
My heart as dry as dust.

I closed my lids, and kept them close,
And the balls like pulses beat;
But the sky and the sea, and the sea and the sky,
Lay like a load on my weary eye,
And the dead were at my feet.

The cold sweat melted from their limbs,
Nor rot nor reek did they:
The look with which they look'd on me
Had never pass'd away.

But the curse liveth for him in the eye of the dead men.

An orphan's curse would drag to hell
A spirit from on high;
But oh! more horrible than that
Is the curse in a dead man's eye!
Seven days, seven nights, I saw that curse,
And yet I could not die.

The moving Moon went up the sky,
And nowhere did abide;
Softly she was going up,
And a star or two beside —

Her beams bemock'd the sultry main,
Like April hoar-frost spread;
But where the ship's huge shadow lay,
The charmèd water burnt alway
A still and awful red.

In his loneliness and fixedness he yearneth towards the journeying Moon, and the stars that still sojourn, yet still move onward; and everywhere the blue sky belongs to them, and is their appointed rest and their native country and their own natural homes, which they enter unannounced, as lords that are certainly expected, and yet there is a silent joy at their arrival.

By the light of the Moon he beholdeth God's creatures of the great calm.

Beyond the shadow of the ship,
I watch'd the water-snakes:
They moved in tracks of shining white,
And when they rear'd, the elfish light
Fell off in hoary flakes.

Within the shadow of the ship
I watch'd their rich attire:
Blue, glossy green, and velvet black,
They coil'd and swam; and every track
Was a flash of golden fire.

Their beauty and their happiness.

O happy living things! no tongue
Their beauty might declare:
A spring of love gush'd from my heart,

He blesseth them in his heart.

And I bless'd them unaware:
Sure my kind saint took pity on me,
And I bless'd them unaware.

The spell begins to break.

The selfsame moment I could pray;
And from my neck so free
The Albatross fell off, and sank
Like lead into the sea.

Part V

'O sleep! it is a gentle thing,
Beloved from pole to pole!
To Mary Queen the praise be given!
She sent the gentle sleep from Heaven,
That slid into my soul.

By grace of the holy Mother, the ancient Mariner is refreshed with rain.

The silly buckets on the deck,
That had so long remain'd,
I dreamt that they were fill'd with dew;
And when I awoke, it rain'd.

My lips were wet, my throat was cold,
My garments all were dank;
Sure I had drunken in my dreams,
And still my body drank.

I moved, and could not feel my limbs:
I was so light — almost
I thought that I had died in sleep,
And was a blessèd ghost.

And soon I heard a roaring wind:
It did not come anear;
But with its sound it shook the sails,
That were so thin and sere.

He heareth sounds and seeth strange sights and commotions in the sky and the element.

The upper air burst into life;
And a hundred fire-flags sheen;
To and fro they were hurried about!
And to and fro, and in and out,
The wan stars danced between.

And the coming wind did roar more loud,
And the sails did sigh like sedge;
And the rain pour'd down from one black cloud;
The Moon was at its edge.

The thick black cloud was cleft, and still
The Moon was at its side;
Like waters shot from some high crag,
The lightning fell with never a jag,
A river steep and wide.

The loud wind never reach'd the ship,
Yet now the ship moved on!
Beneath the lightning and the Moon
The dead men gave a groan.

The bodies of the ship's crew are inspired, and the ship moves on;

They groan'd, they stirr'd, they all uprose,
Nor spake, nor moved their eyes;
It had been strange, even in a dream,
To have seen those dead men rise.

The helmsman steer'd, the ship moved on;
Yet never a breeze up-blew;
The mariners all 'gan work the ropes,
Where they were wont to do;
They raised their limbs like lifeless tools —
We were a ghastly crew.

The body of my brother's son
Stood by me, knee to knee:
The body and I pull'd at one rope,
But he said naught to me.'

But not by the souls of the men, nor by demons of earth or middle air, but by a blessed troop of angelic spirits, sent down by the invocation of the guardian saint.

'I fear thee, ancient Mariner!'
'Be calm, thou Wedding-Guest:
'Twas not those souls that fled in pain,
Which to their corses came again,
But a troop of spirits blest:

For when it dawn'd — they dropp'd their arms,
And cluster'd round the mast;
Sweet sounds rose slowly through their mouths,
And from their bodies pass'd.

Around, around, flew each sweet sound,
Then darted to the Sun;
Slowly the sounds came back again,
Now mix'd, now one by one.

Sometimes a-dropping from the sky
I heard the skylark sing;
Sometimes all little birds that are,
How they seem'd to fill the sea and air
With their sweet jargoning!

And now 'twas like all instruments,
Now like a lonely flute;
And now it is an angel's song,
That makes the Heavens be mute.

It ceased; yet still the sails made on
A pleasant noise till noon,
A noise like of a hidden brook
In the leafy month of June,
That to the sleeping woods all night
Singeth a quiet tune.

Till noon we quietly sail'd on,
Yet never a breeze did breathe:
Slowly and smoothly went the ship,
Moved onward from beneath.

Under the keel nine fathoms deep,
From the land of mist and snow,
The Spirit slid: and it was he
That made the ship to go.
The sails at noon left off their tune,
And the ship stood still also.

The lonesome Spirit from the South Pole carries on the ship as far as the Line, in obedience to the angelic troop, but still requireth vengeance.

The Sun, right up above the mast,
Had fix'd her to the ocean:
But in a minute she 'gan stir,
With a short uneasy motion —
Backwards and forwards half her length
With a short uneasy motion.

Then like a pawing horse let go,
She made a sudden bound:
It flung the blood into my head,
And I fell down in a swound.

The Polar Spirit's fellow demons, the invisible inhabitants of the element, take part in his wrong; and two of them relate, one to the other, that penance long and heavy for the ancient Mariner hath been accorded to the Polar Spirit, who returneth southward.

How long in that same fit I lay,
I have not to declare;
But ere my living life return'd,
I heard, and in my soul discern'd
Two voices in the air.

"Is it he?" quoth one, "is this the man?
By Him who died on cross,
With his cruel bow he laid full low
The harmless Albatross.

The Spirit who bideth by himself
In the land of mist and snow,
He loved the bird that loved the man
Who shot him with his bow."

The other was a softer voice,
As soft as honey-dew;
Quoth he, "The man hath penance done,
And penance more will do."

Part VI

The supernatural motion is retarded; the Mariner awakes, and his penance begins anew.

I woke, and we were sailing on
As in a gentle weather:
'Twas night, calm night, the Moon was high;
The dead men stood together.

All stood together on the deck,
For a charnel-dungeon fitter:
All fix'd on me their stony eyes,
That in the Moon did glitter.

The pang, the curse, with which they died,
Had never pass'd away:
I could not draw my eyes from theirs,
Nor turn them up to pray.

And now this spell was snapt: once more
I viewed the ocean green,
And look'd far forth, yet little saw
Of what had else been seen —

Th curse is finally expiated.

Like one that on a lonesome road
Doth walk in fear and dread,
And having once turn'd round, walks on,
And turns no more his head;
Because he knows a frightful fiend
Doth close behind him tread.

But soon there breathed a wind on me,
Nor sound nor motion made:
Its path was not upon the sea,
In ripple or in shade.

It raised my hair, it fann'd my cheek
Like a meadow-gale of spring —
It mingled strangely with my fears,
Yet it felt like a welcoming.

Swiftly, swiftly flew the ship,
Yet she sail'd softly too:
Sweetly, sweetly blew the breeze —
On me alone it blew.

O dream of joy! is this indeed
The lighthouse top I see?
Is this the hill? is this the kirk?
Is this mine own countree?

And the ancient Mariner beholdeth his native country.

We drifted o'er the harbour-bar,
And I with sobs did pray —
O let me be awake, my God!
Or let me sleep alway.

The harbour-bay was clear as glass,
So smoothly it was strewn!
And on the bay the moonlight lay,
And the shadow of the Moon.

The rock shone bright, the kirk no less
That stands above the rock:
The moonlight steep'd in silentness
The steady weathercock....

Part VII

. . . . .

The ancient Mariner earnestly entreateth the Hermit to shrieve him; and the penance of life falls on him.

"O shrieve me, shrieve me, holy man!"
The Hermit cross'd his brow.
"Say quick," quoth he, "I bid thee say —
What manner of man art thou?"

Forthwith this frame of mine was wrench'd
With a woful agony,
Which forced me to begin my tale;
And then it left me free.

And ever and anon throughout his future life an agony constraineth him to travel from land to land;

Since then, at an uncertain hour,
That agony returns:
And till my ghastly tale is told,
This heart within me burns.

I pass, like night, from land to land;
I have strange power of speech;
That moment that his face I see,
I know the man that must hear me:
To him my tale I teach.

What loud uproar bursts from that door!
The wedding-guests are there:
But in the garden-bower the bride
And bride-maids singing are:
And hark, the little vesper bell,
Which biddeth me to prayer!

O Wedding-Guest! this soul hath been
Alone on a wide, wide sea:
So lonely 'twas, that God Himself
Scarce seemèd there to be.

O sweeter than the marriage-feast,
'Tis sweeter far to me,
To walk together to the kirk
With a goodly company! —

To walk together to the kirk,
And all together pray,
While each to his great Father bends,
Old men, and babes, and loving friends,
And youths and maidens gay!

Farewell, farewell! but this I tell
To thee, thou Wedding-Guest!
He prayeth well, who loveth well
Both man and bird and beast.

And to teach, by his own example, love and reverence to all things that God made and loveth.

He prayeth best, who loveth best
All things both great and small;
For the dear God who loveth us,
He made and loveth all.'

The Mariner, whose eye is bright,
Whose beard with age is hoar,
Is gone: and now the Wedding-Guest
Turn'd from the bridegroom's door.

He went like one that hath been stunn'd,
And is of sense forlorn:
A sadder and a wiser man
He rose the morrow morn.

GUESTS

ANON

YET if His Majesty, our sovereign lord,
Should of his own accord
Friendly himself invite,
And say, 'I'll be your guest to-morrow night,'
How should we stir ourselves, call and command
All hands to work! 'Let no man idle stand!

'Set me fine Spanish tables in the hall;
See they be fitted all;
Let there be room to eat
And order taken that there want no meat.
See every sconce and candlestick made bright,
That without tapers they may give a light.

'Look to the presence: are the carpets spread,
The dazie o'er the head,
The cushions in the chairs,
And all the candles lighted on the stairs?
Perfume the chambers, and in any case
Let each man give attendance in his place!'

Thus, if a king were coming, would we do;
And 'twere good reason too;
For 'tis a duteous thing
To show all honour to an earthly king,
And after all our travail and our cost,
So he be pleased, to think no labour lost.

But at the coming of the King of Heaven
All's set at six and seven;
We wallow in our sin,
Christ cannot find a chamber in the inn.
We entertain Him always like a stranger,
And, as at first, still lodge Him in the manger.

THE PULLEY

George Herbert

WHEN God at first made Man,
Having a glass of blessings standing by —
Let us (said He) pour on him all we can;
Let the world's riches, which dispersèd lie,
    Contract into a span.

So strength first made a way,
Then beauty flow'd, then wisdom, honour, pleasure:
When almost all was out, God made a stay,
Perceiving that, alone of all His treasure,
    Rest in the bottom lay.

For if I should (said He)
Bestow this jewel also on My creature,
He would adore My gifts instead of Me,
And rest in Nature, not the God of Nature:
    So both should losers be.

Yet let him keep the rest,
But keep them with repining restlessness;
Let him be rich and weary, that at least,
If goodness lead him not, yet weariness
    May toss him to My breast.

THE KEY OF THE KINGDOM

Anon

THIS is the Key of the Kingdom:
In that Kingdom there is a city;
In that city is a town;
In that town there is a street;
In that street there winds a lane;
In that lane there is a yard;
In that yard there is a house;

In that house there waits a room;
In that room an empty bed;
And on that bed a basket —
A Basket of Sweet Flowers:
 Of Flowers, of Flowers;
 A Basket of Sweet Flowers.

Flowers in a Basket;
Basket on the bed;
Bed in the chamber;
Chamber in the house;
House in the weedy yard;
Yard in the winding lane;
Lane in the broad street;
Street in the high town;
Town in the city;
City in the Kingdom —
This is the Key of the Kingdom.
 Of the Kingdom this is the Key.

JERUSALEM

from MILTON *by* WILLIAM BLAKE

AND did those feet in ancient time
Walk upon England's mountains green?
And was the holy Lamb of God
On England's pleasant pastures seen?

And did the Countenance Divine
Shine forth upon our clouded hills?
And was Jerusalem builded here
Among these dark Satanic Mills?

Bring me my bow of burning gold!
Bring me my arrows of desire!
Bring me my spear! O clouds, unfold!
Bring me my chariot of fire!

I will not cease from mental fight,
Nor shall my sword sleep in my hand,
Till we have built Jerusalem
In England's green and pleasant land.

Note

It is interesting to contrast Blake's two final magnificent
crusading stanzas with Sir Walter Raleigh's gentle lines:

Give me my scallop-shell of Quiet,
   My Staff of Faith to walk upon,
My scrip of Joy, immortal diet,
   My bottle of salvation,
My gown of Glory, Hope's true gage,
   And thus I'll take my pilgrimage.

So Blake, the man of peace, demands armaments; Raleigh, the
man of war, asks only the emblems of tranquillity.   *A. P. W.*

HYMN ON THE MORNING OF CHRIST'S NATIVITY

John Milton
[*Extracts*]

It was the winter wild,
While the heaven-born Child,
   All meanly wrapt in the rude manger lies;
Nature in awe to him
Had doff'd her gawdy trim,
   With her great Master so to sympathize:
It was no season then for her
To wanton with the sun her lusty paramour.

Only with speeches fair
She woos the gentle air
   To hide her guilty front with innocent snow,
And on her naked shame,
Pollute with sinful blame,

  The saintly veil of maiden white to throw,
Confounded, that her Maker's eyes
Should look so near upon her foul deformities.

But He, her fears to cease,
Sent down the meek-eyed Peace,
 She, crowned with Olive green, came softly sliding
Down through the turning sphere
His ready harbinger,
 With turtle wing the amorous clouds dividing,
And waving wide her myrtle wand,
She strikes a universal peace through sea and land.

No war, or battle's sound
Was heard the world around,
 The idle spear and shield were high uphung;
The hookèd chariot stood
Unstained with hostile blood,
 The trumpet spake not to the armèd throng,
And kings sate still with awful eye,
As if they surely knew their sovran Lord was by.

But peaceful was the night
Wherein the Prince of Light
 His reign of peace upon the earth began:
The winds with wonder whist,
Smoothly the waters kist,
 Whispering new joys to the mild ocean,
Who now hath quite forgot to rave,
While birds of calm sit brooding on the charmèd wave.

The stars with deep amaze
Stand fixt in stedfast gaze,
 Bending one way their precious influence,
And will not take their flight,
For all the morning light,
 Or Lucifer that often warned them thence;
But in their glimmering orbs did glow,
Until their Lord himself bespake, and bid them go.

And though the shady gloom
Had given day her room,
  The sun himself withheld his wonted speed,
And hid his head for shame,
As his inferior flame,
  The new-enlightened world no more should need;
He saw a greater Sun appear
Than his bright throne, or burning axletree could bear.

The shepherds on the lawn,
Or ere the point of dawn,
  Sate simply chatting in a rustic row;
Full little thought they then
That the mighty Pan
  Was kindly come to live with them below;
Perhaps their loves, or else their sheep,
Was all that did their silly thoughts so busy keep.

When such music sweet
Their hearts and ears did greet
  As never was by mortal finger strook,
Divinely-warbled voice
Answering the stringèd noise,
  As all their souls in blissful rapture took
The air, such pleasure loth to lose,
With thousand echoes still prolongs each heavenly close.

Nature that heard such sound
Beneath the hollow round
  Of Cynthia's seat, the airy region thrilling,
Now was almost won
To think her part was done,
  And that her reign had here its last fulfilling;
She knew such harmony alone
Could hold all heaven and earth in happier union.

At last surrounds their sight
A globe of circular light,

That with long beams the shamefaced night arrayed,
The helmèd Cherubim
And sworded Seraphim,
   Are seen in glittering ranks with wings displayed,
Harping in loud and solemn quire,
With unexpressive notes to Heaven's new-born Heir.

Such music (as 'tis said)
Before was never made
   But when of old the sons of morning sung,
While the Creator great
His constellations set,
   And the well-balanced world on hinges hung,
And cast the dark foundations deep,
And bid the weltering waves their oozy channel keep.

Ring out, ye crystal spheres!
Once bless our human ears,
   (If ye have power to touch our senses so)
And let your silver chime
Move in melodious time;
   And let the base of heaven's deep organ blow
And with your ninefold harmony
Make up full consort to th' angelic symphony.

For if such holy song
Enwrap our fancy long,
   Time will run back, and fetch the age of gold,
And speckled vanity
Will sicken soon and die,
   And leprous sin will melt from earthly mould,
And Hell itself will pass away,
And leave her dolorous mansions to the peering day.

Yea, Truth, and Justice then
Will down return to men,
   Th' enamelled arras of the rainbow wearing,
And Mercy set between,
Throned in celestial sheen,

With radiant feet the tissued clouds downsteering,
And Heaven, as at some festival,
Will open wide the gates of her high palace hall.

But wisest Fate says No;
This must not yet be so;
    The Babe lies yet in smiling infancy,
That on the bitter cross
Must redeem our loss;
    So both Himself and us to glorify:
Yet first to those ychain'd in sleep,
The wakeful trump of doom must thunder through the deep,

With such a horrid clang
As on mount Sinai rang
    While the red fire, and smouldering clouds outbrake:
The agèd Earth aghast
With terror of that blast,
    Shall from the surface to the centre shake;
When, at the world's last session,
The dreadful Judge in middle air shall spread His throne.

And then at last our bliss
Full and perfect is,
    But now begins; for from this happy day
Th' old Dragon under ground
In straiter limits bound,
    Not half so far casts his usurpèd sway,
And, wroth to see his kingdom fail,
Swinges the scaly horror of his folded tail.

The oracles are dumb,
No voice or hideous hum
    Runs through the archèd roof in words deceiving.
Apollo from his shrine
Can no more divine,
    With hollow shriek the steep of Delphos leaving.
No nightly trance, or breathèd spell
Inspires the pale-eyed priest from the prophetic cell.

The lonely mountains o'er,
And the resounding shore,
  A voice of weeping heard, and loud lament;
From haunted spring, and dale
Edged with poplar pale,
  The parting Genius is with sighing sent,
With flower-enwoven tresses torn
The nymphs in twilight shade of tangled thickets mourn.

        ·   ·   ·

But see, the Virgin blest,
Hath laid her Babe to rest.
  Time is our tedious song should here have ending:
Heaven's youngest teemèd star,
Hath fixed her polished car,
  Her sleeping Lord with handmaid Lamp attending:
And all about the courtly stable,
Bright-harnessed angels sit in order serviceable.

THE MUSIC-MAKERS

ARTHUR O'SHAUGHNESSY

WE are the music-makers,
  And we are the dreamers of dreams,
Wandering by lone sea-breakers,
  And sitting by desolate streams;
World-losers and world-forsakers,
  On whom the pale moon gleams:
Yet we are the movers and shakers
  Of the world for ever, it seems.

With wonderful deathless ditties
We build up the world's great cities,
  And out of a fabulous story
  We fashion an empire's glory:
One man with a dream, at pleasure,

C

Shall go forth and conquer a crown;
And three with a new song's measure
　　Can trample an empire down.

We, in the ages lying
　　In the buried past of the earth,
Built Nineveh with our sighing,
　　And Babel itself with our mirth;
And o'erthrew them with prophesying
　　To the old of the new world's worth;
For each age is a dream that is dying,
　　Or one that is coming to birth.

TOM O' BEDLAM'S SONG

ANON

FROM the hag and hungry goblin
That into rags would rend ye
And the spirit that stands by the naked man
In the Book of Moons defend ye!
That of your five sound senses
You never be forsaken
Nor wander from your selves with Tom
Abroad to beg your bacon.
　　While I do sing 'Any food, any feeding,
　　Feeding, drink or clothing.'
　　Come dame or maid, be not afraid,
　　Poor Tom will injure nothing....

With a thought I took for Maudlin
And a cruse of cockle pottage,
With a thing thus tall, sky bless you all,
I befell into this dotage.
I slept not since the Conquest,
Till then I never wakèd
Till the roguish boy of love where I lay
Me found and stripped me naked.

And now I sing 'Any food, any feeding,
Feeding, drink or clothing.'
Come dame or maid, be not afraid,
Poor Tom will injure nothing....

When I short have shorn my sour face
And swigged my horny barrel
In an oaken inn I pound my skin
As a suit of gilt apparel.
The moon's my constant Mistress
And the lowly owl my marrow;
The flaming Drake and the Nightcrow make
Me music to my sorrow.
While I do sing 'Any food, any feeding,
Feeding, drink or clothing.'
Come dame or maid, be not afraid,
Poor Tom will injure nothing....

I know more than Apollo,
For oft when he lies sleeping
I see the stars at bloody wars
In the wounded welkin weeping,
The moon embrace her shepherd
And the queen of Love her warrior,
While the first doth horn the star of morn
And the next the heavenly Farrier,
While I do sing 'Any food, any feeding,
Feeding, drink or clothing.'
Come dame or maid, be not afraid,
Poor Tom will injure nothing.

With an host of furious fancies
Whereof I am commander,
With a burning spear, and a horse of air,
To the wilderness I wander.
By a knight of ghosts and shadows
I summoned am to tourney
Ten leagues beyond the wide world's end.
Methinks it is no journey.

Yet will I sing 'Any food, any feeding,
Feeding, drink or clothing.'
Come dame or maid, be not afraid,
Poor Tom will injure nothing.

STRENGTH

from SONG TO DAVID *by*

CHRISTOPHER SMART

STRONG is the horse upon his speed;
Strong in pursuit the rapid glede,
　　Which makes at once his game:
Strong the tall ostrich on the ground;
Strong through the turbulent profound
　　Shoots Xiphias to his aim.

Strong is the lion — like a coal
His eyeball, — like a bastion's mole
　　His chest against the foes:
Strong the gier-eagle on his sail;
Strong against tide th' enormous whale
　　Emerges as he goes.

But stronger still, in earth and air,
And in the sea, the man of prayer,
　　And far beneath the tide:
And in the seat to faith assign'd,
Where ask is have, where seek is find,
　　Where knock is open wide.

LEISURE

W. H. DAVIES

WHAT is this life if, full of care,
We have no time to stand and stare?

No time to stand beneath the boughs
And stare as long as sheep or cows.

No time to see, when woods we pass,
Where squirrels hide their nuts in grass.

No time to see, in broad daylight,
Streams full of stars, like skies at night.

No time to turn at Beauty's glance,
And watch her feet, how they can dance.

No time to wait till her mouth can
Enrich that smile her eyes began.

A poor life this if, full of care,
We have no time to stand and stare.

WEATHERS

Thomas Hardy

I

This is the weather the cuckoo likes,
        And so do I;
When showers betumble the chestnut spikes,
        And nestlings fly:
And the little brown nightingale bills his best,
And they sit outside at 'The Travellers' Rest,'
And maids come forth sprig-muslin drest,
And citizens dream of the south and west,
        And so do I.

II

This is the weather the shepherd shuns,
        And so do I;

When beeches drip in browns and duns,
     And thresh, and ply;
And hill-hid tides throb, throe on throe,
And meadow rivulets overflow,
And drops on gate-bars hang in a row,
And rooks in families homeward go,
     And so do I.

MARCH

from THE EARTHLY PARADISE *by*

WILLIAM MORRIS

SLAYER of the winter, art thou here again?
O welcome, thou that bring'st the summer nigh!
The bitter wind makes not thy victory vain,
Nor will we mock thee for thy faint blue sky.
Welcome, O March! whose kindly days and dry
Make April ready for the throstle's song.
Thou first redresser of the winter's wrong!

    Yea, welcome March! and though I die ere June,
Yet for the hope of life I give thee praise,
Striving to swell the burden of the tune
That even now I hear thy brown birds raise,
Unmindful of the past or coming days;
Who sing: 'O joy! a new year is begun:
What happiness to look upon the sun!'

    Ah, what begetteth all this storm of bliss
But Death himself, who crying solemnly,
E'en from the heart of sweet Forgetfulness,
Bids us 'Rejoice, lest pleasureless ye die.
Within a little time must ye go by.
Stretch forth your open hands, and while ye live
Take all the gifts that Death and Life may give.'

HOME-THOUGHTS, FROM ABROAD
Robert Browning

O to be in England
Now that April's there,
And whoever wakes in England
Sees, some morning, unaware,
That the lowest boughs and the brushwood sheaf
Round the elm-tree bole are in tiny leaf,
While the chaffinch sings on the orchard bough
In England — now!

And after April, when May follows,
And the whitethroat builds, and all the swallows!
Hark, where my blossom'd pear-tree in the hedge
Leans to the field and scatters on the clover
Blossoms and dewdrops — at the bent spray's edge —
That's the wise thrush; he sings each song twice over,
Lest you should think he never could recapture
The first fine careless rapture!
And though the fields look rough with hoary dew,
All will be gay when noontide wakes anew
The buttercups, the little children's dower
— Far brighter than this gaudy melon-flower!

SONNET XXXIII
William Shakespeare

Full many a glorious morning have I seen
   Flatter the mountain-tops with sovereign eye,
Kissing with golden face the meadows green,
   Gilding pale streams with heavenly alchemy;
Anon permit the basest clouds to ride
   With ugly rack on his celestial face,
And from the forlorn world his visage hide,
   Stealing unseen to west with this disgrace:
Even so my sun one early morn did shine,

With all-triumphant splendour on my brow;
But, out! alack! he was but one hour mine,
The region cloud hath masked him from me now.
    Yet him for this my love no whit disdaineth;
    Suns of the world may stain when heaven's sun staineth.

COURTESY

Hilaire Belloc

Of Courtesy, it is much less
Than Courage of Heart or Holiness,
Yet in my Walks it seems to me
That the Grace of God is in Courtesy.

On Monks I did in Storrington fall,
They took me straight into their Hall;
I saw Three Pictures on a wall,
And Courtesy was in them all.

The first the Annunciation;
The second the Visitation;
The third the Consolation,
Of God that was Our Lady's Son.

The first was of Saint Gabriel;
On Wings a-flame from Heaven he fell;
And as he went upon one knee
He shone with Heavenly Courtesy.

Our Lady out of Nazareth rode —
It was Her month of heavy load;
Yet was Her face both great and kind,
For Courtesy was in Her Mind.

The third it was our Little Lord,
Whom all the Kings in arms adored;
He was so small you could not see
His large intent of Courtesy.

Our Lord, that was Our Lady's Son,
Go bless you, People, one by one;
My Rhyme is written, my work is done.

A CHARM

RUDYARD KIPLING

TAKE of English earth as much
As either hand may rightly clutch.
In the taking of it breathe
Prayer for all who lie beneath.
Not the great nor well-bespoke,
But the mere uncounted folk
Of whose life and death is none
Report or lamentation.
  Lay that earth upon thy heart,
  And thy sickness shall depart!

It shall sweeten and make whole
Fevered breath and festered soul.
It shall mightily restrain
Over-busied hand and brain.
It shall ease thy mortal strife
'Gainst the immortal woe of life,
Till thyself, restored, shall prove
By what grace the Heavens do move.

Take of English flowers these —
Spring's full-facèd primroses,
Summer's wild wide-hearted rose,
Autumn's wall-flower of the close,
And, thy darkness to illume,
Winter's bee-thronged ivy-bloom.
Seek and serve them where they bide
From Candlemas to Christmas-tide,
  For these simples, used aright,
  Can restore a failing sight.

These shall cleanse and purify
Webbed and inward-turning eye;
These shall show thee treasure hid,
Thy familiar fields amid;
And reveal (which is thy need)
Every man a King indeed!

THE FAIRIES' FAREWELL

RICHARD CORBET

[Extract]

FAREWELL rewards and fairies,
  Good housewives now may say,
For now foul sluts in dairies
  Do fare as well as they.
And though they sweep their hearths no less
  Than maids were wont to do,
Yet who of late for cleanliness
  Finds sixpence in her shoe?

Lament, lament, old abbeys,
  The fairies lost command;
They did but change priests' babies,
  But some have changed your land:
And all your children stol'n from thence
  Are now grown puritans,
Who live as changelings ever since
  For love of your demains.

At morning and at evening both
  You merry were and glad,
So little care of sleep and sloth
  These pretty ladies had;
When Tom came home from labour,
  Or Ciss to milking rose,
Then merrily merrily went their tabor,
  And nimbly went their toes.

Witness those rings and roundelays
   Of theirs, which yet remain,
Were footed in Queen Mary's days
   On many a grassy plain;
But since of late Elizabeth,
   And later James, came in,
They never danced on any heath
   As when the time hath been.

By which we note the fairies
   Were of the old profession;
Their songs were Ave Maries,
   Their dances were procession:
But now, alas! they all are dead
   Or gone beyond the seas,
Or farther for religion fled,
   Or else they take their ease.

A tell-tale in their company
   They never could endure,
And whoso kept not secretly
   Their mirth was punished sure;
It was a just and Christian deed
   To pinch such black and blue:
O how the Commonwealth doth need
   Such Justices as you!...

THE HUNDREDTH PSALM
(Metrical Version)

All people that on earth do dwell,
Sing to the Lord with cheerful voice.
Him serve with mirth, his praise forth tell
Come ye before him and rejoice.

Know that the Lord is God indeed;
Without our aid he did us make:

We are his flock, he doth us feed,
And for his sheep he doth us take.

O enter then his gates with praise,
Approach with joy his courts unto;
Praise, laud, and bless his name always,
For it is seemly so to do.

For why? the Lord our God is good.
His mercy is for ever sure;
His truth at all times firmly stood,
And shall from age to age endure.

PROLOGUE

from THE EARTHLY PARADISE *by*

WILLIAM MORRIS

OF Heaven or Hell I have no power to sing,
I cannot ease the burden of your fears,
Or make quick-coming death a little thing,
Or bring again the pleasure of past years,
Nor for my words shall ye forget your tears,
Or hope again for aught that I can say,
The idle singer of an empty day.

But rather, when aweary of your mirth,
From full hearts still unsatisfied ye sigh,
And, feeling kindly unto all the earth,
Grudge every minute as it passes by,
Made the more mindful that the sweet days die —
Remember me a little then I pray,
The idle singer of an empty day.

The heavy trouble, the bewildering care
That weighs us down who live and earn our bread,
These idle verses have no power to bear;

So let me sing of names rememberèd,
Because they, living not, can ne'er be dead,
Or long time take their memory quite away
From us poor singers of an empty day.

Dreamer of dreams, born out of my due time,
Why should I strive to set the crooked straight?
Let it suffice me that my murmuring rhyme
Beats with light wing against the ivory gate,
Telling a tale not too importunate
To those who in the sleepy region stay,
Lulled by the singer of an empty day.

Folk say, a wizard to a northern king
At Christmas-tide such wondrous things did show,
That through one window men beheld the spring,
And through another saw the summer glow,
And through a third the fruited vines a-row,
While still, unheard, but in its wonted way,
Piped the drear wind of that December day.

So with this Earthly Paradise it is,
If ye will read aright, and pardon me,
Who strive to build a shadowy isle of bliss
Midmost the beating of the steely sea,
Where tossed about all hearts of men must be;
Whose ravening monsters mighty men shall slay,
Not the poor singer of an empty day.

UPHILL

Christina Rossetti

Does the road wind uphill all the way?
    Yes, to the very end.
Will the day's journey take the whole long day?
    From morn to night, my friend.

But is there for the night a resting-place?
   A roof for when the slow, dark hours begin.
May not the darkness hide it from my face?
   You cannot miss that inn.

Shall I meet other wayfarers at night?
   Those who have gone before.
Then must I knock, or call when just in sight?
   They will not keep you waiting at that door.

Shall I find comfort, travel-sore and weak?
   Of labour you shall find the sum.
Will there be beds for me and all who seek?
   Yea, beds for all who come.

EVE

Ralph Hodgson

Eve, with her basket, was
Deep in the bells and grass,
Wading in bells and grass
Up to her knees,
Picking a dish of sweet
Berries and plums to eat,
Down in the bells and grass
Under the trees.

Mute as a mouse in a
Corner the cobra lay,
Curled round a bough of the
Cinnamon tall....
Now to get even and
Humble proud heaven and —
Now was the moment or
Never at all.

'Eva!' Each syllable
Light as a flower fell,
'Eva!' he whispered the
Wondering maid,
Soft as a bubble sung
Out of a linnet's lung,
Soft and most silverly
'Eva!' he said.

Picture that orchard sprite,
Eve, with her body white,
Supple and smooth to her
Slim finger tips,
Wondering, listening,
Listening, wondering,
Eve with a berry
Half-way to her lips.

Oh, had our simple Eve
Seen through the make-believe!
Had she but known the
Pretender he was!
Out of the boughs he came,
Whispering still her name,
Tumbling in twenty rings
Into the grass.

Here was the strangest pair
In the world anywhere,
Eve in the bells and grass
Kneeling, and he
Telling his story low....
Singing birds saw them go
Down the dark path to
The Blasphemous Tree.

Oh, what a clatter when
Titmouse and Jenny Wren
Saw him successful and
Taking his leave!
How the birds rated him!
How they all hated him!
How they all pitied
Poor motherless Eve!

Picture her crying,
Outside in the lane,
Eve, with no dish of sweet
Berries and plums to eat,
Haunting the gate of the
Orchard in vain....
Picture that lewd delight
Under the hill to-night —
'Eva!' the toast goes round,
'Eva!' again.

ALL THAT'S PAST

WALTER DE LA MARE

VERY old are the woods;
  And the buds that break
Out of the brier's boughs,
  When March winds wake,
So old with their beauty are —
  Oh, no man knows
Through what wild centuries
  Roves back the rose.

Very old are the brooks;
  And the rills that rise
Where snow sleeps cold beneath
  The azure skies

Sing such a history
   Of come and gone,
Their every drop is as wise
   As Solomon.

Very old are we men;
   Our dreams are tales
Told in dim Eden
   By Eve's nightingales;
We wake and whisper awhile,
   But, the day gone by,
Silence and sleep like fields
   Of amaranth lie.

VAIN QUESTIONING

WALTER DE LA MARE

WHAT needest thou? — a few brief hours of rest
Wherein to seek thyself in thine own breast;
A transient silence wherein truth could say
Such was thy constant hope, and this thy way? —
   O burden of life that is
   A livelong tangle of perplexities!

What seekest thou? — a truce from that thou art;
Some steadfast refuge from a fickle heart;
Still to be thou, and yet no thing of scorn,
To find no stay here, and yet not forlorn? —
   O riddle of life that is
   An endless war 'twixt contrarieties.

Leave this vain questioning. Is not sweet the rose?
Sings not the wild bird ere to rest he goes?
Hath not in miracle brave June returned?
Burns not her beauty as of old it burned?
   O foolish one to roam
   So far in thine own mind away from home!

Where blooms the flower when her petals fade,
Where sleepeth echo by earth's music made,
Where all things transient to the changeless win,
There waits the peace thy spirit dwelleth in.

CITIES AND THRONES AND POWERS

RUDYARD KIPLING

Cities and Thrones and Powers,
Stand in Time's eye,
Almost as long as flowers,
Which daily die.
But, as new buds put forth
To glad new men,
Out of the spent and unconsidered Earth
The Cities rise again.

This season's Daffodil,
She never hears
What change, what chance, what chill,
Cut down last year's:
But with bold countenance,
And knowledge small,
Esteems her seven days' continuance
To be perpetual.

So Time that is o'er-kind,
To all that be,
Ordains us e'en as blind,
As bold as she:
That in our very death,
And burial sure,
Shadow to shadow, well persuaded, saith,
'See how our works endure!'

2 . GOOD FIGHTING

FIGHTING — or anyway soldiering — is my profession and I might be presumed to have memorized a large and representative collection of battle songs. Looking over these military trophies of my poetical memory, as one might spread out from the game-bag the results of a day's shooting, I find them rather a mixed lot; and some of them are perhaps of the type that get entered in the 'various' column of a game-book. War is not only a grim but mainly a dull business and does not tend to inspire poetry in those who practise it. Love poems are usually written by those who have been in love; battle poems are seldom written by those who have been in battle. The three poems which head this section, written by men who fought and died in the last war (*Into Battle*, *Magpies in Picardy*, and *Rendezvous*), deal with nature more than with fighting. Only one great general wrote poetry, so far as my recollection serves — Montrose, unless we include Sir Walter Raleigh, who was certainly a poet and a very dashing commander. Montrose was a good general and not a bad poet; his best known lines will be found in Section 8 of this anthology. Horace once had a command of troops, but I feel that it must have been a small one; and at his only serious battle, Philippi, he was on the losing side and had to take to his heels. He fought, as he remarks in one of his Odes, 'not without glory'; but that was on the fields of love. 'Gentleman Johnny' Burgoyne, of the Saratoga disaster, dabbled in literature and wrote plays and verses. He must have been an amusing companion, but was not a great general — though a very gallant soldier — nor a good poet. Coleridge was a great but rather an odd poet; he must have been a very odd trooper of Dragoons.[1] The outlook towards poetry of the traditional English general (who has no greater reality than Colonel Blimp) is illustrated by a certain gallant and distinguished general of the Indian Wars who never quoted, or apparently knew, any other poetry than these two lines of his own composition:

> Damn your writing,
> Mind your fighting.

[1] I have since found other rather unexpected soldier poets. Ben Jonson served in Flanders. That strange unhappy genius E. A. Poe enlisted in the United States Army, and after two years in the ranks went to West Point from which he was dismissed in a few months.

No bad motto for the old times: even in these enlightened days a commander sometimes feels he could do with less correspondence.

The sonorous highly coloured battle-pieces (such as *Lepanto* or *Naseby*) are usually written by those who have never seen steel drawn or shot fired. The *Battle Hymn of the Republic* (an American national anthem), however, was written, not quite on the battlefield, but certainly within sight of 'the watch fires of a hundred circling camps'. The authoress wrote it during a visit to a Federal training camp in the American Civil War, taking the tune of *John Brown's Body*, the soldiers' marching song of the day. It may be more religion than battle, but it has a fire to match the spirit of the authoress, who said on her ninetieth birthday: 'I march to the brave music still.' So may we all.

The prototype of the poet, the tribal ballad-maker, had battle as his main theme; but as civilization progressed and the wandering fighting tribe became a peaceful settled people, the ballad-maker became a poet and dwelt rather on nature and love.

> Four things greater than all things are —
> Women and Horses and Power and War,

wrote Kipling in one of his ballads; but he ended the ballad thus:

> Two things greater than all things are,
> The first is Love, and the second War.
> And since we know not how War may prove,
> Heart of my heart, let us talk of Love!

And so the poet talks of love rather than of war; but all true men — and most poets are true men — feel at some time the supposed glamour of fighting and of the fighting man; and write lusty battle verses, good to read or declaim but singularly unlike the real thing. Of such are Chesterton's *Last Hero*; Macaulay's Lays (*Horatius* and *Lake Regillus*); and Flecker's *War Song of the Saracens*. Even Oscar Wilde wrote a martial poem (*Ave Imperatrix*) with some fine stanzas in it.

There are no examples here of the songs sung by the soldier himself. The British soldier's songs are usually too crude or too ribald to look well in print. I remember the first I heard when I joined my regiment in the South African War, at a period when the infantry trekked wearily and reluctantly over the veldt after far too mobile Boer commandos. It began plaintively:

> Oh why did I leave my little back room
> In Blooms-bur-ee,
> Where I could live for a pound a week
> In lux-ur-ee.

For some reason it used to drive my Commanding Officer to fury and he finally issued an order forbidding it. As a very young officer I thought he was wrong; as a Commander-in-Chief I am sure he was. It had its counterpart in the last war in such verses as:

> Why did we join the Army, boys?
> Why did we join the Army?
> Why did we come to France to fight?
> We must have been b————y well barmy.

Or the interminable:

> We're here because we're here
> Because we're here, because we're here,
> Oh, here we are, oh, here we are,
> Oh, here we are again.

Thackeray surely had little personal acquaintance with the fighting man, yet his *Chronicle of the Drum* is no bad representation of the point of view of the rank and file. Perhaps Butler was right when he wrote in *Hudibras*:

> There's but the twinkling of a star
> Between a man of peace and war.

A. P. W.

INTO BATTLE

Julian Grenfell

The naked earth is warm with spring,
  And with green grass and bursting trees
Leans to the sun's gaze glorying,
  And quivers in the sunny breeze;

And life is colour and warmth and light,
  And a striving evermore for these;
And he is dead who will not fight;
  And who dies fighting has increase.

The fighting man shall from the sun
  Take warmth, and life from the glowing earth;
Speed with the light-foot winds to run,
  And with the trees to newer birth;
And find, when fighting shall be done,
  Great rest, and fullness after dearth.

All the bright company of Heaven
  Hold him in their high comradeship,
The Dog-star, and the Sisters Seven,
  Orion's Belt and sworded hip.

The woodland trees that stand together,
  They stand to him each one a friend;
They gently speak in the windy weather;
  They guide to valley and ridge's end.

The kestrel hovering by day,
  And the little owls that call by night,
Bid him be swift and keen as they,
  As keen of ear, as swift of sight.
The blackbird sings to him, 'Brother, brother,
  If this be the last song you shall sing,
Sing well, for you may not sing another;
  Brother, sing.'

In dreary, doubtful, waiting hours,
  Before the brazen frenzy starts,
The horses show him nobler powers;
  O patient eyes, courageous hearts!

And when the burning moment breaks,
  And all things else are out of mind,

And only joy of battle takes
  Him by the throat, and makes him blind,

Through joy and blindness he shall know,
  Not caring much to know, that still
Nor lead nor steel shall reach him, so
  That it be not the Destined Will.

The thundering line of battle stands,
  And in the air death moans and sings;
But Day shall clasp him with strong hands,
  And Night shall fold him in soft wings.

MAGPIES IN PICARDY

T. P. CAMERON WILSON

THE magpies in Picardy
Are more than I can tell.
They flicker down the dusty roads
And cast a magic spell
On the men who march through Picardy,
Through Picardy to hell.

(The blackbird flies with panic,
The swallow goes with light,
The finches move like ladies,
The owl floats by at night;
But the great and flashing magpie
He flies as artists might.)

A magpie in Picardy
Told me secret things —
Of the music in white feathers,
And the sunlight that sings
And dances in deep shadows —
He told me with his wings.

(The hawk is cruel and rigid,
He watches from a height;
The rook is slow and sombre,
The robin loves to fight;
But the great and flashing magpie
He flies as lovers might.)

He told me that in Picardy,
An age ago or more,
While all his fathers still were eggs,
These dusty highways bore
Brown, singing soldiers marching out
Through Picardy to war.

He said that still through chaos
Works on the ancient plan,
And two things have altered not
Since first the world began —
The beauty of the wild green earth
And the bravery of man.

(For the sparrow flies unthinking
And quarrels in his flight.
The heron trails his legs behind,
The lark goes out of sight;
But the great and flashing magpie
He flies as poets might.)

RENDEZVOUS

Alan Seeger

I HAVE a rendezvous with Death
At some disputed barricade,
When Spring comes back with rustling shade
And apple-blossoms fill the air —
I have a rendezvous with Death
When Spring brings back blue days and fair.

It may be he shall take my hand
And lead me into his dark land
And close my eyes and quench my breath —
It may be I shall pass him still.
I have a rendezvous with Death
On some scarred slope of battered hill,
When Spring comes round again this year
And the first meadow-flowers appear.

God knows 'twere better to be deep
Pillowed in silk and scented down,
Where love throbs out in blissful sleep,
Pulse nigh to pulse, and breath to breath,
Where hushed awakenings are dear ...
But I've a rendezvous with Death
At midnight in some flaming town,
When Spring trips north again this year,
And I to my pledged word am true,
I shall not fail that rendezvous.

THE PILGRIM

John Bunyan

Who would true valour see,
Let him come hither;
One here will constant be,
Come wind, come weather.
There's no discouragement
Shall make him once relent
His first avowed intent
To be a Pilgrim.

Who so beset him round
With dismal stories
Do but themselves confound;
His strength the more is.

No lion can him fright,
He'll with a giant fight,
But he will have a right
To be a Pilgrim.

Hobgoblin nor foul fiend
Can daunt his spirit:
He knows he at the end
Shall life inherit.
Then fancies fly away,
He'll fear not what men say,
He'll labour night and day
To be a Pilgrim.

INVICTUS

W. E. HENLEY

Out of the night that covers me,
   Black as the pit from pole to pole,
I thank whatever gods may be
   For my unconquerable soul.

In the fell clutch of circumstance
   I have not winced nor cried aloud.
Under the bludgeonings of chance
   My head is bloody, but unbow'd.

Beyond this place of wrath and tears
   Looms but the Horror of the shade,
And yet the menace of the years
   Finds and shall find me unafraid.

It matters not how strait the gate,
   How charged with punishments the scroll,
I am the master of my fate:
   I am the captain of my soul.

BOXING

from VERSES ON GAMES *by*

RUDYARD KIPLING

READ here the moral roundly writ
  For him who into battle goes —
Each soul that hitting hard or hit,
  Endureth gross or ghostly foes.
  Prince, blown by many overthrows,
Half blind with shame, half choked with dirt,
  Man cannot tell, but Allah knows
  How much the other side was hurt!

Note

The last two lines illustrate my favourite military maxim, that when things are going badly in battle the best tonic is to take one's mind off one's own troubles by considering what a rotten time one's opponent must be having.   *A. P. W.*

BATTLE HYMN OF THE AMERICAN REPUBLIC

JULIA WARD HOWE

MINE eyes have seen the glory of the coming of the Lord:
He is trampling out the vintage where the grapes of wrath are stored;
He hath loosed the fatal lightning of his terrible swift sword:
      His truth is marching on.

I have seen Him in the watchfires of a hundred circling camps;
They have builded Him an altar in the evening dews and damps;
I can read His righteous sentence by the dim and flaring lamps:
      His day is marching on.

I have read a fiery gospel writ in burnish'd rows of steel:
'As ye deal with my contemners, so with you my grace shall deal;
Let the Hero, born of woman, crush the serpent with His heel!
      Since God is marching on.'

He has sounded forth the trumpet that shall never call retreat;
He is sifting out the hearts of men before His judgment seat;
O, be swift, my soul to answer Him, be jubilant, my feet!
       Our God is marching on.

In the beauty of the lilies Christ was born, across the sea,
With a glory in His bosom that transfigures you and me:
As He died to make men holy, let us die to make men free,
       While God is marching on.

LEPANTO

G. K. CHESTERTON

WHITE founts falling in the courts of the sun,
And the Soldan of Byzantium is smiling as they run;
There is laughter like the fountains in that face of all men feared,
It stirs the forest darkness, the darkness of his beard,
It curls the blood-red crescent, the crescent of his lips,
For the inmost sea of all the earth is shaken with his ships.
They have dared the white republics up the capes of Italy,
They have dashed the Adriatic round the Lion of the Sea,
And the Pope has cast his arms abroad for agony and loss,
And called the kings of Christendom for swords about the Cross,
The cold queen of England is looking in the glass;
The shadow of the Valois is yawning at the Mass;
From evening isles fantastical rings faint the Spanish gun,
And the Lord upon the Golden Horn is laughing in the sun.

Dim drums throbbing, in the hills half heard,
Where only on a nameless throne a crownless prince has stirred,
Where, risen from a doubtful seat and half-attainted stall,
The last knight of Europe takes weapons from the wall,
The last and lingering troubadour to whom the bird has sung,
That once went singing southward when all the world was young,
In that enormous silence, tiny and unafraid,
Comes up along a winding road the noise of the Crusade.
Strong gongs groaning as the guns boom far,

Don John of Austria is going to the war,
Stiff flags straining in the night-blasts cold
In the gloom black-purple, in the glint old-gold,
Torchlight crimson on the copper kettle-drums,
Then the tuckets, then the trumpets, then the cannon, and he comes.
Don John laughing in the brave beard curled,
Spurning of his stirrups like the thrones of all the world,
Holding his head up for a flag of all the free.
Love-light of Spain — hurrah!
Death-light of Africa!
Don John of Austria
Is riding to the sea.

Mahound is in his paradise above the evening star,
(*Don John of Austria is going to the war.*)
He moves a mighty turban on the timeless houri's knees,
His turban that is woven of the sunsets and the seas.
He shakes the peacock gardens as he rises from his ease,
And he strides among the tree-tops and is taller than the trees,
And his voice through all the garden is a thunder sent to bring
Black Azrael and Ariel and Ammon on the wing.
Giants and the Genii,
Multiplex of wing and eye,
Whose strong obedience broke the sky
When Solomon was king.

They rush in red and purple from the red clouds of the morn,
From temples where the yellow gods shut up their eyes in scorn;
They rise in green robes roaring from the green hells of the sea
Where fallen skies and evil hues and eyeless creatures be;
On them the sea-valves cluster and the grey sea-forests curl,
Splashed with a splendid sickness, the sickness of the pearl;
They swell in sapphire smoke out of the blue cracks of the ground, —
They gather and they wonder and give worship to Mahound.
And he saith, 'Break up the mountains where the hermit-folk may
And sift the red and silver sands lest bone of saint abide,   [hide.
And chase the Giaours flying night and day, not giving rest,
For that which was our trouble comes again out of the west.

We have set the seal of Solomon on all things under sun,
Of knowledge and of sorrow and endurance of things done,
But a noise is in the mountains, in the mountains, and I know
The voice that shook our palaces — four hundred years ago:
It is he that saith not 'Kismet': it is he that knows not Fate;
It is Richard, it is Raymond, it is Godfrey in the gate!
It is he whose loss is laughter when he counts the wager worth,
Put down your feet upon him, that our peace be on the earth.'
For he heard drums groaning and he heard guns jar,
(*Don John of Austria is going to the war.*)
Sudden and still — hurrah!
Bolt from Iberia!
Don John of Austria
Is gone by Alcalar.

St Michael's on his Mountain in the sea-roads of the north
(*Don John of Austria is girt and going forth.*)
Where the grey seas glitter and the sharp tides shift
And the sea folk labour and the red sails lift.
He shakes his lance of iron and he claps his wings of stone;
The noise is gone through Normandy; the noise is gone alone;
The North is full of tangled things and texts and aching eyes
And dead is all the innocence of anger and surprise,
And Christian killeth Christian in a narrow dusty room,
And Christian dreadeth Christ that hath a newer face of doom,
And Christian hateth Mary that God kissed in Galilee,
But Don John of Austria is riding to the sea.
Don John calling through the blast and the eclipse,
Crying with the trumpet, with the trumpet of his lips,
Trumpet that sayeth ha!
    Domino Gloria!
Don John of Austria
Is shouting to the ships.

King Philip's in his closet with the Fleece about his neck,
(*Don John of Austria is armed upon the deck.*)
The walls are hung with velvet that is black and soft as sin,
And little dwarfs creep out of it and little dwarfs creep in.

He holds a crystal phial that has colours like the moon,
He touches, and it tingles, and he trembles very soon,
And his face is as a fungus of a leprous white and grey
Like plants in the high houses that are shuttered from the day,
And death is in the phial, and the end of noble work,
But Don John of Austria has fired upon the Turk.
Don John's hunting, and his hounds have bayed —
Booms away past Italy the rumour of his raid.
Gun upon gun, ha! ha!
Gun upon gun, hurrah!
Don John of Austria
Has loosed the cannonade.

The Pope was in his chapel before day or battle broke,
(*Don John of Austria is hidden in the smoke.*)
The hidden room in a man's house where God sits all the year,
The secret window whence the world looks small and very dear.
He sees as in a mirror on the monstrous twilight sea
The crescent of his cruel ships whose name is mystery;
They fling great shadows foe-wards, making Cross and Castle dark,
They veil the plumèd lions on the galleys of St Mark;
And above the ships are palaces of brown, black-bearded chiefs,
And below the ships are prisons, where with multitudinous griefs,
Christian captives sick and sunless, all a labouring race repines
Like a race in sunken cities, like a nation in the mines.
They are lost like slaves that swat, and in the skies of morning hung
The stairways of the tallest gods when tyranny was young.
They are countless, voiceless, hopeless as those fallen or fleeing on
Before the high Kings' horses in the granite of Babylon.
And many a one grows witless in his quiet room in hell
Where a yellow face looks inward through the lattice of his cell,
And he finds his God forgotten, and he seeks no more a sign —
(*But Don John of Austria has burst the battle-line!*)
Don John pounding from the slaughter-painted poop,
Purpling all the ocean like a bloody pirate's sloop,
Scarlet running over on the silvers and the golds,
Breaking of the hatches up and bursting of the holds,
Thronging of the thousands up that labour under sea,

White for bliss and blind for sun and stunned for liberty.
Vivat Hispania!
Domino Gloria!
Don John of Austria
Has set his people free!

Cervantes on his galley sets the sword back in the sheath
(*Don John of Austria rides homeward with a wreath.*)
And he sees across a weary land a straggling road in Spain,
Up which a lean and foolish knight forever rides in vain,
And he smiles, but not as Sultans smile, and settles back the blade ...
(*But Don John of Austria rides home from the Crusade.*)

Note

A family of my acquaintance is fond of declaiming this poem in
chorus on festive occasions. Don John is a great hero of theirs
consequently; but I am afraid he was not always the high-souled
crusader of Chesterton's stirring poem; perhaps success at Le-
panto turned his head. Certainly in the latter part of his short life
he was an ambitious schemer whose favourite plan was to land a
Spanish force in Scotland or England, to marry Mary Queen of
Scots, and in her name displace Elizabeth on the throne of
England. He was a natural son of the famous Emperor Charles V
by an amorous lady called Barbara Blomberg, and so half-brother
to Philip II of Spain, the Philip of the Armada, who seems to have
been jealous of Don John's enterprises and discouraged them. It
was not till after Don John's death that he launched the Armada,
under command of a land-lubber. Don John would have been a
better match on the high seas for Drake than the many-syllabled
Medina-Sidonia.

Lepanto was the last great battle in which the motive power was
supplied by galley slaves.

Cervantes of the final stanza, who according to Byron 'smiled
Spain's chivalry away', was badly wounded at Lepanto, and had
one hand maimed for life. He would therefore have had some
difficulty in settling his sword back into its sheath — certainly in
doing so with a smile. If the image of the 'lean and foolish knight',

Don Quixote, was in his brain at Lepanto, it took a long time to emerge; it was more than thirty years later before he and Sancho Panza were created in print. Meantime Cervantes had had many adventures which included capture by Barbary Corsairs and imprisonment for some years in Algiers; a government post which entailed fitting out the Armada; and imprisonment in Spain.   *A. P. W.*

LONDON UNDER BOMBARDMENT

GRETA BRIGGS

I, who am known as London, have faced stern times before,
Having fought and ruled and traded for a thousand years and more;
I knew the Roman legions and the harsh-voiced Danish hordes;
I heard the Saxon revels, saw blood on the Norman swords.
But, though I am scarred by battle, my grim defenders vow
Never was I so stately nor so well-beloved as now.
The lights that burn and glitter in the exile's lonely dream,
The lights of Piccadilly, and those that used to gleam
Down Regent-street and Kingsway may now no longer shine,
But other lights keep burning, and their splendour, too, is mine,
Seen in the work-worn faces and glimpsed in the steadfast eyes
When little homes lie broken and death descends from the skies.
The bombs have shattered my churches, have torn my streets apart,
But they have not bent my spirit and they shall not break my heart.
For my people's faith and courage are lights of London town
Which still would shine in legends though my last broad bridge were
down.

Note

I read these verses in an Egyptian newspaper while flying from Cairo to Barce in Cyrenaica at the beginning of April 1941, to try to deal with Rommel's counter-attack. I was uncomfortable in body — for the bomber was cramped and draughty — and in mind for I knew I had been caught with insufficient strength to meet a heavy counter-attack; reading this poem and committing it to memory did something to relieve my discomforts of body and mind.   *A. P. W.*

D

A ST HELENA LULLABY

RUDYARD KIPLING

'How far is St Helena from a little child at play?'
What makes you want to wander there with all the world between?
Oh, Mother, call your son again or else he'll run away.
(*No one thinks of winter when the grass is green!*)

'How far is St Helena from a fight in Paris street?'
I haven't time to answer now — the men are falling fast.
The guns begin to thunder, and the drums begin to beat.
(*If you take the first step, you will take the last!*)

'How far is St Helena from the field of Austerlitz?'
You couldn't hear me if I told — so loud the cannons roar.
But not so far for people who are living by their wits.
(*'Gay go up' means 'Gay go down' the wide world o'er!*)

'How far is St Helena from an Emperor of France?'
I cannot see — I cannot tell — the crowns they dazzle so.
The Kings sit down to dinner, and the Queens stand up to dance.
(*After open weather you may look for snow!*)

'How far is St Helena from the Capes of Trafalgar?'
A longish way — a longish way — with ten year more to run.
It's South across the water underneath a falling star.
(*What you cannot finish you must leave undone!*)

'How far is St Helena from the Beresina ice?'
An ill way — a chill way — the ice begins to crack.
But not so far for gentlemen who never took advice.
(*When you can't go forward you must e'en come back!*)

'How far is St Helena from the field of Waterloo?'
A near way — a clear way — the ship will take you soon
A pleasant place for gentlemen with little left to do.
(*Morning never tries you till the afternoon!*)

'How far from St Helena to the Gate of Heaven's Grace?'
That no one knows — that no one knows — and no one ever will.
But fold your hands across your heart and cover up your face,
And after all your trapesings, child, lie still!

Note

Many hundreds of books have been written about Napoleon's career but I know of no better summing up in a short space than Kipling's verses, though they are in wrong order chronologically; Austerlitz was after Napoleon was crowned Emperor and after Trafalgar, so that verse three ought logically (or should it be 'logistically', following the idiom of our American allies?) to come after the two verses that follow it. Did Kipling deliberately alter the order for dramatic effect, or did he just forget to verify his references? De la Mare's comment on Napoleon's monstrous egotism follows; it may have been inspired by the well-known conclusion of the letter in which Napoleon recorded the complete destruction of his army in 1812 — 'The Emperor is in excellent health'.   *A. P. W.*

NAPOLEON

WALTER DE LA MARE

'What is the world, O soldiers?
  It is I:
I, this incessant snow,
  This northern sky;
Soldiers, this solitude
  Through which we go
    Is I.'

THE REVEILLE

BRET HARTE

HARK! I hear the tramp of thousands,
  And of armèd men the hum;
Lo! a nation's hosts have gathered
  Round the quick alarming drum, —

Saying, 'Come,
  Freemen, come!
Ere your heritage be wasted,' said the quick alarming drum.

'Let me of my heart take counsel:
    War is not of life the sum;
Who shall stay and reap the harvest
    When the autumn days shall come?'
      But the drum
      Echoed, 'Come!
Death shall reap the braver harvest,' said the solemn sounding drum.

'But when won the coming battle,
    What of profit springs therefrom?
What if conquest, subjugation,
    Even greater ills become?
      But the drum
      Answered, 'Come!
You must do the sum to prove it,' said the Yankee-answering drum.

'What if, 'mid the cannons' thunder,
    Whistling shot and bursting bomb,
When my brothers fall around me,
    Should my heart grow cold and numb?'
      But the drum
      Answered, 'Come!
Better there in death united, than in life a recreant, Come!'

Thus they answered, — hoping, fearing,
    Some in faith, and doubting some,
Till a trumpet-voice proclaiming,
    Said, 'My chosen people, come!'
      Then the drum,
      Lo! was dumb,
For the great heart of the nation, throbbing, answered, 'Lord we,
                                                          come!'

THE LAST HERO

G. K. CHESTERTON

THE wind blew out from Bergen from the dawning to the day,
There was a wreck of trees and fall of towers a score of miles away,
And drifted like a livid leaf I go before its tide,
Spewed out of house and stable, beggared of flag and bride.
The heavens are bowed about my head, shouting like seraph wars,
With rains that might put out the sun and clean the sky of stars,
Rains like the fall of ruined seas from secret worlds above,
The roaring of the rains of God none but the lonely love.
Feast in my hall, O foemen, and eat and drink and drain,
You never loved the sun in heaven as I have loved the rain.

The chance of battle changes — so may all battle be;
I stole my lady bride from them, they stole her back from me.
I rent her from her red-roofed hall, I rode and saw arise
More lovely than the living flowers the hatred in her eyes.
She never loved me, never bent, never was less divine;
The sunset never loved me; the wind was never mine.
Was it all nothing that she stood imperial in duresse?
Silence itself made softer with the sweeping of her dress.
O you who drain the cup of life, O you who wear the crown,
You never loved a woman's smile as I have loved her frown.

The wind blew out from Bergen from the dawning to the day,
They ride and run with fifty spears to break and bar my way,
I shall not die alone, alone, but kin to all the powers,
As merry as the ancient sun and fighting like the flowers.
How white their steel, how bright their eyes! I love each laughing
                                                            knave,
Cry high and bid him welcome to the banquet of the brave.
Yea, I will bless them as they bend and love them where they lie,
When on their skulls the sword I swing falls shattering from the sky.
The hour when death is like a light and blood is like a rose, —
You never loved your friends, my friends, as I shall love my foes.

Know you what earth shall lose to-night, what rich uncounted loans,
What heavy gold of tales untold you bury with my bones?
My loves in deep dim meadows, my ships that rode at ease,
Ruffling the purple plumage of strange and secret seas.
To see this fair earth as it is to me alone was given,
The blow that breaks my brow to-night shall break the dome of
The skies I saw, the trees I saw after no eyes shall see.   [heaven.
To-night I die the death of God: the stars shall die with me:
One sound shall sunder all the spears and break the trumpet's breath:
You never laughed in all your life as I shall laugh in death.

A CONSECRATION

John Masefield

Not of the princes and prelates with periwigged charioteers
Riding triumphantly laurelled to lap the fat of the years,
Rather the scorned — the rejected — the men hemmed in with spears;

The men of the tattered battalion which fights till it dies,
Dazed with the dust of the battle, the din and the cries,
The men with the broken heads and the blood running into their eyes.

Not the be-medalled Commander, beloved of the throne,
Riding cock-horse to parade when the bugles are blown,
But the lads who carried the koppie and cannot be known.

Not the ruler for me, but the ranker, the tramp of the road,
The slave with the sack on his shoulders pricked on with the goad,
The man with too weighty a burden, too weary a load.

The sailor, the stoker of steamers, the man with the clout,
The chantyman bent at the halliards putting a tune to the shout,
The drowsy man at the wheel and the tired look-out.

Others may sing of the wine and the wealth and the mirth,
The portly presence of potentates goodly in girth; —
Mine be the dirt and the dross, the dust and scum of the earth!

Theirs be the music, the colour, the glory, the gold;
Mine be a handful of ashes, a mouthful of mould.
Of the maimed, of the halt and the blind in the rain and the cold —

Of these shall my songs be fashioned, my tale be told. Amen.

SAY NOT THE STRUGGLE

ARTHUR HUGH CLOUGH

Say not the struggle naught availeth,
    The labour and the wounds are vain,
The enemy faints not, nor faileth,
    And as things have been they remain.

If hopes were dupes, fears may be liars;
    It may be, in yon smoke concealed,
Your comrades chase e'en now the fliers,
    And, but for you, possess the field.

For while the tired waves, vainly breaking,
    Seem here no painful inch to gain,
Far back, through creeks and inlets making,
    Comes silent, flooding in, the main,

And not by eastern windows only,
    When daylight comes, comes in the light,
In front, the sun climbs slow, how slowly,
    But westward, look, the land is bright.

TO-MORROW

JOHN MASEFIELD

Oh yesterday the cutting edge drank thirstily and deep,
The upland outlaws ringed us in and herded us as sheep,
They drove us from the stricken field and bayed us into keep;
    But to-morrow,
  By the living God, we'll try the game again!

Oh yesterday our little troop was ridden through and through,
Our swaying, tattered pennons fled, a broken, beaten few,
And all a summer afternoon they hunted us and slew;
                    But to-morrow,
    By the living God, we'll try the game again!

And here upon the turret-top the bale-fire glowers red,
The wake-lights burn and drip about our hacked, disfigured dead,
And many a broken heart is here and many a broken head;
                    But to-morrow,
    By the living God, we'll try the game again!

THE EVE OF WATERLOO

from CHILDE HAROLD'S PILGRIMAGE *by*

LORD BYRON

THERE was a sound of revelry by night,
And Belgium's capital had gathered then
Her Beauty and her Chivalry, and bright
The lamps shone o'er fair women and brave men;
A thousand hearts beat happily; and when
Music arose with its voluptuous swell,
Soft eyes looked love to eyes which spake again,
And all went merry as a marriage bell;
But hush! hark! a deep sound strikes like a rising knell!

Did ye not hear it? — No; 'twas but the wind,
Or the car rattling o'er the stony street;
On with the dance! let joy be unconfined;
No sleep till morn, when Youth and Pleasure meet
To chase the glowing Hours with flying feet —
But hark! — that heavy sound breaks in once more,
As if the clouds its echo would repeat;
And nearer, clearer, deadlier than before!
Arm! Arm! it is — it is — the cannon's opening roar!

Within a windowed niche of that high hall
Sate Brunswick's fated chieftain; he did hear
That sound the first amidst the festival,
And caught its tone with Death's prophetic ear,
And when they smiled because he deemed it near,
His heart more truly knew that peal too well
Which stretched his father on a bloody bier,
And roused the vengeance blood alone could quell;
He rushed into the field, and, foremost fighting, fell.

Ah! then and there was hurrying to and fro,
And gathering tears, and tremblings of distress,
And cheeks all pale, which but an hour ago
Blushed at the praise of their own loveliness;
And there were sudden partings, such as press
The life from out young hearts, and choking sighs
Which ne'er might be repeated; who could guess
If ever more should meet those mutual eyes,
Since upon night so sweet such awful morn could rise?

And there was mounting in hot haste: the steed,
The mustering squadron, and the clattering car,
Went pouring forward with impetuous speed,
And swiftly forming in the ranks of war;
And the deep thunder peal on peal afar;
And near, the beat of the alarming drum
Roused up the soldier ere the morning star;
While thronged the citizens with terror dumb,
Or whispering, with white lips — 'The foe! they come! they come!'

And wild and high the 'Cameron's gathering' rose!
The war-note of Lochiel, which Albyn's hills
Have heard, and heard, too, have her Saxon foes:—
How in the noon of night that pibroch thrills,
Savage and shrill! But with the breath which fills
Their mountain-pipe, so fill the mountaineers
With the fierce native daring which instils
The stirring memory of a thousand years,
And Evan's, Donald's fame rings in each clansman's ears!

And Ardennes waves above them her green leaves,
Dewy with nature's tear-drops as they pass,
Grieving, if aught inanimate e'er grieves,
Over the unreturning brave, — alas!
Ere evening to be trodden like the grass
Which now beneath them, but above shall grow
In its next verdure, when this fiery mass
Of living valour, rolling on the foe
And burning with high hope, shall moulder cold and low.

Last noon beheld them full of lusty life,
Last eve in Beauty's circle proudly gay,
The midnight brought the signal-sound of strife,
The morn the marshalling in arms, — the day
Battle's magnificently stern array!
The thunder-clouds close o'er it, which when rent
The earth is covered thick with other clay,
Which her own clay shall cover, heaped and pent,
Rider and horse, — friend, foe, — in one red burial blent!

Note

The Duchess of Richmond's so-called 'Waterloo' ball has been
somewhat hyperbolically described by one biographer of Welling-
ton as 'more widely celebrated than any entertainment since
Belshazzar poured libations to his gods or Thaïs lighted Alexander
on his way to overwhelm the towers of Babylon'. Actually, the
ball took place on the night of Thursday, June 15th, three days
before Waterloo, on the eve of the battles of Ligny and Quatre
Bras. These engagements took place about twenty miles from
Brussels; and while it is possible to assume that cannon fire could
have been heard at that distance, the fighting did not begin till the
afternoon of the 16th; so that the Duke of Brunswick and other
guests would have required highly anticipatory ears to hear any
cannon fire at midnight; and in fact none was heard that night in
Brussels. Wellington himself attended the ball, and told his host
as he left: 'Napoleon has humbugged me, by Gad.'   *A. P. W.*

THE FIGHT AT THE BRIDGE

from HORATIUS *by*

LORD MACAULAY

MEANWHILE the Tuscan army,
  Right glorious to behold,
Came flashing back the noonday light,
Rank behind rank, like surges bright
  Of a broad sea of gold.
Four hundred trumpets sounded
  A peal of warlike glee,
As that great host, with measured tread,
And spears advanced, and ensigns spread,
Rolled slowly towards the bridge's head,
  Where stood the dauntless Three.

The Three stood calm and silent,
  And looked upon the foes,
And a great shout of laughter
  From all the vanguard rose:
And forth three chiefs came spurring
  Before that deep array;
To earth they sprang, their swords they drew,
And lifted high their shields, and flew
To win the narrow way;

Aunus from green Tifernum,
  Lord of the Hill of Vines;
And Seius, whose eight hundred slaves
  Sicken in Ilva's mines;
And Picus, long to Clusium
  Vassal in peace and war,
Who led to fight his Umbrian powers
From that grey crag where, girt with towers,
The fortress of Nequinum lowers
  O'er the pale waves of Nar.

Stout Lartius hurled down Aunus
  Into the stream beneath:

Herminius struck at Seius,
    And clove him to the teeth:
At Picus brave Horatius
    Darted one fiery thrust;
And the proud Umbrian's gilded arms
    Clashed in the bloody dust.

Then Ocnus of Falerii
    Rushed on the Roman Three;
And Lausulus of Urgo,
    The rover of the sea;
And Aruns of Volsinium,
    Who slew the great wild boar,
The great wild boar that had his den
Amidst the reeds of Cosa's fen,
And wasted fields, and slaughtered men,
    Along Albinia's shore.

Herminius smote down Aruns:
    Lartius laid Ocnus low:
Right to the heart of Lausulus
    Horatius sent a blow.
'Lie there,' he cried, 'fell pirate!
    No more, aghast and pale,
From Ostia's walls the crowd shall mark
The track of thy destroying bark.
No more Campania's hinds shall fly
To woods and caverns when they spy
    Thy thrice accursed sail.'

But now no sound of laughter
    Was heard among the foes.
A wild and wrathful clamour
    From all the vanguard rose.
Six spears' lengths from the entrance
    Halted that deep array,
And for a space no man came forth
    To win the narrow way.

But hark! the cry is Astur:
  And lo! the ranks divide;
And the great Lord of Luna
  Comes with his stately stride.
Upon his ample shoulders
  Clangs loud the four-fold shield,
And in his hand he shakes the brand
  Which none but he can wield.

He smiled on those bold Romans
  A smile serene and high;
He eyed the flinching Tuscans,
  And scorn was in his eye.
Quoth he, 'The she-wolf's litter
  Stand savagely at bay:
But will ye dare to follow,
  If Astur clears the way?'

Then, whirling up his broadsword
  With both hands to the height,
He rushed against Horatius,
  And smote with all his might.
With shield and blade Horatius
  Right deftly turned the blow.
The blow, though turned, came yet too nigh;
It missed his helm, but gashed his thigh:
The Tuscans raised a joyful cry
  To see the red blood flow.

He reeled, and on Herminius
  He leaned one breathing space;
Then, like a wild cat mad with wounds,
  Sprang right at Astur's face.
Through teeth, and skull, and helmet
  So fierce a thrust he sped,
The good sword stood a hand-breadth out
  Behind the Tuscan's head.

And the great Lord of Luna
 Fell at that deadly stroke,
As falls on Mount Alvernus
 A thunder-smitten oak.
Far o'er the crashing forest
 The giant arms lie spread;
And the pale augurs, muttering low,
 Gaze on the blasted head.

On Astur's throat Horatius
 Right firmly pressed his heel,
And thrice and four times tugged amain,
 Ere he wrenched out the steel.
'And see,' he cried, 'the welcome,
 Fair guests, that waits you here!
What noble Lucumo comes next
 To taste our Roman cheer?'

But at his haughty challenge
 A sullen murmur ran,
Mingled of wrath, and shame, and dread,
 Along that glittering van.
There lacked not men of prowess,
 Nor men of lordly race;
For all Etruria's noblest
 Were round the fatal place.

But all Etruria's noblest
 Felt their hearts sink to see
On the earth the bloody corpses,
 In the path the dauntless Three:
And, from the ghastly entrance
 Where those bold Romans stood,
All shrank, like boys who unaware,
Ranging the woods to start a hare,
Come to the mouth of the dark lair
Where, growling low, a fierce old bear
 Lies amidst bones and blood.

Was none who would be foremost
  To lead such dire attack:
But those behind cried 'Forward!'
  And those before cried 'Back!'
And backward now and forward
  Wavers the deep array;
And on the tossing sea of steel,
To and fro the standards reel;
And the victorious trumpet-peal
  Dies fitfully away.

THE FIGHT IN THE CENTRE

from THE BATTLE OF THE LAKE REGILLUS *by*

LORD MACAULAY

BUT meanwhile in the centre
  Great deeds of arms were wrought;
There Aulus the Dictator
  And there Valerius fought.
Aulus with his good broadsword
  A bloody passage cleared
To where, amidst the thickest foes,
  He saw the long white beard.
Flat lighted that good broadsword
  Upon proud Tarquin's head.
He dropped the lance: he dropped the reins
  He fell as fall the dead.
Down Aulus springs to slay him,
  With eyes like coals of fire;
But faster Titus hath sprung down,
  And hath bestrode his sire.
Latian captains, Roman knights,
  Fast down to earth they spring,
And hand to hand they fight on foot
  Around the ancient king.
First Titus gave tall Cæso

A death wound in the face;
Tall Cæso was the bravest man
   Of the brave Fabian race:
Aulus slew Rex of Gabii,
   The priest of Juno's shrine:
Valerius smote down Julius,
   Of Rome's great Julian line;
Julius, who left his mansion
   High on the Velian hill,
And through all turns of weal and woe
   Followed proud Tarquin still.
Now right across proud Tarquin
   A corpse was Julius laid;
And Titus groaned with rage and grief,
   And at Valerius made.
Valerius struck at Titus,
   And lopped off half his crest;
But Titus stabbed Valerius
   A span deep in the breast.
Like a mast snapped by the tempest,
   Valerius reeled and fell.
Ah! woe is me for the good house
   That loves the people well!
Then shouted loud the Latines;
   And with one rush they bore
The struggling Romans backward
   Three lances' length and more:
And up they took proud Tarquin,
   And laid him on a shield,
And four strong yeomen bare him,
   Still senseless, from the field.

But fiercer grew the fighting
   Around Valerius dead;
For Titus dragged him by the foot,
   And Aulus by the head.
'On, Latines, on!' quoth Titus,
   'See how the rebels fly!'

'Romans, stand firm!' quoth Aulus,
  'And win this fight or die!
They must not give Valerius
  To raven and to kite;
For aye Valerius loathed the wrong,
  And aye upheld the right:
And for your wives and babies
  In the front rank he fell.
Now play the men for the good house
  That loves the people well!'

Then tenfold round the body
  The roar of battle rose,
Like the roar of a burning forest,
  When a strong north wind blows.
Now backward, and now forward,
  Rocked furiously the fray,
Till none could see Valerius,
  And none wist where he lay.
For shivered arms and ensigns
  Were heaped there in a mound,
And corpses stiff, and dying men
  That writhed and gnawed the ground;
And wounded horses kicking,
  And snorting purple foam:
Right well did such a couch befit
  A Consular of Rome.

THE DEATH OF HERMINIUS

from THE BATTLE OF THE LAKE REGILLUS *by*

LORD MACAULAY

'HERMINIUS! Aulus greets thee;
  He bids thee come with speed,
To help our central battle;
  For sore is there our need.

There wars the youngest Tarquin,
   And there the Crest of Flame,
The Tusculan Mamilius,
   Prince of the Latian name.
Valerius hath fallen fighting
   In front of our array;
And Aulus of the seventy fields
   Alone upholds the day.'

Herminius beat his bosom:
   But never a word he spake.
He clapped his hand on Auster's mane:
   He gave the reins a shake.
Away, away, went Auster,
   Like an arrow from the bow:
Black Auster was the fleetest steed
   From Aufidus to Po.

Right glad were all the Romans
   Who, in that hour of dread,
Against great odds bare up the war
   Around Valerius dead,
When from the south the cheering
   Rose with a mighty swell;
'Herminius comes, Herminius,
   Who kept the bridge so well!'

Mamilius spied Herminius,
   And dashed across the way.
'Herminius! I have sought thee
   Through many a bloody day.
One of us two, Herminius,
   Shall never more go home.
I will lay on for Tusculum,
   And lay thou on for Rome!'

All round them paused the battle,
   While met in mortal fray

The Roman and the Tusculan,
  The horses black and grey.
Herminius smote Mamilius
  Through breast-plate and through breast;
And fast flowed out the purple blood
  Over the purple vest.
Mamilius smote Herminius
  Through head-piece and through head;
And side by side those chiefs of pride
  Together fell down dead.
Down fell they dead together
  In a great lake of gore;
And still stood all who saw them fall
  While men might count a score.

Fast, fast, with heels wild spurning,
  The dark-grey charger fled:
He burst through ranks of fighting men;
  He sprang o'er heaps of dead.
His bridle far out-streaming,
  His flanks all blood and foam,
He sought the southern mountains,
  The mountains of his home.
The pass was steep and rugged,
  The wolves they howled and whined;
But he ran like a whirlwind up the pass,
  And he left the wolves behind.
Through many a startled hamlet
  Thundered his flying feet;
He rushed through the gate of Tusculum,
  He rushed up the long white street;
He rushed by tower and temple,
  And paused not from his race
Till he stood before his master's door
  In the stately market-place.
And straightway round him gathered
  A pale and trembling crowd,
And when they knew him, cries of rage

Brake forth, and wailing loud:
And women rent their tresses
    For their great prince's fall;
And old men girt on their old swords,
    And went to man the wall.

But, like a graven image,
    Black Auster kept his place,
And ever wistfully he looked
    Into his master's face.
The raven-mane that daily,
    With pats and fond caresses,
The young Herminia washed and combed,
    And twined in even tresses,
And decked with coloured ribands
    From her own gay attire,
Hung sadly o'er her father's corpse
    In carnage and in mire.
Forth with a shout sprang Titus,
    And seized black Auster's rein.
Then Aulus sware a fearful oath,
    And ran at him amain.
'The furies of thy brother
    With me and mine abide,
If one of your accursed house
    Upon black Auster ride!'
As on an Alpine watch-tower
    From heaven comes down the flame,
Full on the neck of Titus
    The blade of Aulus came:
And out the red blood spouted,
    In a wide arch and tall,
As spouts a fountain in the court
    Of some rich Capuan's hall.
The knees of all the Latines
    Were loosened with dismay,
When dead, on dead Herminius,
    The bravest Tarquin lay.

ENGLAND'S STANDARD

from THE ARMADA *by*

LORD MACAULAY

WITH his white hair unbonneted, the stout old sheriff comes;
Behind him march the halberdiers; before him sound the drums;
His yeomen round the market cross make clear an ample space;
For there behoves him to set up the standard of Her Grace.
And haughtily the trumpets peal, and gaily dance the bells,
As slow upon the labouring wind the royal blazon swells.
Look how the Lion of the sea lifts up his ancient crown,
And underneath his deadly paw treads the gay lilies down.
So stalked he when he turned to flight, on that famed Picard field,
Bohemia's plume, and Genoa's bow, and Cæsar's eagle shield.
So glared he when at Agincourt in wrath he turned to bay,
And crushed and torn beneath his claws the princely hunters lay.
Ho! strike the flagstaff deep, sir Knight: ho! scatter flowers, fair maids:
Ho! gunners, fire a loud salute: ho! gallants, draw your blades:
Thou sun, shine on her joyously; ye breezes, waft her wide;
Our glorious SEMPER EADEM, the banner of our pride.
The freshening breeze of eve unfurled that banner's massy fold;
The parting gleam of sunshine kissed that haughty scroll of gold;
Night sank upon the dusky beach, and on the purple sea,
Such night in England ne'er had been, nor e'er again shall be.

THE RED THREAD OF HONOUR

Told to the Author by the late Sir Charles James Napier

SIR FRANCIS HASTINGS DOYLE

ELEVEN men of England
   A breast-work charged in vain;
Eleven men of England
   Lie stripped, and gashed, and slain.
Slain; but of foes that guarded
   Their rock-built fortress well,
Some twenty had been mastered,
   When the last soldier fell.

Whilst Napier piloted his wondrous way
   Across the sand-waves of the desert sea,
Then flashed at once, on each fierce clan, dismay,
   Lord of their wild Truckee.

These missed the glen to which their steps were bent,
   Mistook a mandate, from afar half heard,
And, in that glorious error, calmly went
   To death, without a word.

    The robber-chief mused deeply,
      Above those daring dead;
    'Bring here,' at length he shouted,
      'Bring quick, the battle thread.
    Let Eblis blast for ever
      Their souls, if Allah will:
    But WE must keep unbroken
      The old rules of the Hill.

    'Before the Ghuznee tiger
      Leapt forth to burn and slay;
    Before the holy Prophet
      Taught our grim tribes to pray;
    Before Secunder's lances
      Pierced through each Indian glen;
    The mountain laws of honour
      Were framed for fearless men.

    'Still, when a chief dies bravely,
      We bind with green *one* wrist —
    Green for the brave, for heroes
      ONE crimson thread we twist.
    Say ye, oh gallant Hillmen,
      For these, whose life has fled,
    Which is the fitting colour,
      The green one or the red?'

'Our brethren, laid in honoured graves, may wear
   Their green reward,' each noble savage said;
'To these, whom hawks and hungry wolves shall tear,
   Who dares deny the red?'

Thus, conquering hate, and steadfast to the right,
   Fresh from the heart that haughty verdict came;
Beneath a waning moon, each spectral height
   Rolled back its loud acclaim.

    Once more the chief gazed keenly
      Down on those daring dead;
    From his good sword their heart's blood
      Crept to that crimson thread.
    Once more he cried, 'The judgment,
      Good friends, is wise and true,
    But though the red be given,
      Have we not more to do?

    'These were not stirred by anger,
      Nor yet by lust made bold;
    Renown they thought above them,
      Nor did they look for gold.
    To them their leader's signal
      Was as the voice of God:
    Unmoved, and uncomplaining,
      The path it showed they trod.

    'As, without sound or struggle,
      The stars unhurrying march,
    Where Allah's finger guides them,
      Through yonder purple arch,
    These Franks, sublimely silent,
      Without a quickened breath,
    Went, in the strength of duty,
      Straight to their goal of death.

'If I were now to ask you,
    To name our bravest man,
Ye all at once would answer,
    They called him Mehrab Khan.
He sleeps among his fathers,
    Dear to our native land,
With the bright mark he bled for
    Firm round his faithful hand.

'The songs they sing of Rustum
    Fill all the past with light;
If truth be in their music,
    He was a noble knight.
But were those heroes living,
    And strong for battle still,
Would Mehrab Khan or Rustum
    Have climbed, like these, the Hill?'

And they replied, 'Though Mehrab Khan was brave
    As chief, he chose himself what risks to run;
Prince Rustum lied, his forfeit life to save,
    Which these had never done.'

'Enough!' he shouted fiercely;
    'Doomed though they be to hell,
Bind fast the crimson trophy
    Round *both* wrists — bind it well.
Who knows but that great Allah
    May grudge such matchless men,
With none so decked in heaven,
    To the fiend's flaming den?'

Then all those gallant robbers
    Shouted a stern 'Amen!'
They raised the slaughtered sergeant,
    They raised his mangled ten.

> And when we found their bodies
>   Left bleaching in the wind,
> Around *both* wrists in glory
>   That crimson thread was twined.
>
>
> Then Napier's knightly heart, touched to the core,
>   Rung, like an echo, to that knightly deed;
> He bade its memory live for evermore,
>   That those who run may read.

Note

Sir Charles Napier is supposed to have announced his conquest of Scinde with the one word 'Peccavi'. This is a myth, but Doyle's tale has good historical warrant, and is based on the following passage from Sir Charles Napier's account of his administration in Scinde.

'Those commanders had, as before related, entered a short way into the defile, but from some error, a sergeant and sixteen privates of the 13th Volunteers got on the wrong side of what appeared a small chasm and went against a height crowned by the enemy, where the chasm suddenly deepened so as to be impassable. The company from which the sergeant had separated was on the other side, and his officer, seeing how strong the hillmen were on the rock, made signs to retire, which the sergeant mistook for gestures to attack, and with inexpressible intrepidity scaled the precipitous height. The robbers waited concealed behind a breastwork on a landing-place until eleven of the party came up, and then, being seventy in number, closed on them. All the eleven had medals, some had three, and in that dire moment proved that their courage at Jellalabad had not been exaggerated by fame. Six of them fell stark, and the others being wounded, were shoved back over the edge and rolled down the almost perpendicular side of the hill; but this did not happen until seventeen of the robbers and their commander were laid dead above.

'There is a custom with the hillmen, that when a great champion dies in battle, his comrades, after stripping his body, tie a red or green thread round his right or left wrist according to the greatness of his exploit — the red being most honourable. Here those brave warriors stripped the British dead, and cast the bodies over; but with this testimony of their own chivalric sense of honour and the greatness of the fallen soldiers' courage — each body had a red thread on both wrists!'

The 13th are now the Somerset Light Infantry. The author of the poem came from a very distinguished fighting family. The poem is said to have become the theme of a Pushtu ballad, but I have been unable to find that it still exists on the Indian frontier.

A. P. W.

WAR SONG OF THE SARACENS

JAMES ELROY FLECKER

WE are they who come faster than fate: we are they who ride early
        or late:
We storm at your ivory gate: Pale Kings of the Sunset, beware!
Not on silk nor in samet we lie, not in curtained solemnity die
Among women who chatter and cry, and children who mumble a
        prayer.
But we sleep by the ropes of the camp, and we rise with a shout, and
        we tramp
With the sun or the moon for a lamp and the spray of the wind in
        our hair.

From the lands, where the elephants are, to the forts of Merou and
        Balghar,
Our steel we have brought and our star to shine on the ruins of Rum.
We have marched from the Indus to Spain, and by God we will go
        there again;
We have stood on the shore of the plain where the Waters of Destiny
        boom.
A mart of destruction we made at Jalula where men were afraid,
For death was a difficult trade, and the sword was a broker of doom;

And the Spear was a Desert Physician who cured not a few of ambition,
And drave not a few to perdition with medicine bitter and strong:
And the shield was a grief to the fool and as bright as a desolate pool,
And as straight as the rock of Stamboul when their cavalry thundered
along:
For the coward was drowned with the brave when our battle sheered
up like a wave,
And the dead to the desert we gave, and the glory to God in our song.

HERVÉ RIEL

Robert Browning

On the sea and at the Hogue, sixteen hundred ninety-two,
    Did the English fight the French, — woe to France!
And, the thirty-first of May, helter-skelter through the blue,
Like a crowd of frightened porpoises a shoal of sharks pursue,
    Came crowding ship on ship to Saint-Malo on the Rance,
With the English fleet in view.
'Twas the squadron that escaped, with the victor in full chase;
    First and foremost of the drove, in his great ship, Damfreville;
        Close on him fled, great and small,
        Twenty-two good ships in all;
And they signalled to the place
'Help the winners of a race!
    Get us guidance, give us harbour, take us quick — or, quicker still,
    Here's the English can and will!'

Then the pilots of the place put out brisk and leapt on board;
    'Why, what hope or chance have ships like these to pass?' laughed
they:
'Rocks to starboard, rocks to port, all the passage scarred and scored, —
Shall the "Formidable" here, with her twelve and eighty guns,
    Think to make the river-mouth by the single narrow way,
Trust to enter — where 'tis ticklish for a craft of twenty tons,
        And with flow at full beside?
        Now, 'tis slackest ebb of tide.
    Reach the mooring? Rather say,

While rock stands or water runs,
    Not a ship will leave the bay!'

Then was called a council straight.
Brief and bitter the debate:
'Here's the English at our heels; would you have them take in tow
All that's left us of the fleet, linked together stern and bow,
For a prize to Plymouth Sound?
Better run the ships aground!'
    (Ended Damfreville his speech.)
'Not a minute more to wait!
    Let the Captains all and each,
    Shove ashore, then blow up, burn the vessels on the beach!
France must undergo her fate.

Give the word!' But no such word
Was ever spoke or heard;
    For up stood, for out stepped, for in struck amid all these
— A Captain? A Lieutenant? A Mate — first, second, third?
    No such man of mark, and meet
    With his betters to compete!
    But a simple Breton sailor pressed by Tourville for the fleet,
A poor coasting-pilot he, Hervé Riel the Croisickese.

And 'What mockery or malice have we here?' cries Hervé Riel:
    'Are you mad, you Malouins? Are you cowards, fools, or rogues?
Talk to me of rocks and shoals, me who took the soundings, tell
On my fingers every bank, every shallow, every swell
    'Twixt the offing here and Grève where the river disembogues?
Are you bought by English gold? Is it love the lying's for?
    Morn and eve, night and day,
    Have I piloted your bay,
Entered free and anchored fast at the foot of Solidor.
    Burn the fleet and ruin France? That were worse than fifty Hogues!
    Sirs, they know I speak the truth! Sirs, believe me there's a way.
Only let me lead the line,
    Have the biggest ship to steer,
    Get this "Formidable" clear,

Make the others follow mine,
And I lead them, most and least, by a passage I know well,
  Right to Solidor past Grève,
    And there lay them safe and sound;
  And if one ship misbehave, —
    — Keel so much as grate the ground,
Why, I've nothing but my life, — here's my head!' cries Hervé Riel.

Not a minute more to wait.
'Steer us in, then, small and great!
  Take the helm, lead the line, save the squadron!' cries its chief.
Captains, give the sailor place!
  He is Admiral, in brief.
Still the north-wind, by God's grace
See the noble fellow's face
As the big ship, with a bound,
Clears the entry like a hound,
Keeps the passage, as its inch of way were the wide sea's profound!
  See, safe thro' shoal and rock,
  How they follow in a flock,
Not a ship that misbehaves, not a keel that grates the ground,
  Not a spar that comes to grief!
The peril, see, is past.
All are harboured to the last,
And just as Hervé Riel hollas 'Anchor!' — sure as fate,
Up the English come, — too late!

So, the storm subsides to calm:
  They see the green trees wave
  On the heights o'erlooking Grève.
Hearts that bled are stanched with balm.
'Just our rapture to enhance,
  Let the English rake the bay,
Gnash their teeth and glare askance
  As they cannonade away!
'Neath rampired Solidor pleasant riding on the Rance!'
How hope succeeds despair on each Captain's countenance!
Out burst all with one accord,

'This is Paradise for Hell!
Let France, let France's King
    Thank the man that did the thing!'
What a shout, and all one word,
    'Hervé Riel!'
As he stepped in front once more,
    Not a symptom of surprise
    In the frank blue Breton eyes,
Just the same man as before.

Then said Damfreville, 'My friend,
I must speak out at the end,
    Though I find the speaking hard.
Praise is deeper than the lips:
You have saved the King his ships,
    You must name your own reward.
'Faith, our sun was near eclipse!
Demand whate'er you will,
France remains your debtor still.
Ask to heart's content and have! or my name's not Damfreville.'
Then a beam of fun outbroke
On the bearded mouth that spoke,
As the honest heart laughed through
Those frank eyes of Breton blue:
'Since I needs must say my say,
    Since on board the duty's done,
    And from Malo Roads to Croisic Point, what is it but a run? —
Since 'tis ask and have, I may —
    Since the others go ashore —
Come! A good whole holiday!
    Leave to go and see my wife, whom I call the Belle Aurore!'
That he asked and that he got, — nothing more.

Name and deed alike are lost:
Not a pillar nor a post
    In his Croisic keeps alive the feat as it befell;
Not a head in white and black
On a single fishing-smack,

In memory of the man but for whom had gone to wrack
   All that France saved from the fight whence England bore the bell.
Go to Paris: rank on rank
   Search the heroes flung pell-mell
On the Louvre, face and flank!
   You shall look long enough ere you come to Hervé Riel.
So, for better and for worse,
Hervé Riel, accept my verse!
In my verse, Hervé Riel, do thou once more
Save the squadron, honour France, love thy wife the Belle Aurore!

Note

This story is true, though all France, including the French
Admiralty, had forgotten it till Browning's poem caused the
records to be searched. One item is incorrect: Hervé Riel did not
simply ask for a day's holiday but for *congé absolu* — release from the
Service, to rejoin his Belle Aurore.

Hervé Riel was written during an earlier period of eclipse for
France, when Germany's dark shadow lay over her in 1871. By
reminding her of a forgotten feat of the past Browning may have
helped her to emerge into the light again. He gave the money he
received from the poem to the Paris Relief Fund to provide food
for the starving people after the Siege of Paris.   *A. P. W.*

DRAKE'S DRUM

Sir Henry Newbolt

Drake he's in his hammock an' a thousand mile away,
   (Capten, art tha sleepin' there below?)
Slung atween the round shot in Nombre Dios Bay,
   An' dreamin' arl the time o' Plymouth Hoe.
Yarnder lumes the Island, yarnder lie the ships,
   Wi' sailor lads a-dancin' heel-an'-toe,
An' the shore-lights flashin', an' the night-tide dashin',
   He sees et arl so plainly as he saw et long ago.

Drake he was a Devon man, an' rüled the Devon seas,
   (Capten, art tha sleepin' there below?)
Rovin' tho' his death fell, he went wi' heart at ease,
   An' dreamin' arl the time o' Plymouth Hoe.
'Take my drum to England, hang et by the shore,
   Strike et when your powder's runnin' low;
If the Dons sight Devon, I'll quit the port o' Heaven,
   An' drum them up the Channel as we drumm'd them long ago.'

Drake he's in his hammock till the great Armadas come,
   (Capten, art tha sleepin' there below?)
Slung atween the round shot, listenin' for the drum,
   An' dreamin' arl the time o' Plymouth Hoe.
Call him on the deep sea, call him up the Sound,
   Call him when ye sail to meet the foe;
Where the old trade's plyin' an' the old flag vlyin'
   They shall find him ware an' wakin', as they found him long ago!

THE FAIRIES' SIEGE

Rudyard Kipling

I HAVE been given my charge to keep —
Well have I kept the same!
Playing with strife for the most of my life,
But this is a different game.
I'll not fight against swords unseen,
Or spears that I cannot view —
Hand him the keys of the place on your knees —
'Tis the Dreamer whose dreams come true!

Ask him his terms and accept them at once.
Quick, ere we anger him, go!
Never before have I flinched from the guns,
But this is a different show.
I'll not fight with the Herald of God.

(I know what his Master can do!)
Open the gate, he must enter in state,
'Tis the Dreamer whose dreams come true!

I'd not give way for an Emperor,
I'd hold my road for a King —
To the Triple Crown I would not bow down —
But this is a different thing.
I'll not fight with the Powers of Air,
Sentry, pass him through!
Drawbridge let fall, 'tis the Lord of us all,
The Dreamer whose dreams come true!

LEADERS

I. OLD STYLE

from MARMION *by*

SIR WALTER SCOTT

FOR though, with men of high degree,
The proudest of the proud was he,
Yet, train'd in camps, he knew the art
To win the soldier's hardy heart.
They love a captain to obey
Boisterous as March, yet fresh as May;
With open hand, and brow as free,
Lover of wine and minstrelsy;
Ever the first to scale a tower,
As venturous in a lady's bower: —
Such buxom chief shall lead his host
From India's fires to Zembla's frost.

F

II. NEW STYLE

THE GENERAL (1917)

SIEGFRIED SASSOON

'GOOD-MORNING; good-morning!' the General said
When we met him last week on our way to the Line.
Now the soldiers he smiled at are most of 'em dead,
And we're cursing his staff for incompetent swine.
'He's a cheery old card,' grunted Harry to Jack
As they slogged up to Arras with rifle and pack.

But he did for them both with his plan of attack.

THE STAFF OFFICER

from HENRY IV, Pt. I, Act I, Sc. 3, *by*

WILLIAM SHAKESPEARE

BUT I remember when the fight was done,
When I was dry with rage and extreme toil,
Breathless and faint, leaning upon my sword,
Came there a certain lord, neat, trimly dress'd,
Fresh as a bridegroom; and his chin new reap'd
Show'd like a stubble-land at harvest-home; —
He was perfumèd like a milliner;
And 'twixt his finger and his thumb he held
A pouncet-box, which ever and anon
He gave his nose, and took 't away again;
Who therewith angry, when it next came there,
Took it in snuff: and still he smil'd and talk'd;
And as the soldiers bore dead bodies by,
He call'd them untaught knaves, unmannerly,
To bring a slovenly unhandsome corse
Betwixt the wind and his nobility.
With many holiday and lady terms

He question'd me; among the rest, demanded
My prisoners in your majesty's behalf.
I, then all smarting with my wounds being cold,
To be so pester'd with a popinjay,
Out of my grief and my impatience,
Answer'd neglectingly, I know not what, —
He should, or he should not; — for he made me mad
To see him shine so brisk, and smell so sweet,
And talk so like a waiting-gentlewoman
Of guns, and drums, and wounds, — God save the mark! —
And telling me the sovereign'st thing on earth
Was parmaceti for an inward bruise;
And that it was great pity, so it was,
This villanous saltpetre should be digg'd
Out of the bowels of the harmless earth,
Which many a good tall fellow had destroy'd
So cowardly; and but for these vile guns —
He would himself have been a soldier.

Note

The feeling between the regimental officer and the staff officer
is as old as the history of fighting. I have been a regimental officer
in two minor wars and realized what a poor hand the staff made
of things and what a safe luxurious life they led; I was a staff officer
in the first World War and realized that the staff were worked to
the bone to try and keep the regimental officer on the rails; I
have been a Higher Commander in one minor and one major war
and have sympathized with the views of both staff and regimental
officer. Shakespeare's description in this passage of the fighting
officer's view of the popinjays on the staff is extreme, but amusing.
Hotspur, by the way, described poetry contemptuously as 'minc-
ing poetry, like the forced gait of a shuffling nag'.   *A. P. W.*

THE ENGLISH WAR

DOROTHY L. SAYERS

PRAISE God, now, for an English **war** —
  The grey tide and the sullen coast,
The menace of the urgent hour,
The single island, like a tower,
  Ringed with an angry host.

This is the war that England knows,
  When all the world holds but one man —
King Philip of the galleons,
Louis, whose light outshone the sun's,
  The conquering Corsican.

When Europe, like a prison door,
  Clangs; and the swift, enfranchised sea
Runs narrower than a village brook;
And men who love us not, yet look
  To us for liberty;

When no allies are left, no help
  To count upon from alien hands,
No waverers remain to woo,
No more advice to listen to,
  And only England stands.

This is the war we always knew,
  When every county keeps her own,
When Kent stands sentry in the lane
And Fenland guards her dyke and drain,
  Cornwall, her cliffs of stone;

When from the Cinque Ports and the Wight,
  From Plymouth Sound and Bristol Town,
There comes a noise that breaks our sleep,
Of the deep calling to the deep
  Where the ships go up and down,

And near and far across the world
   Hold open wide the water-gates,
And all the tall adventurers come
Homeward to England, and Drake's drum
   Is beaten through the Straits.

This is the war that we have known
   And fought in every hundred years,
Our sword, upon the last, steep path,
Forged by the hammer of our wrath
   On the anvil of our fears.

Send us, O God, the will and power
   To do as we have done before;
The men that ride the sea and air
Are the same men their fathers were
   To fight the English war.

And send, O God, an English peace –
   Some sense, some decency, perhaps
Some justice, too, if we are able,
With no sly jackals round our table,
   Cringing for blood-stained scraps;

No dangerous dreams of wishful men
   Whose homes are safe, who never feel
The flying death that swoops and stuns,
The kisses of the curtseying guns
   Slavering their streets with steel;

No dreams, Lord God, but vigilance,
   That we may keep, by might and main,
Inviolate seas, inviolate skies; —
But, if another tyrant rise,
   Then we shall fight again.

THE BATTLE OF NASEBY

Lord Macaulay

Oh! wherefore come ye forth, in triumph from the North,
  With your hands, and your feet, and your raiment all red?
And wherefore doth your rout sent forth a joyous shout?
  And whence be the grapes of the wine-press which ye tread?

Oh evil was the root, and bitter was the fruit,
  And crimson was the juice of the vintage that we trod;
For we trampled on the throng of the haughty and the strong,
  Who sate in the high places, and slew the saints of God.

It was about the noon of a glorious day in June,
  That we saw their banners dance, and their cuirasses shine,
And the Man of Blood was there, with his long essenced hair,
  And Astley, and Sir Marmaduke, and Rupert of the Rhine.

Like a servant of the Lord, with his Bible and his sword,
  The General rode along us to form us to the fight,
When a murmuring sound broke out, and swell'd into a shout,
  Among the godless horsemen upon the tyrant's right.

And hark! like the roar of the billows on the shore,
  The cry of battle rises along their charging line!
For God! for the Cause! for the Church, for the Laws!
  For Charles King of England, and Rupert of the Rhine!

The furious German comes, with his clarions and his drums,
  His bravoes of Alsatia, and pages of Whitehall;
They are bursting on our flanks. Grasp your pikes, close your ranks;
  For Rupert never comes but to conquer or to fall.

They are here! They rush on! We are broken! We are gone!
  Our left is borne before them like stubble on the blast.
O Lord, put forth thy might! O Lord, defend the right!
  Stand back to back, in God's name, and fight it to the last.

Stout Skippon hath a wound; the centre hath given ground:
   Hark! hark! — What means the trampling of horsemen on our rear?
Whose banner do I see, boys? 'Tis he, thank God! 'tis he, boys,
   Bear up another minute: brave Oliver is here.

Their heads all stooping low, their points all in a row,
   Like a whirlwind on the trees, like a deluge on the dykes,
Our cuirassiers have burst on the ranks of the accurst,
   And at a shock have scattered the forest of his pikes.

Fast, fast, the gallants ride, in some safe nook to hide
   Their coward heads, predestined to rot on Temple Bar:
And he — he turns, he flies: — shame on those cruel eyes
   That bore to look on torture, and dare not look on war.

Ho! comrades, scour the plain; and, ere ye strip the slain,
   First give another stab to make your search secure,
Then shake from sleeves and pockets their broad pieces and lockets,
   The tokens of the wanton, the plunder of the poor.

Fools, your doublets shone with gold, and your hearts were gay and
   When you kissed your lily hands to your lemans to-day;   [bold,
And to-morrow shall the fox, from her chambers in the rocks,
   Lead forth her tawny cubs to howl above the prey.

Where be your tongues that late mocked at heaven and hell and fate,
   And the fingers that once were so busy with your blades,
Your perfumed satin clothes, your catches and your oaths,
   Your stage-plays and your sonnets, your diamonds and your spades?

Down, down, for ever down with the mitre and the crown,
   With the Belial of the Court, and the Mammon of the Pope;
There is woe in Oxford Halls; there is wail in Durham's Stalls:
   The Jesuit smites his bosom; the Bishop rends his cope.

And She of the seven hills shall mourn her children's ills,
   And tremble when she thinks of the edge of England's sword;
And the Kings of earth in fear shall shudder when they hear
   What the hand of God hath wrought for the Houses and the Word.

HIC JACET ARTHURUS REX QUONDAM REXQUE FUTURUS...

from THE ISLAND *by*

FRANCIS BRETT YOUNG

ARTHUR is gone ... Tristram in Careol
Sleeps, with a broken sword — and Yseult sleeps
Beside him, where the westering waters roll
Over drowned Lyonesse to the outer deeps.

Lancelot is fallen ... The ardent helms that shone
So knightly and the splintered lances rust
In the anonymous mould of Avalon:
Gawain and Gareth and Galahad — all are dust!

Where do the vanes and towers of Camelot
And tall Tintagil crumble? where do those tragic
Lovers and all their bright-eyed ladies rot?
We cannot tell — for lost is Merlin's magic.

And Guinevere — call her not back again
Lest she betray the loveliness Time lent
A name that blends the rapture and the pain
Linked in the lovely nightingale's lament,

Nor pry too deeply, lest you should discover
The bower of Astolat a smoky hut
Of mud and wattle — find the knightliest lover
A braggart, and his Lily Maid a slut;

And all that coloured tale a tapestry
Woven by poets. As the spider's skeins
Are spun of its own substance, so have they
Embroidered empty legend. What remains?

This: That when Rome fell, like a writhen oak
That age had sapped and cankered at the root,
Resistant, from her topmost bough there broke
The miracle of one unwithering shoot

Which was the spirit of Britain — that certain men,
Uncouth, untutored, of our island brood
Loved freedom better than their lives; and when
The tempest crashed about them, rose and stood

And charged into the storm's black heart, with sword
Lifted, or lance in rest, and rode there, helmed
With a strange majesty that the heathen horde
Remembered after all were overwhelmed;

And made of them a legend, to their chief,
Arthur, Ambrosius — no man knows his name –
Granting a gallantry beyond belief,
And to his knights imperishable fame.

They were so few ... We know not in what manner
Or where or when they fell — whether they went
Riding into the dark under Christ's banner
Or died beneath the blood-red dragon of Gwent;

But this we know: That, when the Saxon rout
Swept over them, the sun no longer shone
On Britain, and the last lights flickered out;
And men in darkness murmured: Arthur is gone ...

Note

The truth at the root of the Arthurian legend, so far as it can
now be guessed at, is well summed up in the lines above, i.e.
that in the dark ages which followed the Roman withdrawal from
Britain, some man, perhaps a Romanized Briton, put up such a
fight for civilization and freedom against the barbarian invaders
as to be remembered for ever in a legend of gallant doings.

I carried a pocket edition of Malory with me in the early days of the late war. Malory is excellent reading, but only a court or fancy dress version of the real story which no man knows. Arthur was probably a grim figure in a grim unromantic struggle in a dark period of history. A lately published reconstruction, *The Bear of Britain* by Frankland, comes perhaps as near the truth as we are ever likely to get.   *A. P. W.*

ATLANTIC CHARTER

from THE ISLAND *by*

FRANCIS BRETT YOUNG

WHAT were you carrying, Pilgrims, Pilgrims?
What did you carry beyond the sea?
    We carried the Book, we carried the Sword,
    A steadfast heart in the fear of the Lord,
    And a living faith in His plighted word
    That all men should be free.

What were your memories, Pilgrims, Pilgrims?
What of the dreams you bore away?
    We carried the songs our fathers sung
    By the hearths of home when they were young,
    And the comely words of the mother-tongue
    In which they learnt to pray.

What did you find there, Pilgrims, Pilgrims?
What did you find beyond the waves?
    A stubborn land and a barren shore,
    Hunger and want and sickness sore;
    All these we found and gladly bore
    Rather than be slaves.

How did you fare there, Pilgrims, Pilgrims?
What did you build in that stubborn land?
    We felled the forest and tilled the sod
    Of a continent no man had trod
    And we established there, in the Grace of God,
    The rights whereby we stand.

What are you bringing us, Pilgrims, Pilgrims?
Bringing us back in this bitter day?
    The selfsame things we carried away;
    The book, The Sword,
    The fear of the Lord,
    And the boons our fathers dearly bought:
    Freedom of Worship, Speech and Thought,
    Freedom from Want, Freedom from Fear,
    The Liberties we hold most dear,
    And who shall say us Nay?

3 . LOVE AND ALL THAT

Love is almost as universal an experience as death, with the advantage from a poet's point of view that it is possible to write of it from personal experience. Hence a large proportion of poetry deals with love in one of its many aspects, such as love young and simple (*O Mistress Mine*; *A Red, Red Rose*); love romantic (*Rudel to the Lady of Tripoli*); love practical (*To His Coy Mistress*); love uxorious (*One Word More*); love gay and willing (*Kiss'd Yestreen*; *O Whistle and I'll come to you*); love oriental (*Arab Love-Song*, with the two most beautiful last lines of any love song); love explanatory, as of the poet who was unfaithful to Cynara in his fashion; love valedictory (Drayton's *Parting*); love submissive (Browning's *One Way of Love*, as likely to succeed as the methods of Suckling's sad lover); curtain-lecture love (*Any Wife to Any Husband*); love misdirected and betrayed (*The Banks o' Doon*; *La Belle Dame Sans Merci*); love in the twilight (*John Anderson*; *When you are old and gray*); and many others.

Burns is, I suppose, the best poet of love, simple unsophisticated country love. I like Browning's lovers, but they come from books, while those of Burns came from experience; Chesterton's come from pure imagination — except perhaps *The Strange Music*, which sounds like experience — and Kipling never wrote a real love poem (his *Love Song of Har Dyal* is only a drawing-room ditty); I have included one other here, but it expresses Kipling's love of England rather than love of woman.

Should a poet, or any man, have one love or many? Shelley (*The Longest Journey*) has given his unequivocal answer; Browning, himself the most faithful of lovers, has put forward in a favourite stanza of mine, which begins 'Ah, but the fresher faces', a disarming plea for inconstancy; other poets and other men have pointed out, musically or crudely, that a singleton heart is seldom a satisfactory holding. The question seems to me almost equivalent to asking: 'Should a man have mumps as well as measles, pleurisy as well as bronchitis?' The answer to the one question depends on his temperament and his opportunities, to the other on his constitution and the risks he takes. A man who goes into a tropical country in the rainy season without quinine or mosquito net will almost surely contract malaria; one who goes to some haunt of lovelies in spring without a wife or conscience is apt to fall in love. Some catch malaria even with quinine and net and all reasonable precautions; they must avoid tropical climates. Some fall in love in season or out of season; for them there is no cure, nor do they often desire one. Perhaps an Elizabethan, who first amused and then shocked his royal Mistress, phrased it most succinctly: 'It is better to love two too many than one too few.' Or as a music-hall song of my youth put it rather more crudely:

> 'If you can't be true to one or two
> You are much better off with three.'
>
> *A. P. W.*

O MISTRESS MINE

WILLIAM SHAKESPEARE

O MISTRESS mine, where are you roaming?
O, stay and hear! your true love's coming,
　That can sing both high and low:
Trip no further, pretty sweeting;
Journeys end in lovers meeting,
　Every wise man's son doth know.

What is love? 'tis not hereafter;
Present mirth hath present laughter;
　What's to come is still unsure:
In delay there lies no plenty;
Then come kiss me, sweet-and-twenty!
　Youth's a stuff will not endure.

A RED, RED ROSE

ROBERT BURNS

O MY Luve's like a red, red rose
　That's newly sprung in June:
O my Luve's like the melodie
　That's sweetly play'd in tune!

As fair art thou, my bonnie lass,
　　So deep in luve am I:
And I will luve thee still, my dear,
　　Till a' the seas gang dry:

Till a' the seas gang dry, my dear,
　　And the rocks melt wi' the sun;
I will luve thee still, my dear,
　　While the sands o' life shall run.

And fare thee weel, my only Luve,
　　And fare thee weel a while!
And I will come again, my Luve,
　　Tho' it were ten thousand mile.

TO HIS COY MISTRESS

Andrew Marvell

HAD we but world enough, and time,
This coyness, Lady, were no crime.
We would sit down and think which way
To walk and pass our long love's day.
Thou by the Indian Ganges' side
Shouldst rubies find: I by the tide
Of Humber would complain. I would
Love you ten years before the Flood,
And you should, if you please, refuse
Till the conversion of the Jews.
My vegetable love should grow
Vaster than empires, and more slow;
An hundred years should go to praise
Thine eyes and on thy forehead gaze;
Two hundred to adore each breast,
But thirty thousand to the rest;
An age at least to every part,
And the last age should show your heart.
For, Lady, you deserve this state,

Nor would I love at lower rate.
   But at my back I always hear
Time's wingèd chariot hurrying near;
And yonder all before us lie
Deserts of vast eternity.
Thy beauty shall no more be found,
Nor, in thy marble vault, shall sound
My echoing song: then worms shall try
That long preserved virginity,
And your quaint honour turn to dust,
And into ashes all my lust:
The grave's a fine and private place,
But none, I think, do there embrace.
   Now therefore, while the youthful hue
Sits on thy skin like morning dew,
And while thy willing soul transpires
At every pore with instant fires,
Now let us sport us while we may,
And now, like amorous birds of prey,
Rather at once our time devour
Than languish in his slow-chapt power.
Let us roll all our strength and all
Our sweetness up into one ball,
And tear our pleasures with rough strife
Thorough the iron gates of life:
Thus, though we cannot make our sun
Stand still, yet we will make him run.

RUDEL TO THE LADY OF TRIPOLI

Robert Browning

I

I KNOW a Mount, the gracious Sun perceives
First when he visits, last, too, when he leaves
The world; and, vainly favoured, it repays
The day-long glory of his steadfast gaze
By no change of its large calm front of snow.

And underneath the Mount, a Flower I know,
He cannot have perceived, that changes ever
At his approach; and, in the lost endeavour
To live his life, has parted, one by one,
With all a flower's true graces, for the grace
Of being but a foolish mimic sun,
With ray-like florets round a disk-like face.
Men nobly call by many a name the Mount
As over many a land of theirs its large
Calm front of snow like a triumphal targe
Is reared, and still with old names, fresh ones vie,
Each to its proper praise and own account:
Men call the Flower, the Sunflower, sportively.

II

Oh, Angel of the East, one, one gold look
Across the waters to this twilight nook,
— The far sad waters, Angel, to this nook!

III

Dear Pilgrim, art thou for the East indeed?
Go! Saying ever as thou dost proceed,
That I, French Rudel, choose for my device
A sunflower outspread like a sacrifice
Before its idol. See! These inexpert
And hurried fingers could not fail to hurt
The woven picture: 'tis a woman's skill
Indeed; but nothing baffled me, so, ill
Or well, the work is finished. Say, men feed
On songs I sing, and therefore bask the bees
On my flower's breast as on a platform broad:
But, as the flower's concern is not for these
But solely for the sun, so men applaud
In vain this Rudel, he not looking here
But to the East — the East! Go, say this, Pilgrim dear!

Note

This beautiful lyric is one of my favourite love poems and it
enshrines a romantic love story. Geoffrey de Rudel, Prince of

Blaye, was a twelfth-century troubadour from Provence. In the spirit of his class, land and time he fell in love with the Countess of Tripoli, a daughter of King Baldwin of Jerusalem, merely on the reports of her beauty and charm brought home by Crusaders (Rudel's was the Syrian Tripoli, not the African Tripoli of Rommel). After some years of singing the perfections of the distant lady up and down the land after the fashion of troubadours he induced a fellow troubadour to make a voyage with him to find her. Rudel fell ill on the way and was dying when he reached Tripoli, but lived just long enough to see his long-loved lady.

Rostand, the creator of *Cyrano*, used the story in a play, *La Princesse Lointaine*. In it the lady was named Mélisande and was played by Sarah Bernhardt, so was worth a long voyage, perhaps even with a funeral at the end of it.

Rudel's constancy to a distant and unseen mistress has been much praised; but to many it is easier to be true to an unseen ideal whose qualities can be imagined in perfection than to a present, possibly a petulant or peevish, beauty; and it is well known that the pleasures of anticipation so often exceed those of realization. Perhaps that is the moral of Rudel's story.

For some reason or other — ignorance of the Syrian Tripoli, I suppose — I used to think when I first read and loved the poem in youth that Rudel's mount was Mount Atlas; it must really have been one of the Alps overlooking his native Provence.

A. P. W.

ARAB LOVE-SONG

Francis Thompson

The hunchèd camels of the night
Trouble the bright
And silver waters of the moon.
The Maiden of the Morn will soon
Through Heaven stray and sing,
Star gathering.

Now while the dark about our loves is strewn,
Light of my dark, blood of my heart, O come!
And night will catch her breath up, and be dumb.

Leave thy father, leave thy mother
And thy brother;
Leave the black tents of thy tribe apart!
Am I not thy father and thy brother,
And thy mother?
And thou — what needest with thy tribe's black tents
Who hast the red pavilion of my heart?

WE'LL GO NO MORE A-ROVING

Lord Byron

So, we'll go no more a-roving
  So late into the night,
Though the heart be still as loving,
  And the moon be still as bright.

For the sword outwears its sheath,
  And the soul wears out the breast,
And the heart must pause to breathe,
  And love itself have rest.

Though the night was made for loving,
  And the day returns too soon,
Yet we'll go no more a-roving
  By the light of the moon.

THE BARGAIN

Sir Philip Sidney

My true love hath my heart, and I have his,
  By just exchange one for another given:
I hold his dear, and mine he cannot miss,
  There never was a better bargain driven:
    My true love hath my heart, and I have his.

His heart in me keeps him and me in one,
　My heart in him his thoughts and senses guides:
He loves my heart, for once it was his own,
　I cherish his because in me it bides:
　　My true love hath my heart, and I have his.

ONE WORD MORE
[To E. B. B.]
ROBERT BROWNING

I

THERE they are, my fifty men and women
Naming me the fifty poems finished!
Take them, Love, the book and me together:
Where the heart lies, let the brain lie also.

II

Rafael made a century of sonnets,
Made and wrote them in a certain volume
Dinted with the silver-pointed pencil
Else he only used to draw Madonnas;
These, the world might view — but One, the volume,
Who that one, you ask? Your heart instructs you.
Did she live and love it all her lifetime?
Did she drop, his lady of the sonnets,
Die, and let it drop beside her pillow
Where it lay in place of Rafael's glory,
Rafael's cheek so duteous and so loving —
Cheek, the world was wont to hail a painter's,
Rafael's cheek, her love had turned a poet's?

III

You and I would rather read that volume,
(Taken to his beating bosom by it)
Lean and list the bosom-beats of Rafael,
Would we not? than wonder at Madonnas —
Her, San Sisto names, and Her, Foligno,

Her, that visits Florence in a vision,
Her, that's left with lilies in the Louvre —
Seen by us and all the world in circle.

IV

You and I will never read that volume.
Guido Reni, like his own eye's apple
Guarded long the treasure-book and loved it.
Guido Reni dying, all Bologna
Cried, and the world cried too, 'Ours — the treasure!'
Suddenly, as rare things will, it vanished.

V

Dante once prepared to paint an angel:
Whom to please? You whisper 'Beatrice'.
While he mused and traced it and retraced it,
(Peradventure with a pen corroded
Still by drops of that hot ink he dipped for,
When, his left-hand i' the hair o' the wicked,
Back he held the brow and pricked its stigma,
Bit into the live man's flesh for parchment,
Loosed him, laughed to see the writing rankle,
Let the wretch go festering through Florence) —
Dante, who loved well because he hated,
Hated wickedness that hinders loving,
Dante standing, studying his angel, —
In there broke the folk of his Inferno.
Says he — 'Certain people of importance'
(Such he gave his daily, dreadful line to)
'Entered and would seize, forsooth, the poet.'
Says the poet — 'Then I stopped my painting.'

VI

You and I would rather see that angel,
Painted by the tenderness of Dante,
Would we not? — than read a fresh Inferno.

VII

You and I will never see that picture.
While he mused on love and Beatrice,
While he softened o'er his outlined angel,
In they broke, those 'people of importance':
We and Bice bear the loss for ever.

VIII

What of Rafael's sonnets, Dante's picture?
This: no artist lives and loves, that longs not
Once, and only once, and for One only,
(Ah, the prize!) to find his love a language
Fit and fair and simple and sufficient —
Using nature that's an art to others,
Not, this one time, art that's turned his nature.
Ay, of all the artists living, loving,
None but would forego his proper dowry, —
Does he paint? he fain would write a poem, —
Does he write? he fain would paint a picture,
Put to proof art alien to the artist's,
Once, and only once, and for One only,
So to be the man and leave the artist,
Gain the man's joy, miss the artist's sorrow.

IX

Wherefore? Heaven's gift takes earth's abatement!
He who smites the rock and spreads the water,
Bidding drink and live a crowd beneath him,
Even he, the minute makes immortal,
Proves, perchance, his mortal in the minute,
Desecrates, belike, the deed in doing.
While he smites, how can he but remember,
So he smote before, in such a peril,
When they stood and mocked — 'Shall smiting help us?'
When they drank and sneered — 'A stroke is easy!'
When they wiped their mouths and went their journey,
Throwing him for thanks — 'But drought was pleasant.'
Thus old memories mar the actual triumph;

Thus the doing savours of disrelish;
Thus achievement lacks a gracious somewhat;
O'er-importuned brows becloud the mandate,
Carelessness or consciousness, the gesture.
For he bears an ancient wrong about him,
Sees and knows again those phalanxed faces,
Hears, yet one time more, the 'customed prelude —
'How shouldst thou, of all men, smite, and save us?'
Guesses what is like to prove the sequel —
'Egypt's flesh-pots — nay, the drought was better.'

X

Oh, the crowd must have emphatic warrant!
Theirs, the Sinai-forehead's cloven brilliance,
Right-arm's rod-sweep, tongue's imperial fiat.
Never dares the man put off the prophet.

XI

Did he love one face from out the thousands,
(Were she Jethro's daughter, white and wifely,
Were she but the Aethiopian bond-slave,)
He would envy yon dumb patient camel,
Keeping a reserve of scanty water
Meant to save his own life in the desert;
Ready in the desert to deliver
(Kneeling down to let his breast be opened)
Hoard and life together for his mistress.

XII

I shall never, in the years remaining,
Paint you pictures, no, nor carve you statues,
Make you music that should all-express me;
So it seems: I stand on my attainment.
This of verse alone, one life allows me:
Verse and nothing else have I to give you.
Other heights in other lives, God willing —
All the gifts from all the heights, your own, Love!

XIII

Yet a semblance of resource avails us —
Shade so finely touched, love's sense must seize it.
Take these lines, look lovingly and nearly,
Lines I write the first time and the last time.
He who works in fresco, steals a hair-brush,
Curbs the liberal hand, subservient proudly,
Cramps his spirit, crowds its all in little,
Makes a strange art of an art familiar,
Fills his lady's missal-marge with flowerets.
He who blows thro' bronze, may breathe thro' silver,
Fitly serenade a slumbrous princess.
He who writes, may write for once, as I do.

XIV

Love, you saw me gather men and women,
Live or dead or fashioned by my fancy,
Enter each and all, and use their service,
Speak from every mouth, — the speech, a poem.
Hardly shall I tell my joys and sorrows,
Hopes and fears, belief and disbelieving:
I am mine and yours — the rest be all men's,
Karshook, Cleon, Norbert and the fifty.
Let me speak this once in my true person,
Not as Lippo, Roland or Andrea,
Though the fruit of speech be just this sentence —
Pray you, look on these my men and women,
Take and keep my fifty poems finished;
Where my heart lies, let my brain lie also!
Poor the speech; be how I speak, for all things.

XV

Not but that you know me! Lo, the moon's self!
Here in London, yonder late in Florence,
Still we find her face, the thrice-transfigured,
Curving on a sky imbrued with colour,
Drifted over Fiesole by twilight,
Came she, our new crescent of a hair's-breadth.

Full she flared it, lamping Samminiato,
Rounder 'twixt the cypresses and rounder,
Perfect till the nightingales applauded.
Now, a piece of her old self, impoverished,
Hard to greet, she traverses the house-roofs,
Hurries with unhandsome thrift of silver,
Goes dispiritedly, glad to finish.

XVI

What, there's nothing in the moon note-worthy?
Nay — for if that moon could love a mortal,
Use, to charm him (so to fit a fancy)
All her magic ('tis the old sweet mythos)
She would turn a new side to her mortal,
Side unseen of herdsman, huntsman, steersman —
Blank to Zoroaster on his terrace,
Blind to Galileo on his turret,
Dumb to Homer, dumb to Keats — him, even!
Think, the wonder of the moonstruck mortal —
When she turns round, comes again in heaven,
Opens out anew for worse or better?
Proves she like some portent of an iceberg
Swimming full upon the ship it founders,
Hungry with huge teeth of splintered crystals?
Proves she as the paved-work of a sapphire
Seen by Moses when he climbed the mountain?
Moses, Aaron, Nadab and Abihu
Climbed and saw the very God, the Highest,
Stand upon the paved-work of a sapphire.
Like the bodied heaven in his clearness
Shone the stone, the sapphire of that paved-work,
When they ate and drank and saw God also!

XVII

What were seen? None knows, none ever shall know.
Only this is sure — the sight were other,
Not the moon's same side, born late in Florence,
Dying now impoverished here in London.

God be thanked, the meanest of his creatures
Boasts two soul-sides, one to face the world with,
One to show a woman when he loves her.

XVIII

This I say of me, but think of you, Love!
This to you — yourself my moon of poets!
Ah, but that's the world's side, there's the wonder,
Thus they see you, praise you, think they know you.
There, in turn I stand with them and praise you,
Out of my own self, I dare to phrase it.
But the best is when I glide from out them,
Cross a step or two of dubious twilight,
Come out on the other side, the novel
Silent silver lights and darks undreamed of,
Where I hush and bless myself with silence.

XIX

Oh, their Rafael of the dear Madonnas,
Oh, their Dante of the dread Inferno,
Wrote one song — and in my brain I sing it,
Drew one angel — borne, see, on my bosom!

Note

'And they lived happily ever afterwards.' Of all the great love stories of history or literature, that of the Brownings is almost the only one of which the fairy tale ending is true. Most of the great love romances end in tragedy or parting: Antony and Cleopatra, Abélard and Héloïse, Tristram and Iseult, Romeo and Juliet, Dante and Beatrice. Perhaps it is that happiness has no history, or very seldom. 'Browning', said Francis Thompson, 'stooped and picked up a fair-coined soul that lay rusting in a pool of tears.' This tribute of Browning to his wife is to my mind a great poem, though it would have been better without the rather petulant and self-conscious stanzas IX-XI — and camels of my acquaintance have been neither dumb nor patient. Mrs Browning's tribute 'Sonnets from the Portuguese' has some unforgettable lines, such as:

'Guess now who holds thee — "Death", I said, but there
The silver answer rang: "Not Death but Love".' *A. P. W.*

CYNARA
('NON SUM QUALIS ERAM BONAE SUB REGNO CYNARAE')
ERNEST DOWSON

LAST night, ah, yesternight, betwixt her lips and mine
There fell thy shadow, Cynara! thy breath was shed
Upon my soul between the kisses and the wine;
And I was desolate and sick of an old passion,
   Yea, I was desolate and bowed my head:
I have been faithful to thee, Cynara! in my fashion.

All night upon mine heart I felt her warm heart beat,
Night-long within mine arms in love and sleep she lay;
Surely the kisses of her bought red mouth were sweet;
But I was desolate and sick of an old passion,
   When I awoke and found the dawn was grey:
I have been faithful to thee, Cynara! in my fashion.

I have forgot much, Cynara! gone with the wind,
Flung roses, roses, riotously with the throng,
Dancing, to put thy pale, lost lilies out of mind;
But I was desolate and sick of an old passion,
   Yea, all the time, because the dance was long:
I have been faithful to thee, Cynara! in my fashion.

I cried for madder music and for stronger wine,
But when the feast is finished and the lamps expire,
Then falls thy shadow, Cynara! the night is thine;
And I am desolate and sick of an old passion,
   Yea, hungry for the lips of my desire:
I have been faithful to thee, Cynara! in my fashion.

THE BANKS O' DOON
ROBERT BURNS

YE flowery banks o' bonnie Doon,
  How can ye blume sae fair!
How can ye chant, ye little birds,
  And I sae fu' o' care!

Thou'll break my heart, thou bonnie bird,
  That sings upon the bough;
Thou minds me o' the happy days
  When my fause luve was true.

Thou'll break my heart, thou bonnie bird,
  That sings beside thy mate;
For sae I sat, and sae I sang,
  And wistna o' my fate.

Aft hae I roved by bonnie Doon,
  To see the woodbine twine;
And ilka bird sang o' its luve,
  And sae did I o' mine.

Wi' lightsome heart I pu'd a rose
  Upon a morn in June;
And sae I flourish'd on the morn,
  And sae was pu'd or' noon.

Wi' lightsome heart I pu'd a rose
  Upon its thorny tree;
But my fause luver staw my rose,
  And left the thorn wi' me.

THE LONGEST JOURNEY

from EPIPSYCHIDION *by*
PERCY BYSSHE SHELLEY

I NEVER was attached to that great sect,
Whose doctrine is, that each one should select
Out of the crowd a mistress or a friend,
And all the rest, though fair and wise, commend
To cold oblivion, though it is in the code
Of modern morals, and the beaten road
Which those poor slaves with weary footsteps tread,
Who travel to their home among the dead
By the broad highway of the world, and so
With one chained friend, perhaps a jealous foe,
The dreariest and the longest journey go.

KISS'D YESTREEN

ANON

KISS'D yestreen, and kiss'd yestreen,
Up the Gallowgate, down the Green:
I've woo'd wi' lords, and woo'd wi' lairds,
I've mool'd wi' carles and mell'd wi' cairds,
I've kiss'd wi' priests — 'twas done i' the dark,
Twice in my gown, and thrice in my sark:
But priest, nor lord, nor loon can gie
Sic kindly kisses as he gae me.

ANY WIFE TO ANY HUSBAND

ROBERT BROWNING

I

MY love, this is the bitterest, that thou
Who art all truth and who dost love me now
  As thine eyes say, as thy voice breaks to say —
Shouldst love so truly and couldst love me still
A whole long life through, had but love its will,
  Would death that leads me from thee brook delay!

II

I have but to be by thee, and thy hand
Would never let mine go, nor heart withstand
  The beating of my heart to reach its place.
When should I look for thee and feel thee gone?
When cry for the old comfort and find none?
  Never, I know! Thy soul is in thy face.

III

Oh, I should fade — 'tis willed so! might I save,
Gladly I would, whatever beauty gave
  Joy to thy sense, for that was precious too.
It is not to be granted. But the soul
Whence the love comes, all ravage leaves that whole;
  Vainly the flesh fades: soul makes all things new.

IV

And 'twould not be because my eye grew dim
Thou couldst not find the love there, thanks to Him
   Who never is dishonoured in the spark
He gave us from His fire of fires, and bade
Remember whence it sprang nor be afraid
   While that burns on, though all the rest grow dark.

V

So, how thou wouldst be perfect, white and clean
Outside as inside, soul and soul's demesne
   Alike, this body given to show it by!
Oh, three-parts through the worst of life's abyss,
What plaudits from the next world after this,
   Couldst thou repeat a stroke and gain the sky!

VI

And is it not the bitterer to think
That, disengage our hands and thou wilt sink
   Although thy love was love in very deed?
I know that nature! Pass a festive day
Thou dost not throw its relic-flower away
   Nor bid its music's loitering echo speed.

VII

Thou let'st the stranger's glove lie where it fell;
If old things remain old things all is well,
   For thou art grateful as becomes man best:
And hadst thou only heard me play one tune,
Or viewed me from a window, not so soon
   With thee would such things fade as with the rest.

VIII

I seem to see! we meet and part; 'tis brief;
The book I opened keeps a folded leaf,
   The very chair I sat on, breaks the rank;
That is a portrait of me on the wall —
Three lines, my face comes at so slight a call:
   And for all this, one little hour's to thank.

IX

But now, because the hour through years was fixed,
Because our inmost beings met and mixed,
    Because thou once hast loved me — wilt thou dare
Say to thy soul and Who may list beside,
'Therefore she is immortally my bride,
    Chance cannot change my love, nor time impair.

X

'So, what if in the dusk of life that's left,
I, a tired traveller, of my sun bereft,
    Look from my path when, mimicking the same,
The fire-fly glimpses past me, come and gone?
— Where was it till the sunset? where anon
    It will be at the sunrise! what's to blame?'

XI

Is it so helpful to thee? canst thou take
The mimic up, nor, for the true thing's sake,
    Put gently by such efforts at a beam?
Is the remainder of the way so long
Thou need'st the little solace, thou the strong?
    Watch out thy watch, let weak ones doze and dream!

XII

'— Ah, but the fresher faces! Is it true,'
Thou'lt ask, 'some eyes are beautiful and new?
    Some hair, — how can one choose but grasp such
And if a man would press his lips to lips   [wealth?
Fresh as the wilding hedge-rose cup there slips
    The dew-drop out of, must it be by stealth?

XIII

'It cannot change the love still kept for Her,
Much more than, such a picture to prefer
    Passing a day with, to a room's bare side:
The painted form takes nothing she possessed,
Yet, while the Titian's Venus lies at rest,
    A man looks. Once more, what is there to chide?'

XIV

So must I see, from where I sit and watch,
My own self sell myself, my hand attach
    Its warrant to the very thefts from me —
Thy singleness of soul that made me proud,
Thy purity of heart I loved aloud,
    Thy man's-truth I was bold to bid God see!

XV

Love so, then, if thou wilt! Give all thou canst
Away to the new faces — disentranced,
    (Say it and think it) obdurate no more,
Re-issue looks and words from the old mint,
Pass them afresh, no matter whose the print
    Image and superscription once they bore!

XVI

Re-coin thyself and give it them to spend, —
It all comes to the same thing at the end,
    Since mine thou wast, mine art and mine shalt be,
Faithful or faithless, sealing up the sum
Or lavish of my treasure, thou must come
    Back to the heart's place here I keep for thee!

XVII

Only, why should it be with stain at all?
Why must I, 'twixt the leaves of coronal,
    Put any kiss of pardon on thy brow?
Why need the other women know so much,
And talk together, 'Such the look and such
    The smile he used to love with, then as now!'

XVIII

Might I die last and show thee! Should I find
Such hardship in the few years left behind,
    If free to take and light my lamp, and go
Into thy tomb, and shut the door and sit
Seeing thy face on those four sides of it
    The better that they are so blank, I know!

XIX

Why, time was what I wanted, to turn o'er
'Within my mind each look, get more and more
   By heart each word, too much to learn at first;
And join thee all the fitter for the pause
'Neath the low door-way's lintel. That were cause
   For lingering, though thou calledst, if I durst!

XX

And yet thou art the nobler of us two:
What dare I dream of, that thou canst not do,
   Outstripping my ten small steps with one stride?
I'll say then, here's a trial and a task —
Is it to bear? — if easy, I'll not ask:
   Though love fail, I can trust on in thy pride.

XXI

Pride? — when those eyes forestall the life behind
The death I have to go through! — when I find,
   Now that I want thy help most, all of thee!
What did I fear? Thy love shall hold me fast
Until the little minute's sleep is past
   And I wake saved. — And yet it will not be!

WHISTLE, AND I'LL COME TO YOU, MY LAD

ROBERT BURNS

O WHISTLE, and I'll come to you, my lad;
O whistle, and I'll come to you, my lad:
Tho' father and mither and a' should gae mad,
O whistle, and I'll come to you, my lad.

But warily tent, when ye come to court me,
And come na unless the back-yett be a-jee;
Syne up the back-stile, and let naebody see,
And come as ye were na comin' to me.
And come as ye were na comin' to me.

At kirk, or at market, whene'er ye meet me,
Gang by me as tho' that ye car'd na a flee:
But steal me a blink o' your bonnie black ee,
Yet look as ye were na lookin' at me.
Yet look as ye were na lookin' at me.

Aye vow and protest that ye care na for me,
And whiles ye ma lightly my beauty a wee;
But court na anither, tho' jokin' ye be,
For fear that she wyle your fancy frae me.
For fear that she wyle your fancy frae me.

SONNET CXXIX

William Shakespeare

Th'expense of Spirit in a waste of shame
Is lust in action; and till action, lust
Is perjured, murderous, bloody, full of blame,
Savage, extreme, rude, cruel, not to trust;
Enjoy'd no sooner but despisèd straight;
Past reason hunted; and, no sooner had,
Past reason hated, as a swallow'd bait
On purpose laid to make the taker mad:
Mad in pursuit, and in possession so;
Had, having, and in quest to have, extreme;
A bliss in proof, and proved, a very woe;
Before, a joy proposed; behind, a dream.
  All this the world well knows; yet none knows well
  To shun the heaven that leads men to this hell.

THE PRAISE OF DUST

G. K. Chesterton

'What of vile dust?' the preacher said.
  Methought the whole world woke,
The dead stone lived beneath my foot,
  And my whole body spoke.

F

'You, that play tyrant to the dust,
    And stamp its wrinkled face,
This patient star that flings you not
    Far into homeless space.

'Come down out of your dusty shrine
    The living dust to see,
The flowers that at your sermon's end
    Stand blazing silently.

'Rich white and blood-red blossom; stones,
    Lichens like fire encrust;
A gleam of blue, a glare of gold,
    The vision of the dust.

'Pass them all by: till, as you come
    Where, at the city's edge,
Under a tree — I know it well —
    Under a lattice ledge,

'The sunshine falls on one brown head.
    You, too, O cold of clay,
Eater of stones, may haply hear
    The trumpets of that day.

'When God to all his paladins
    By his own splendour swore
To make a fairer face than heaven,
    Of dust and nothing more.'

TO HELEN

EDGAR ALLAN POE

HELEN, thy beauty is to me
    Like those Nicèan barks of yore
That gently, o'er a perfumed sea,
    The weary way-worn wanderer bore
    To his own native shore.

On desperate seas long wont to roam,
　Thy hyacinth hair, thy classic face,
Thy Naiad airs have brought me home
　To the glory that was Greece,
And the grandeur that was Rome.

Lo, in yon brilliant window-niche
　How statue-like I see thee stand,
　The agate lamp within thy hand!
Ah! Psyche, from the regions which
　Are holy land!

THE STRANGE MUSIC

G. K. Chesterton

Other loves may sink and settle, other loves may loose and slack,
But I wander like a minstrel with a harp upon his back,
Though the harp be on my bosom, though I finger and I fret,
Still, my hope is all before me: for I cannot play it yet.

In your strings is hid a music that no hand hath e'er let fall,
In your soul is sealed a pleasure that you have not known at all;
Pleasure subtle as your spirit, strange and slender as your frame,
Fiercer than the pain that folds you, softer than your sorrow's name.

Not as mine, my soul's anointed, not as mine the rude and light
Easy mirth of many faces, swaggering pride of song and fight;
Something stranger, something sweeter, something waiting you afar,
Secret as your stricken senses, magic as your sorrows are.

But on this, God's harp supernal, stretched but to be stricken once,
Hoary time is a beginner, Life a bungler, Death a dunce.
But I will not fear to match them — no, by God, I will not fear,
I will learn you, I will play you and the stars stand still to hear.

WHEN I WAS ONE-AND-TWENTY

A. E. HOUSMAN

When I was one-and-twenty
   I heard a wise man say,
'Give crowns and pounds and guineas
   But not your heart away;
Give pearls away and rubies
   But keep your fancy free.'
But I was one-and-twenty,
   No use to talk to me.

When I was one-and-twenty
   I heard him say again,
'The heart out of the bosom
   Was never given in vain;
'Tis paid with sighs a plenty
   And sold for endless rue.'
And I am two-and-twenty,
   And oh, 'tis true, 'tis true.

ROMANCE

ROBERT LOUIS STEVENSON

I will make you brooches and toys for your delight
Of bird-song at morning and star-shine at night.
I will make a palace fit for you and me,
Of green days in forests and blue days at sea.

I will make my kitchen, and you shall keep your room,
Where white flows the river and bright blows the broom,
And you shall wash your linen and keep your body white
In rainfall at morning and dewfall at night.

And this shall be for music when no one else is near,
The fine song for singing, the rare song to hear!
That only I remember, that only you admire,
Of the broad road that stretches and the roadside fire.

LOCHINVAR

from MARMION *by*

SIR WALTER SCOTT

O, YOUNG Lochinvar is come out of the west,
Through all the wide Border his steed was the best;
And save his good broadsword he weapons had none,
He rode all unarm'd, and he rode all alone.
So faithful in love, and so dauntless in war,
There never was knight like the young Lochinvar.

He staid not for brake, and he stopp'd not for stone,
He swam the Eske river where ford there was none;
But ere he alighted at Netherby gate,
The bride had consented, the gallant came late:
For a laggard in love, and a dastard in war,
Was to wed the fair Ellen of brave Lochinvar.

So boldly he enterd the Netherby Hall,
Among bride's-men, and kinsmen, and brothers, and all:
Then spoke the bride's father, his hand on his sword,
(For the poor craven bridegroom said never a word,)
'O come ye in peace here, or come ye in war,
Or to dance at our bridal, young Lord Lochinvar?' —

'I long woo'd your daughter, my suit you denied; —
Love swells like the Solway, but ebbs like its tide —
And now am I come, with this lost love of mine,
To lead but one measure, drink one cup of wine.
There are maidens in Scotland more lovely by far,
That would gladly be bride to the young Lochinvar.'

The bride kiss'd the goblet: the knight took it up,
He quaff'd off the wine, and he threw down the cup.
She look'd down to blush, and she look'd up to sigh,
With a smile on her lips, and a tear in her eye.
He took her soft hand, ere her mother could bar, —
'Now tread we a measure!' said young Lochinvar.

So stately his form, and so lovely her face,
That never a hall such a galliard did grace;
While her mother did fret, and her father did fume,
And the bridegroom stood dangling his bonnet and plume,
And the bride-maidens whisper'd, "Twere better by far,
To have match'd our fair cousin with young Lochinvar.'

One touch to her hand, and one word in her ear,
When they reach'd the hall-door, and the charger stood near;
So light to the croupe the fair lady he swung,
So light to the saddle before her he sprung!
'She is won! we are gone, over bank, bush, and scaur:
They'll have fleet steeds that follow,' quoth young Lochinvar.

There was mounting 'mong Graemes of the Netherby clan;
Forsters, Fenwicks, and Musgraves, they rode and they ran;
There was racing and chasing, on Cannobie Lee,
But the lost bride of Netherby ne'er did they see.
So daring in love, and so dauntless in war,
Have ye e'er heard of gallant like young Lochinvar?

THE LOVE SONG OF HAR DYAL

RUDYARD KIPLING

ALONE upon the housetops to the North
I turn and watch the lightning in the sky —
The glamour of thy footsteps in the North —
Come back to me, Belovèd, or I die!

Below my feet the still bazar is laid;
Far, far below the weary camels lie —
The camels and the captives of thy raid —
Come back to me, Belovèd, or I die!

My father's wife is old and harsh with years,
And drudge of all my father's house am I;
My bread is sorrow and my drink is tears —
Come back to me, Belovèd, or I die!

ME HEART

G. K. CHESTERTON

I COME from Castlepatrick, and me heart is on me sleeve,
And any sword or pistol boy can hit it with me leave,
It shines there for an epaulette, as golden as a flame,
And naked as me ancestors, as noble as me name.
For I come from Castlepatrick and me heart is on me sleeve,
But a lady stole it from me on St Gallowglass's Eve.

The folk that live in Liverpool, their heart is in their boots;
They go to hell like lambs, they do, because the hooter hoots.
Where men may not be dancin', though the wheels may dance all day;
And men may not be smokin'; but only chimneys may.
But I come from Castlepatrick, and me heart is on me sleeve,
But a lady stole it from me on St Poleander's Eve.

The folk that live in black Belfast, their heart is in their mouth,
They see us making murders in the meadows of the South;
They think a plough's a rack, they do, and cattle-calls are creeds,
And they think we're burnin' witches when we're only burnin' weeds;
But I come from Castlepatrick, and me heart is on me sleeve,
But a lady stole it from me on St Barnabas's Eve.

SONNET CXXX

WILLIAM SHAKESPEARE

My mistress' eyes are nothing like the sun;
Coral is far more red than her lips' red:
If snow be white, why then her breasts are dun;
If hairs be wires, black wires grow on her head.
I have seen roses damasked, red and white,
But no such roses see I in her cheeks;
And in some perfumes is there more delight
Than in the breath that from my mistress reeks.
I love to hear her speak, — yet well I know

That music hath a far more pleasing sound;
I grant I never saw a goddess go, —
My mistress when she walks, treads on the ground;
   And yet, by heavens, I think my love as rare
   As any she belied with false compare.

SIR RICHARD'S SONG

A.D. 1066

RUDYARD KIPLING

I FOLLOWED my Duke ere I was a lover,
   To take from England fief and fee;
But now this game is the other way over —
   But now England hath taken me!

I had my horse, my shield and banner,
   And a boy's heart, so whole and free.
But now I sing in another manner —
   But now England hath taken me!

As for my Father in his tower,
   Asking news of my ship at sea,
He will remember his own hour —
   Tell him England hath taken me!

As for my Mother in her bower,
   That rules my Father so cunningly,
She will remember a maiden's power —
   Tell her England hath taken me!

As for my Brother in Rouen City,
   A nimble and naughty page is he,
But he will come to suffer and pity —
   Tell him England hath taken me!

As for my little Sister waiting
   In the pleasant orchards of Normandie,
Tell her youth is the time for mating —
   Tell her England hath taken me!

As for my comrades in camp and highway,
   That lift their eyebrows scornfully,
Tell them their way is not my way —
   Tell them England hath taken me!

Kings and Princes and Barons famèd,
   Knights and Captains in your degree;
Hear me a little before I am blamèd —
   Seeing England hath taken me!

Howso great man's strength be reckoned,
   There are two things he cannot flee.
Love is the first, and Death is the second —
   And Love in England hath taken me!

ONE WAY OF LOVE
ROBERT BROWNING

I

ALL June I bound the rose in sheaves.
Now, rose by rose, I strip the leaves
And strew them where Pauline may pass.
She will not turn aside? Alas!
Let them lie. Suppose they die?
The chance was they might take her eye.

II

How many a month I strove to suit
These stubborn fingers to the lute!
To-day I venture all I know.
She will not hear my music? So!
Break the string; fold music's wing:
Suppose Pauline had bade me sing!

III

My whole life long I learned to love.
This hour my utmost art I prove
And speak my passion. — Heaven or Hell?
She will not give me Heaven? 'Tis well!
Lose who may — I still can say,
Those who win Heaven, blest are they!

WHY SO PALE AND WAN?

SIR JOHN SUCKLING

WHY so pale and wan, fond lover?
    Prithee, why so pale?
Will, when looking well can't move her,
    Looking ill prevail?
    Prithee, why so pale?

Why so dull and mute, young sinner?
    Prithee, why so mute?
Will, when speaking well can't win her,
    Saying nothing do 't?
    Prithee, why so mute?

Quit, quit for shame! This will not move;
    This cannot take her.
If of herself she will not love,
    Nothing can make her:
    The devil take her!

LOVE'S SECRET

WILLIAM BLAKE

NEVER seek to tell thy love,
    Love that never told can be;
For the gentle wind doth move
    Silently, invisibly.

I told my love, I told my love,
    I told her all my heart,
Trembling, cold, in ghastly fears.
    Ah! she did depart!

Soon after she was gone from me,
    A traveller came by,
Silently, invisibly:
    He took her with a sigh.

THE CLOD AND THE PEBBLE

William Blake

'LOVE seeketh not Itself to please,
Nor for Itself hath any care,
But for another gives its ease,
And builds a Heaven in Hell's despair.'

So sung a little Clod of Clay
Trodden with the cattle's feet,
But a Pebble of the brook
Warbled out these metres meet:

'Love seeketh only Self to please,
To bind another to Its delight,
Joys in another's loss of ease,
And builds a Hell in Heaven's despite.'

THE PARTING

Michael Drayton

SINCE there's no help, come let us kiss and part —
Nay, I have done, you get no more of me;
And I am glad, yea, glad with all my heart,
That thus so cleanly I myself can free.

Shake hands for ever, cancel all our vows,
And when we meet at any time again,
Be it not seen in either of our brows
That we one jot of former love retain.
Now at the last gasp of Love's latest breath,
When, his pulse failing, Passion speechless lies,
When Faith is kneeling by his bed of death,
And Innocence is closing up his eyes,
　— Now if thou wouldst, when all have given him over,
　From death to life thou might'st him yet recover.

WHEN YOU ARE OLD

W. B. Yeats

When you are old and gray and full of sleep
　And nodding by the fire, take down this book,
　And slowly read, and dream of the soft look
Your eyes had once, and of their shadows deep;

How many loved your moments of glad grace,
　And loved your beauty with love false or true;
　But one man loved the pilgrim soul in you,
And loved the sorrows of your changing face.

And bending down beside the glowing bars,
　Murmur, a little sadly, how love fled
　And paced upon the mountains overhead,
And hid his face amid a crowd of stars.

JOHN ANDERSON, MY JO

Robert Burns

John Anderson, my jo, John,
　When we were first acquent,
Your locks were like the raven,
　Your bonnie brow was brent;

But now your brow is beld, John,
 Your locks are like the snow;
But blessings on your frosty pow,
 John Anderson, my jo!

John Anderson, my jo, John,
 We clamb the hill thegither;
And monie a canty day, John,
 We've had wi' ane anither:
Now we maun totter down, John,
 But hand in hand we'll go,
And sleep thegither at the foot,
 John Anderson, my jo.

LA BELLE DAME SANS MERCI

John Keats

'O what can ail thee, knight-at-arms,
 Alone and palely loitering?
The sedge is wither'd from the lake,
 And no birds sing.

O what can ail thee, knight-at-arms,
 So haggard and so woe-begone?
The squirrel's granary is full,
 And the harvest's done.

I see a lily on thy brow
 With anguish moist and fever dew;
And on thy cheek a fading rose
 Fast withereth too.'

'I met a lady in the meads,
 Full beautiful — a faery's child,
Her hair was long, her foot was light,
 And her eyes were wild.

I made a garland for her head,
   And bracelets too, and fragrant zone;
She look'd at me as she did love,
   And made sweet moan.

I set her on my pacing steed
   And nothing else saw all day long,
For sideways would she lean, and sing
   A faery's song.

She found me roots of relish sweet,
   And honey wild and manna dew,
And sure in language strange she said,
   "I love thee true!"

She took me to her elfin grot,
   And there she wept and sigh'd full sore;
And there I shut her wild, wild eyes
   With kisses four.

And there she lullèd me asleep,
   And there I dream'd — Ah! woe betide!
The latest dream I ever dream'd
   On the cold hill's side.

I saw pale kings and princes too,
   Pale warriors, death-pale were they all;
Who cried — "La belle Dame sans Merci
   Hath thee in thrall!"

I saw their starved lips in the gloam
   With horrid warning gapèd wide,
And I awoke and found me here
   On the cold hill's side.

And this is why I sojourn here
   Alone and palely loitering,
Though the sedge is wither'd from the lake,
   And no birds sing.'

ANNABEL LEE

Edgar Allan Poe

It was many and many a year ago,
 In a kingdom by the sea,
That a maiden there lived whom you may know
 By the name of Annabel Lee.
And this maiden she lived with no other thought
 Than to love and be loved by me.

I was a child and she was a child
 In this kingdom by the sea:
But we loved with a love that was more than love —
 I and my Annabel Lee,
With a love that the wingèd seraphs of heaven
 Coveted her and me.

And this was the reason that, long ago,
 In this kingdom by the sea,
A wind blew out of a cloud, chilling
 My beautiful Annabel Lee,
So that her high-born kinsmen came
 And bore her away from me,
To shut her up in a sepulchre
 In this kingdom by the sea.

The angels, not half so happy in heaven,
 Went envying her and me —
Yes! that was the reason (as all men know,
 In this kingdom by the sea)
That the wind came out of the cloud one night,
 Chilling and killing my Annabel Lee.

But our love it was stronger by far than the love
 Of those who were older than we —
 Of many far wiser than we —
And neither the angels in heaven above,
 Nor the demons down under the sea,
Can ever dissever my soul from the soul
 Of the beautiful Annabel Lee:

    For the moon never beams without bringing me dreams
      Of the beautiful Annabel Lee;
And the stars never rise, but I feel the bright eyes
      Of the beautiful Annabel Lee;
And so, all the night-tide, I lie down by the side
Of my darling — my darling — my life and my bride,
    In the sepulchre there by the sea,
    In her tomb by the sounding sea.

TAM I' THE KIRK

VIOLET JACOB

O JEAN, my Jean, when the bell ca's the congregation
    Owre valley an' hill wi' the ding frae its iron mou'.
When a' body's thochts is set on his ain salvation,
    Mine's set on you.

There's a reid rose lies on the Buik o' the Word 'afore ye
    That was growin' braw on its bush at the keek o' day,
But the lad that pu'd yon flower i' the mornin's glory,
    He canna pray.

He canna pray; but there's nane i' the Kirk will heed him
    Whaur he sits sae still his lane at the side of the wa',
For nane but the reid rose kens what my lassie gie'd him,
    It an' us twa!

He canna sing for the sang that his ain he'rt raises,
    He canna see for the mist that's 'afore his een,
And a voice drouns the hale o' the psalms an' the paraphrases,
    Cryin' 'Jean, Jean, Jean!'

LOVE

GEORGE HERBERT

LOVE bade me welcome; yet my soul drew back,
  Guilty of dust and sin.
But quick-eyed Love, observing me grow slack
  From my first entrance in,
Drew nearer to me, sweetly questioning
  If I lack'd anything.

'A guest,' I answer'd, 'worthy to be here':
  Love said, 'You shall be he.'
'I, the unkind, ungrateful? Ah, my dear,
  I cannot look on Thee.'
Love took my hand and smiling did reply,
  'Who made the eyes but I?'

'Truth, Lord: but I have marr'd them: let my shame
  Go where it doth deserve.'
'And know you not,' says Love, 'Who bore the blame?'
  'My dear, then I will serve.'
'You must sit down,' says Love, 'and taste my meat.'
  So I did sit and eat.

PARTING AT DAWN

from JOHN ATTYE's First Book of Airs, 1622

ANON

ON a time the amorous Silvy
Said to her shepherd, 'Sweet, how do you?
Kiss me this once, and then God be wi' you,
               My sweetest dear!
Kiss me this once and then God be wi' you,
For now the morning draweth near.'

With that, her fairest bosom showing,
Opening her lips, rich perfumes blowing,
She said, 'Now kiss me and be going,
                              My sweetest dear!
Kiss me this once and then be going,
For now the morning draweth near.'

With that the shepherd waked from sleeping,
And, spying where the day was peeping,
He said, 'Now take my soul in keeping,
                              My sweetest dear!
Kiss me, and take my soul in keeping,
Since I must go, now day is near.'

THE CAP AND BELLS

W. B. YEATS

THE jester walked in the garden:
The garden had fallen still;
He bade his soul rise upward
And stand on her window-sill.

It rose in a straight blue garment,
When owls began to call:
It had grown wise-tongued by thinking
Of a quiet and light footfall;

But the young queen would not listen;
She rose in her pale night gown;
She drew in the heavy casement
And pushed the latches down.

He bade his heart go to her,
When the owls called out no more;
In a red and quivering garment
It sang to her through the door.

It had grown sweet-tongued by dreaming,
Of a flutter of flower-like hair;
But she took up her fan from the table
And waved it off on the air.

'I have cap and bells,' he pondered,
'I will send them to her and die';
And when the morning whitened
He left them where she went by.

She laid them upon her bosom,
Under a cloud of her hair,
And her red lips sang them a love-song:
Till stars grew out of the air.

She opened her door and her window,
And the heart and the soul came through,
To her right hand came the red one,
To her left hand came the blue.

They set up a noise like crickets,
A chattering wise and sweet,
And her hair was a folded flower
And the quiet of love in her feet.

4. THE CALL OF THE WILD

THIS section contains poetry of the sea, the road, the hills, the chase — the poetry of youth and adventure.

Comparatively few of our best known poets have themselves experienced travel and adventure. Milton, Donne, Blake, Keats, Tennyson, A. E. Housman, to name a few, are indoor hearth-side poets. Tennyson wrote much of adventure but his heroes and adventurers are of the type who figure in coloured supplements for Xmas numbers. His ballad of the *Revenge* makes a romantic gentlemanly hero of a savage Elizabethan tough. Compare too his self-consciously heroic Ulysses — drawn from the same model as his Round Table Knights — with Flecker's 'talkative bald-headed seaman' and his 'great lies about his wooden horse'. Flecker had seen the real Greek mariner and knew the type.

Byron wrote much of adventure and experienced some, but was more at home in a drawing-room than on the poop of a ship or in a bivouac. Shelley, Browning, Flecker, Kipling, Masefield, Belloc are more of the overseas, outdoor type. Shakespeare can hardly be written down as a traveller, but all life was adventure in Elizabethan days.

That spirit of adventure which once ran so high in the young men of the British Isles grew thin and sluggish in the years between the wars. They preferred to experience their adventure vicariously by way of Hollywood-made films and cheap sensational fiction, also largely from America; their travels abroad were by Cook's Tours and 'luxury' cruises. They marry younger and become 'domesticated' — the process by which man, to serve his purposes, has turned far-ranging wild-fowl into barndoor hens, and woman, to serve hers, has turned nomad man into the black-coated clerk. They are open to the taunt thrown by Juvenal at the Roman people more than 1800 years ago that their main desire was 'panem et circenses' — cake and cinemas.

Perhaps the enervating march of civilization is as inevitable as old age, but it seems to have come on us as a nation somewhat suddenly. Forty years ago, when I joined the Army, almost every subaltern sought service abroad in the hope of sport and adventure; twenty years later almost every subaltern did all he could to avoid foreign service. Even our airmen, who must surely have the spirit of adventure, risk death lightly but complain bitterly of discomfort. It seems to me that prosperity slackened our fibres and that we are very definitely less tough in mind and in body than we were even twenty years ago. It is a law of life which has yet to be broken that a nation can only earn the right to live soft by being prepared to die hard in defence of its living. Our seamen at least in the fleet and in the merchant navy are still doing so, as they have always done. Our soldiers, our airmen, John Citizen and Jill Citizen are relearning the lesson; in the silken East some of our merchants and administrators have it still to learn. May the spirit of adventure and self-sacrifice be rekindled and stay with us after the war, when we undertake the greatest adventure yet laid on the human race, to refashion a shattered world. *A. P. W.*

SESTINA OF THE TRAMP-ROYAL

Rudyard Kipling

Speakin' in general, I 'ave tried 'em all,
The 'appy roads that take you o'er the world.
Speakin' in general, I 'ave found them good
For such as cannot use one bed too long,
But must get 'ence, the same as I 'ave done,
An' go observin' matters till they die.

What do it matter where or 'ow we die,
So long as we've our 'ealth to watch it all —
The different ways that different things are done,
An' men an' women lovin' in this world —
Takin' our chances as they come along,
An' when they ain't, pretendin' they are good?

In cash or credit — no, it aren't no good;
You 'ave to 'ave the 'abit or you'd die,
Unless you lived your life but one day long,
Nor didn't prophesy nor fret at all,

But drew your tucker some'ow from the world,
An' never bothered what you might ha' done.

But, Gawd, what things are they I 'aven't done?
I've turned my 'and to most, an' turned it good,
In various situations round the world —
For 'im that doth not work must surely die;
But that's no reason man should labour all
'Is life on one same shift; life's none so long.

Therefore, from job to job I've moved along.
Pay couldn't 'old me when my time was done,
For something in my 'ead upset me all,
Till I 'ad dropped whatever 'twas for good,
An', out at sea, be'eld the dock-lights die,
An' met my mate — the wind that tramps the world!

It's like a book, I think, this bloomin' world,
Which you can read and care for just so long,
But presently you feel that you will die
Unless you get the page you're readin' done,
An' turn another — likely not so good;
But what you're after is to turn 'em all.

Gawd bless this world! Whatever she 'ath done —
Excep' when awful long — I've found it good.
So write, before I die, "E liked it all!'

THE SONG OF HONOUR

Ralph Hodgson

I climbed a hill as light fell short,
And rooks came home in scramble sort,
And filled the trees and flapped and fought,
And sang themselves to sleep;
An owl from nowhere with no sound

Swung by and soon was nowhere found,
I heard him calling half-way round,
Holloing loud and deep;
A pair of stars, faint pins of light,
Then many a star, sailed into sight,
And all the stars, the flower of night,
Were round me at a leap;
To tell how still the valleys lay
I heard a watchdog miles away,
And bells of distant sheep.

I heard no more of bird or bell,
The mastiff in a slumber fell,
I stared into the sky,
As wondering men have always done
Since beauty and the stars were one,
Though none so hard as I.

It seemed, so still the valleys were,
As if the whole world knelt at prayer,
Save me and me alone;
So pure and wide that silence was
I feared to bend a blade of grass,
And there I stood like stone.

There, sharp and sudden, there I heard —
    Ah! some wild lovesick singing bird
    Woke singing in the trees?
    The nightingale and babble-wren
    Were in the English greenwood then,
    And you heard one of these?

The babble-wren and nightingale
Sang in the Abyssinian vale
That season of the year!
Yet, true enough, I heard them plain,
I heard them both again, again,
As sharp and sweet and clear

As if the Abyssinian tree
Had thrust a bough across the sea,
Had thrust a bough across to me
With music for my ear!

I heard them both, and oh! I heard
The song of every singing bird
That sings beneath the sky,
And with the song of lark and wren
The song of mountains, moths and men
And seas and rainbows vie!

I heard the universal choir,
The Sons of Light exalt their Sire
With universal song,
Earth's lowliest and loudest notes,
Her million times ten million throats
Exalt Him loud and long,
And lips and lungs and tongues of Grace
From every part and every place
Within the shining of His face,
The universal throng.

I heard the hymn of being sound
From every well of honour found
In human sense and soul:
The song of poets when they write
The testament of Beautysprite
Upon a flying scroll,
The song of painters when they take
A burning brush for Beauty's sake
And limn her features whole —

The song of men divinely wise
Who look and see in starry skies
Not stars so much as robins' eyes,
And when these pale away
Hear flocks of shiny pleiades
Among the plums and apple trees
Sing in the summer day —

The song of all both high and low
To some blest vision true,
The song of beggars when they throw
The crust of pity all men owe
To hungry sparrows in the snow,
Old beggars hungry too —
The song of kings of kingdoms when
They rise above their fortune Men,
And crown themselves anew —

The song of courage, heart and will
And gladness in a fight,
Of men who face a hopeless hill
With sparking and delight,
The bells and bells of song that ring
Round banners of a cause or king
From armies bleeding white —

The song of sailors every one
When monstrous tide and tempest run
At ships like bulls at red,
When stately ships are twirled and spun
Like whipping tops and help there's none
And mighty ships ten thousand ton
Go down like lumps of lead —

And song of fighters stern as they
At odds with fortune night and day,
Crammed up in cities grim and grey
As thick as bees in hives,
Hosannas of a lowly throng
Who sing unconscious of their song,
Whose lips are in their lives —

And song of some at holy war
With spells and ghouls more dread by far
Than deadly seas and cities are
Or hordes of quarrelling kings —

The song of fighters great and small,
The song of pretty fighters all
And high heroic things —

The song of lovers — who knows how
Twitched up from place and time
Upon a sigh, a blush, a vow,
A curve or hue of cheek or brow,
Borne up and off from here and now
Into the void sublime!

And crying loves and passions still
In every key from soft to shrill
And numbers never done,
Dog-loyalties to faith and friend,
And loves like Ruth's of old no end,
And intermission none —

And burst on burst for beauty and
For numbers not behind,
From men whose love of motherland
Is like a dog's for one dear hand,
Sole, selfless, boundless, blind —
And song of some with hearts beside
For men and sorrows far and wide,
Who watch the world with pity and pride
And warm to all mankind —

And endless joyous music rise
From children at their play,
And endless soaring lullabies
From happy, happy mothers' eyes,
And answering crows and baby-cries,
How many who shall say!
And many a song as wondrous well
With pangs and sweets intolerable
From lonely hearths too grey to tell,
God knows how utter grey!

And song from many a house of care
When pain has forced a footing there
And there's a Darkness on the stair
Will not be turned away —
And song — that song whose singers come
With old kind tales of pity from
The Great Compassion's lips,
That make the bells of Heaven to peal
Round pillows frosty with the feel
Of Death's cold finger tips —

The song of men all sorts and kinds,
As many tempers, moods and minds
As leaves are on a tree,
As many faiths and castes and creeds,
As many human bloods and breeds,
As in the world may be;
The song of each and all who gaze
On Beauty in her naked blaze,
Or see her dimly in a haze,
Or get her light in fitful rays
And tiniest needles even,
The song of all not wholly dark,
Not wholly sunk in stupor stark
Too deep for groping Heaven —
And alleluias sweet and clear
And wild with beauty men mishear,
From choirs of song as near and dear
To Paradise as they,
The everlasting pipe and flute
Of wind and sea and bird and brute,
And lips deaf men imagine mute
In wood and stone and clay:

The music of a lion strong
That shakes a hill a whole night long,
A hill as loud as he,
The twitter of a mouse among

Melodious greenery,
The ruby's and the rainbow's song,
The nightingale's — all three,
The song of life that wells and flows
From every leopard, lark and rose
And everything that gleams or goes
Lack-lustre in the sea.

I heard it all, each, every note
Of every lung and tongue and throat,
Ay, every rhythm and rhyme
Of everything that lives and loves
And upward, ever upward moves
From lowly to sublime!
Earth's multitudinous Sons of Light,
I heard them lift their lyric might
With each and every chanting sprite
That lit the sky that wondrous night
As far as eye could climb!

I heard it all, I heard the whole
Harmonious hymn of being roll
Up through the chapel of my soul
And at the altar die,
And in the awful quiet then
Myself I heard, Amen, Amen,
Amen I heard me cry!
I heard it all and then although
I caught my flying senses, Oh,
A dizzy man was I!
I stood and stared; the sky was lit,
The sky was stars all over it,
I stood, I knew not why,
Without a wish, without a will,
I stood upon that silent hill
And stared into the sky until
My eyes were blind with stars and still
I stared into the sky.

SAUL

Robert Browning

[Stanza IX]

'Oh, our manhood's prime vigour! no spirit feels waste,
Not a muscle is stopped in its playing, nor sinew unbraced.
Oh, the wild joys of living! the leaping from rock up to rock —
The strong rending of boughs from the fir-tree, — the cool silver shock
Of the plunge in a pool's living water, — the hunt of the bear,
And the sultriness showing the lion is couched in his lair.
And the meal — the rich dates yellowed over with gold dust divine,
And the locust's-flesh steeped in the pitcher! the full draught of
wine,
And the sleep in the dried river-channel where bulrushes tell
That the water was wont to go warbling so softly and well.
How good is man's life, the mere living! how fit to employ
All the heart and the soul and the senses, for ever in joy!
Hast thou loved the white locks of thy father, whose sword thou
didst guard
When he trusted thee forth with the armies, for glorious reward?
Didst thou see the thin hands of thy mother, held up as men sung
The low song of the nearly-departed, and heard her faint tongue
Joining in while it could to the witness, 'Let one more attest,
I have lived, seen God's hand thro' a lifetime, and all was for best!'
Then they sung thro' their tears in strong triumph, not much — but
the rest.
And thy brothers, the help and the contest, the working whence
grew
Such results as, from seething grape-bundles, the spirit strained true!
And the friends of thy boyhood — that boyhood of wonder and hope,
Present promise, and wealth of the future beyond the eye's scope, —
Till lo, thou art grown to a monarch; a people is thine;
And all gifts, which the world offers singly, on one head combine!
On one head, all the beauty and strength, love and rage (like the
throe
That, a-work in the rock, helps its labour and lets the gold go),
High ambition and deeds which surpass it, fame crowning it, — all
Brought to blaze on the head of one creature — King Saul!'

Note

This is David, the young poet, singing to Saul the king and the warrior to cure him of one of his fits of depression. I have always had great sympathy for the character of Saul and distaste for that of David. I believe Saul was the better man, just as his son Jonathan was a finer character than David's son Solomon. It would surely have gone better, though less brilliantly, for Israel had the simple straightforward Jonathan survived and succeeded his father rather than the subtle, scheming David. Perhaps then the world would never have had the Jewish problem. That fight on Mount Gilboa may have changed the course of history more deeply than is supposed. Both Saul and David committed crimes, but David's were underhand. Murder even in hot blood is a crime, but murder by proxy is surely mean; and David was responsible for three such murders: that of Uriah by the agency of Joab, those of Shimei and Joab himself by the agency of Solomon as David's posthumous act of revenge. I know few more tragic and pitiful pictures in history than that of the aged Commander-in-Chief clinging to the horns of the altar and being butchered there at the instigation of the man to whom he had always been loyal, but for whom he had probably always had some contempt. He had once been handed his bowler hat after his defeat of Absalom's rebellion. But Joab was no man to give up power easily, and Amasa suffered the fate of Abner. Joab is surely the only Commander-in-Chief in history to have bumped off personally two other Commanders-in-Chief.   *A. P. W.*

THE SONG OF DIEGO VALDEZ

RUDYARD KIPLING

THE God of Fair Beginnings
   Hath prospered here my hand —
The cargoes of my lading,
   And the keels of my command.
For out of many ventures
   That sailed with hope as high,

My own have made the better trade,
  And Admiral am I!

To me my King's much honour,
  To me my people's love —
To me the pride of Princes
  And power all pride above;
To me the shouting cities,
  To me the mob's refrain: —
'Who knows not noble Valdez,
  Hath never heard of Spain.'

But I remember comrades —
  Old playmates on new seas —
When as we traded orpiment
  Among the savages —
A thousand leagues to south'ard
  And thirty years removed —
They knew not noble Valdez,
  But me they knew and loved.

Then they that found good liquor,
  They drank it not alone,
And they that found fair plunder,
  They told us every one,
About our chosen islands
  Or secret shoals between,
When, walty from far voyage,
  We gathered to careen.

There burned our breaming-fagots
  All pale along the shore:
There rose our worn pavilions —
  A sail above an oar:
As flashed each yearning anchor
  Through mellow seas afire,
So swift our careless captains
  Rowed each to his desire.

Where lay our loosened harness?
  Where turned our naked feet?
Whose tavern 'mid the palm-trees?
  What quenchings of what heat!
Oh fountain in the desert!
  Oh cistern in the waste!
Oh bread we ate in secret!
  Oh cup we spilled in haste!

The youth new-taught of longing,
  The widow curbed and wan —
The goodwife proud at season,
  And the maid aware of man;
All souls unslaked, consuming,
  Defrauded in delays,
Desire not more their quittance
  Than I those forfeit days!

I dreamed to wait my pleasure
  Unchanged my spring would bide:
Wherefore, to wait my pleasure,
  I put my spring aside
Till, first in face of Fortune,
  And last in mazed disdain,
I made Diego Valdez
  High Admiral of Spain.

Then walked no wind 'neath Heaven
  Nor surge that did not aid —
I dared extreme occasion,
  Nor ever one betrayed.
They wrought a deeper treason —
  (Led seas that served my needs!)
They sold Diego Valdez
  To bondage of great deeds.

The tempest flung me seaward,
  And pinned and bade me hold

The course I might not alter —
 And men esteemed me bold!
The calms embayed my quarry,
 The fog-wreath sealed his eyes;
The dawn-wind brought my topsails —
 And men esteemed me wise!

Yet 'spite my tyrant triumphs
 Bewildered, dispossessed —
My dream held I before me —
 My vision of my rest;
But, crowned by Fleet and people,
 And bound by King and Pope —
Stands here Diego Valdez
 To rob me of my hope!

No prayer of mine shall move him,
 No word of his set free
The Lord of Sixty Pennants
 And the Steward of the Sea.
His will can loose ten thousand
 To seek their loves again —
But not Diego Valdez,
 High Admiral of Spain.

There walks no wind 'neath Heaven
 Nor wave that shall restore
The old careening riot
 And the clamorous, crowded shore —
The fountain in the desert,
 The cistern in the waste,
The bread we ate in secret,
 The cup we spilled in haste!

Now call I to my Captains —
 For council fly the sign,
Now leap their zealous galleys
 Twelve-oared across the brine.

G

> To me the straiter prison,
>   To me the heavier chain –
> To me Diego Valdez,
>   High Admiral of Spain!

Note

I have a great fellow-feeling for Valdez, the irresponsible buccaneer turned Admiral, the sea-gipsy chained to a battleship, the man whom careless daring betrayed to bondage of high place. But for all his regrets I doubt if he would really have gone back, and I expect he found some compensation in the pride of place and power which few men of action really despise. I hope he kept a saving sense of humour and did not become pompous.

I cannot find whether Diego Valdez has any historical background or came from Kipling's imagination. There was a Diego Valdez who commanded one of the squadrons of the Armada but he was never High Admiral; and according to Froude he was a naval designer rather than a sailor, and a timid, unenterprising Commander. He can hardly have been the model for Kipling's dashing seaman. His brother Pedro Valdez, a much stouter fellow, was captured by Drake and spent some time in England before being ransomed. Perhaps Kipling confused the two.

A. P. W.

CHILDE ROLAND TO THE DARK TOWER CAME

See Edgar's song in LEAR

ROBERT BROWNING

I

> MY first thought was, he lied in every word,
>   That hoary cripple, with malicious eye
>   Askance to watch the working of his lie
> On mine, and mouth scarce able to afford
> Suppression of the glee that pursed and scored
>   Its edge at one more victim gained thereby.

II

What else should he be set for, with his staff?
   What, save to waylay with his lies, ensnare
   All travellers that might find him posted there,
And ask the road? I guessed what skull-like laugh
Would break, what crutch 'gin write my epitaph
   For pastime in the dusty thoroughfare,

III

If at his counsel I should turn aside
   Into that ominous tract which, all agree,
   Hides the Dark Tower. Yet acquiescingly
I did turn as he pointed; neither pride
Nor hope rekindling at the end descried,
   So much as gladness that some end might be.

IV

For, what with my whole world-wide wandering,
   What with my search drawn out thro' years, my hope
   Dwindled into a ghost not fit to cope
With that obstreperous joy success would bring, —
I hardly tried now to rebuke the spring
   My heart made, finding failure in its scope.

V

As when a sick man very near to death
   Seems dead indeed, and feels begin and end
   The tears and takes the farewell of each friend,
And hears one bid the others go, draw breath
Freelier outside, ('since all is o'er,' he saith,
   'And the blow fallen no grieving can amend;')

VI

While some discuss if near the other graves
   Be room enough for this, and when a day
   Suits best for carrying the corpse away,
With care about the banners, scarves and staves, —
And still the man hears all, and only craves
   He may not shame such tender love and stay.

VII

Thus, I had so long suffered in this quest,
    Heard failure prophesied so oft, been writ
    So many times among 'The Band' — to wit,
The knights who to the Dark Tower's search addressed
Their steps — that just to fail as they, seemed best,
    And all the doubt was now — should I be fit.

VIII

So, quiet as despair, I turned from him,
    That hateful cripple, out of his highway
    Into the path he pointed. All the day
Had been a dreary one at best, and dim
Was settling to its close, yet shot one grim
    Red leer to see the plain catch its estray.

IX

For mark! no sooner was I fairly found
    Pledged to the plain, after a pace or two,
    Than, pausing to throw backward a last view
To the safe road, 'twas gone; grey plain all round:
Nothing but plain to the horizon's bound.
    I might go on; nought else remained to do.

X

So, on I went. I think I never saw
    Such starved ignoble nature; nothing throve:
    For flowers — as well expect a cedar grove!
But cockle, spurge, according to their law
Might propagate their kind, with none to awe,
    You'd think; a burr had been a treasure-trove.

XI

No! penury, inertness and grimace,
    In some strange sort, were the land's portion. 'See
    Or shut your eyes,' said Nature peevishly,
'It nothing skills: I cannot help my case:
'Tis the Last Judgment's fire must cure this place,
    Calcine its clods and set my prisoners free.'

XII

If there pushed any ragged thistle-stalk
    Above its mates, the head was chopped — the bents
    Were jealous else. What made those holes and rents
In the dock's harsh swarth leaves — bruised as to baulk
All hope of greenness? 'tis a brute must walk
    Pashing their life out, with a brute's intents.

XIII

As for the grass, it grew as scant as hair
    In leprosy; thin dry blades pricked the mud
    Which underneath looked kneaded up with blood.
One stiff blind horse, his every bone a-stare,
Stood stupefied, however he came there:
    Thrust out past service from the devil's stud!

XIV

Alive? he might be dead for aught I know,
    With that red, gaunt and colloped neck a-strain,
    And shut eyes underneath the rusty mane;
Seldom went such grotesqueness with such woe;
I never saw a brute I hated so;
    He must be wicked to deserve such pain.

XV

I shut my eyes and turned them on my heart.
    As a man calls for wine before he fights,
    I asked one draught of earlier, happier sights,
Ere fitly I could hope to play my part.
Think first, fight afterwards — the soldier's art:
    One taste of the old time sets all to rights!

XVI

Not it! I fancied Cuthbert's reddening face
    Beneath its garniture of curly gold,
    Dear fellow, till I almost felt him fold
An arm in mine to fix me to the place,
That way he used. Alas, one night's disgrace!
    Out went my heart's new fire and left it cold.

XVII

Giles, then, the soul of honour — there he stands
    Frank as ten years ago when knighted first.
    What honest men should dare (he said) he durst.
Good — but the scene shifts — faugh! what hangman's hands
Pin to his breast a parchment? his own bands
    Read it. Poor traitor, spit upon and curst!

XVIII

Better this Present than a Past like that;
    Back therefore to my darkening path again.
    No sound, no sight as far as eye could strain.
Will the night send a howlet or a bat?
I asked: when something on the dismal flat
    Came to arrest my thoughts and change their train.

XIX

A sudden little river crossed my path
    As unexpected as a serpent comes.
    No sluggish tide congenial to the glooms —
This, as it frothed by, might have been a bath
For the fiend's glowing hoof — to see the wrath
    Of its black eddy bespate with flakes and spumes.

XX

So petty yet so spiteful! All along,
    Low scrubby alders kneeled down over it;
    Drenched willows flung them headlong in a fit
Of mute despair, a suicidal throng:
The river which had done them all the wrong,
    Whate'er that was, rolled by, deterred no whit.

XXI

Which, while I forded, — good saints, how I feared
    To set my foot upon a dead man's cheek,
    Each step, or feel the spear I thrust to seek
For hollows, tangled in his hair or beard!
— It may have been a water-rat I speared,
    But, ugh! it sounded like a baby's shriek.

XXII

Glad was I when I reached the other bank.
   Now for a better country. Vain presage!
   Who were the strugglers, what war did they wage
Whose savage trample thus could pad the dank
Soil to a plash? toads in a poisoned tank,
   Or wild cats in a red-hot iron cage —

XXIII

The fight must so have seemed in that fell cirque.
   What penned them there, with all the plain to choose?
   No foot-print leading to that horrid mews,
None out of it. Mad brewage set to work
Their brains, no doubt, like galley-slaves the Turk
   Pits for his pastime, Christians against Jews.

XXIV

And more than that — a furlong on — why, there!
   What bad use was that engine for, that wheel,
   Or brake, not wheel — that harrow fit to reel
Men's bodies out like silk? with all the air
Of Tophet's tool, on earth left unaware,
   Or brought to sharpen its rusty teeth of steel.

XXV

Then came a bit of stubbed ground, once a wood,
   Next a marsh, it would seem, and now mere earth
   Desperate and done with; (so a fool finds mirth,
Makes a thing and then mars it, till his mood
Changes and off he goes!) within a rood —
   Bog, clay and rubble, sand and stark black dearth.

XXVI

Now blotches rankling, coloured gay and grim,
   Now patches where some leanness of the soil's
   Broke into moss or substances like boils;
Then came some palsied oak, a cleft in him
Like a distorted mouth that splits its rim
   Gaping at death, and dies while it recoils.

XXVII

And just as far as ever from the end!
    Nought in the distance but the evening, nought
    To point my footstep further! At the thought,
A great black bird, Apollyon's bosom-friend,
Sailed past, nor beat his wide wing dragon-penned
    That brushed my cap — perchance the guide I sought.

XXVIII

For, looking up, aware I somehow grew,
    'Spite of the dusk, the plain had given place
    All round to mountains — with such name to grace
Mere ugly heights and heaps now stolen in view.
How thus they had surprised me, — solve it, you!
    How to get from them was no clearer case.

XXIX

Yet half I seemed to recognize some trick
    Of mischief happened to me, God knows when —
    In a bad dream, perhaps. Here ended, then,
Progress this way. When, in the very nick
Of giving up, one time more, came a click
    As when a trap shuts — you're inside the den!

XXX

Burningly it came on me all at once,
    This was the place! those two hills on the right,
    Crouched like two bulls locked horn in horn in fight;
While to the left, a tall scalped mountain ... Dunce,
Fool, to be dozing at the very nonce,
    After a life spent training for the sight!

XXXI

What in the midst lay but the Tower itself?
    The round squat turret, blind as the fool's heart,
    Built of brown stone, without a counterpart
In the whole world. The tempest's mocking elf
Points to the shipman thus the unseen shelf
    He strikes on, only when the timbers start.

XXXII

Not see? because of night perhaps? — Why, day
   Came back again for that! before it left,
   The dying sunset kindled through a cleft:
The hills, like giants at a hunting, lay,
Chin upon hand, to see the game at bay, —
   'Now stab and end the creature — to the heft!'

XXXIII

Not hear? when noise was everywhere! it tolled
   Increasing like a bell. Names in my ears,
   Of all the lost adventurers my peers,—
How such a one was strong, and such was bold,
And such was fortunate, yet each of old
   Lost, lost! one moment knelled the woe of years.

XXXIV

There they stood, ranged along the hillsides, met
   To view the last of me, a living frame
   For one more picture! in a sheet of flame
I saw them and I knew them all. And yet
Dauntless the slug-horn to my lips I set,
   And blew. '*Childe Roland to the Dark Tower came.*'

Note

This grim poem has always fascinated me. I wonder who the melancholy but persistent Childe Roland was, what was his errand to the Dark Tower, and what happened when he blew the slug-horn. I wonder if Browning knew. He borrowed the title from *King Lear*, but the tale came, I think, simply from his imagination. His Childe Roland was neither the Knight of Roncesvalles, nor the legendary son of Arthur who figures in an old northern ballad. I connect the poem with one I read much later, de la Mare's *The Listeners*; did Childe Roland meet the same silence to his summons, had he too gone to the Dark Tower just to keep his word? It is a melancholy poem but it has one stirring stanza, that beginning: 'I shut my eyes and turned them on my heart.' It is my prescription for trying to get asleep when worried, to ask 'one draught of earlier, happier sights'. Sometimes it works, sometimes it happens as it did to Roland that one only recalls a tragedy.

Note to Revised Edition

A reader has kindly supplied me with the source from which Browning obviously drew his poem. It is an old English fairy tale about one Burd Ellen, who ran 'widdershins' round a church, and thus put herself into the power of the King of Elf Land. Her brothers, who go in turn to rescue her, all fail until Childe Roland has the normal success of youngest sons in fairy tales, favoured as usual by the abnormal advantage of a fairy godmother, or wizard friend – in this tale the warlock Merlin.

Browning slipped up on 'slug-horn'; it sounds the sort of thing that a medieval ogre might well hang at his castle gate, actually it is the corruption of a Gaelic word for the rallying cry of a clan; and its modern form is 'slogan'. *A. P. W.*

THE LISTENERS

Walter de la Mare

'Is there anybody there?' said the Traveller,
  Knocking on the moonlit door;
And his horse in the silence champed the grasses
  Of the forest's ferny floor:
And a bird flew up out of the turret,
  Above the Traveller's head:
And he smote upon the door again a second time;
  'Is there anybody there?' he said.
But no one descended to the Traveller;
  No head from the leaf-fringed sill
Leaned over and looked into his grey eyes,
  Where he stood perplexed and still.

But only a host of phantom listeners
   That dwelt in the lone house then
Stood listening in the quiet of the moonlight
   To that voice from the world of men:
Stood thronging the faint moonbeams on the dark stair,
   That goes down to the empty hall,
Hearkening in an air stirred and shaken
   By the lonely Traveller's call.
And he felt in his heart their strangeness,
   Their stillness answering his cry,
While his horse moved, cropping the dark turf,
   'Neath the starred and leafy sky;
For he suddenly smote on the door, even
   Louder, and lifted his head:—
'Tell them I came, and no one answered,
   That I kept my word,' he said.
Never the least stir made the listeners,
   Though every word he spake
Fell echoing through the shadowiness of the still house
   From the one man left awake:
Ay, they heard his foot upon the stirrup,
   And the sound of iron on stone,
And how the silence surged softly backward,
   When the plunging hoofs were gone.

GIPSY VANS

Rudyard Kipling

Unless you come of the gipsy stock
   That steals by night and day,
Lock your heart with a double lock
   And throw the key away.
Bury it under the blackest stone
   Beneath your father's hearth,
And keep your eyes on your lawful own
   And your feet to the proper path.

Then you can stand at your door and mock
  When the gipsy-vans come through ...
For it isn't right that the Gorgio stock
  Should live as the Romany do.

Unless you come of the gipsy blood
  That takes and never spares,
Bide content with your given good
  And follow your own affairs.
Plough and harrow and roll your land,
  And sow what ought to be sowed;
But never let loose your heart from your hand,
  Nor flitter it down the road!
  Then you can thrive on your boughten food
    As the gipsy-vans come through ...
  For it isn't nature the Gorgio blood
    Should love as the Romany do.

Unless you carry the gipsy eyes
  That see but seldom weep,
Keep your head from the naked skies
  Or the stars'll trouble your sleep.
Watch your moon through your window-pane
  And take what weather she brews;
But don't run out in the midnight rain
  Nor home in the morning dews.
  Then you can huddle and shut your eyes
    As the gipsy-vans come through ...
  For it isn't fitting the Gorgio ryes
    Should walk as the Romany do.

Unless you come of the gipsy race
  That counts all time the same,
Be you careful of Time and Place
  And Judgment and Good Name:
Lose your life for to live your life
  The way that you ought to do;
And when you are finished, your God and your wife
  And the Gipsies 'll laugh at you!

Then you can rot in your burying-place
As the gipsy-vans come through ...
For it isn't reason the Gorgio race
Should die as the Romany do.

Note

The gipsy in real life is usually both dirty and dull. So is war. Yet both gipsy life and war have a supposed glamour and are the subject of much poetry. This is due, I suppose, to the persistence in man's memory of his old past as nomad and warrior. Just so, the house dog turns round several times on the carpet before composing himself to sleep, as if he were still making a couch in the grass; or the stabled horse shies at a ditch because in them wild animals used to lurk and ambush his ancestors.

I like *Gipsy Vans*; it does not idealize the gipsy, but it reminds one that the gipsy is at least free from the fettering conventions of civilization. I should have liked to include Browning's *Flight of the Duchess*; but it is too long and only shreds of it are in my memory.

A. P. W.

THE OLD SHIPS

James Elroy Flecker

I HAVE seen old ships sail like swans asleep
Beyond the village which men still call Tyre,
With leaden age o'ercargoed, dipping deep
For Famagusta and the hidden sun
That rings black Cyprus with a lake of fire;
And all those ships were certainly so old
Who knows how oft with squat and noisy gun,
Questing brown slaves or Syrian oranges,
The pirate Genoese
Hell-raked them till they rolled
Blood, water, fruit, and corpses up the hold.
But now through friendly seas they softly run,
Painted the mid-sea blue or shore-sea green,
Still patterned with the vine and grapes in gold.

But I have seen,
Pointing her shapely shadows from the dawn
And image tumbled on a rose-swept bay,
A drowsy ship of some yet older day;
And, wonder's breath indrawn,
Thought I — who knows — who knows — but in that same
(Fished up beyond Ææa, patched up new
— Stern painted brighter blue —)
That talkative, bald-headed seaman came
(Twelve patient comrades sweating at the oar)
From Troy's doom-crimson shore,
And with great lies about his wooden horse
Set the crew laughing, and forgot his course.
It was so old a ship — who knows — who knows?
— And yet so beautiful, I watched in vain
To see the mast burst open with a rose,
And the whole deck put on its leaves again.

HARP SONG OF THE DANE WOMEN

Rudyard Kipling

WHAT is a Woman that you forsake her,
And the hearth-fire and the home-acre,
To go with the old grey Widow-maker?

She has no house to lay a guest in —
But one chill bed for all to rest in,
That the pale suns and the stray bergs nest in.

She has no strong white arms to fold you,
But the ten-times-fingering weed to hold you —
Out on the rocks where the tide has rolled you.

Yet, when the signs of summer thicken,
And the ice breaks, and the birch-buds quicken,
Yearly you turn from our sides, and sicken —

Sicken again for the shouts and the slaughters.
You steal away to the lapping waters,
And look at your ship in her winter-quarters.

You forget our mirth, and talk at the tables,
The kine in the shed and the horse in the stables —
To pitch her sides and go over her cables.

Then you drive out where the storm-clouds swallow,
And the sound of your oar-blades, falling hollow,
Is all we have left through the months to follow.

Ah, what is Woman that you forsake her,
And the hearth-fire and the home-acre,
To go with the old grey Widow-maker?

WARING

Robert Browning

I

I

WHAT's become of Waring
Since he gave us all the slip,
Chose land-travel or seafaring,
Boots and chest or staff and scrip,
Rather than pace up and down
Any longer London-town?

II

Who'd have guessed it from his lip
Or his brow's accustomed bearing,
On the night he thus took ship
Or started landward? — little caring
For us, it seems, who supped together
(Friends of his too, I remember)
And walked home thro' the merry weather,
The snowiest in all December.

I left his arm that night myself
For what's-his-name's, the new prose-poet
That wrote the book there, on the shelf —
How, forsooth, was I to know it
If Waring meant to glide away
Like a ghost at break of day?
Never looked he half so gay!

III

He was prouder than the Devil:
How he must have cursed our revel!
Ay, and many other meetings,
Indoor visits, outdoor greetings,
As up and down he paced this London,
With no work done, but great works undone,
Where scarce twenty knew his name.
Why not, then, have earlier spoken,
Written, bustled? Who's to blame
If your silence kept unbroken?
'True, but there were sundry jottings,
Stray-leaves, fragments, blurrs and blottings,
Certain first steps were achieved
Already which' — (is that your meaning?)
'Had well borne out whoe'er believed
In more to come!' But who goes gleaning
Hedge-side chance-blades, while full-sheaved
Stand cornfields by him? Pride, o'erweening
Pride alone, puts forth such claims
O'er the day's distinguished names.

IV

Meantime, how much I loved him,
I find out now I've lost him:
I, who cared not if I moved him,
Who could so carelessly accost him,
Henceforth never shall get free
Of his ghostly company,
His eyes that just a little wink

As deep I go into the merit
Of this and that distinguished spirit —
His cheeks' raised colour, soon to sink,
As long I dwell on some stupendous
And tremendous (Heaven defend us!)
Monstr'-inform'-ingens-horrend-ous
Demoniaco-seraphic
Penman's latest piece of graphic.
Nay, my very wrist grows warm
With his dragging weight of arm!
E'en so, swimmingly appears,
Through one's after-supper musings,
Some lost Lady of old years
With her beauteous vain endeavour
And goodness unrepaid as ever;
The face, accustomed to refusings,
We, puppies that we were ... Oh never
Surely, nice of conscience, scrupled
Being aught like false, forsooth, to?
Telling aught but honest truth to?
What a sin, had we centupled
Its possessor's grace and sweetness!
No! she heard in its completeness
Truth, for truth's a weighty matter,
And truth, at issue, we can't flatter!
Well, 'tis done with; she's exempt
From damning us thro' such a sally;
And so she glides, as down a valley,
Taking up with her contempt,
Past our reach; and in, the flowers
Shut her unregarded hours.

v

Oh, could I have him back once more,
This Waring, but one half-day more!
Back, with the quiet face of yore,
So hungry for acknowledgment
Like mine! I'd fool him to his bent!

Feed, should not he, to heart's content?
I'd say, 'to only have conceived
Your great works, though they ne'er make progress,
Surpasses all we've yet achieved!'
I'd lie so, I should be believed.
I'd make such havoc of the claims
Of the day's distinguished names
To feast him with, as feasts an ogress
Her sharp-toothed, golden-crowned child!
Or, as one feasts a creature rarely
Captured here, unreconciled
To capture; and completely gives
Its pettish humours licence, barely
Requiring that it lives.

VI

Ichabod, Ichabod,
The glory is departed!
Travels Waring East away?
Who, of knowledge, by hearsay,
Reports a man upstarted
Somewhere as a God,
Hordes grown European-hearted,
Millions of the wild made tame
On a sudden at his fame?
In Vishnu-land what Avatar?
Or who, in Moscow, toward the Czar,
With the demurest of footfalls
Over the Kremlin's pavement, bright
With serpentine and syenite,
Steps, with five other Generals
That simultaneously take snuff,
For each to have pretext enough
To kerchiefwise unfold his sash
Which, softness' self, is yet the stuff
To hold fast where a steel chain snaps,
And leave the grand white neck no gash?
Waring, in Moscow, to those rough

Cold northern natures borne, perhaps,
Like the lambwhite maiden dear
From the circle of mute kings
Unable to repress the tear,
Each as his sceptre down he flings,
To Dian's fane at Taurica,
Where now a captive priestess she alway
Mingles her tender grave Hellenic speech
With theirs, tuned to the hailstone-beaten beach,
As pours some pigeon, from the myrrhy lands
Rapt by the whirlblast to fierce Scythian strands
Where breed the swallows, her melodious cry
Amid their barbarous twitter!
In Russia? Never! Spain were fitter!
Ay, most likely 'tis in Spain
That we and Waring meet again
Now, while he turns down that cool narrow lane
Into the blackness, out of grave Madrid
All fire and shine, abrupt as when there's slid
Its stiff gold blazing pall
From some black coffin-lid.
Or, best of all,
I love to think
The leaving us was just a feint;
Back here to London did he slink,
And now works on without a wink
Of sleep, and we are on the brink
Of something great in fresco-paint;
Some garret's ceiling, walls and floor,
Up and down and o'er and o'er
He splashes, as none splashed before
Since great Caldara Polidore.
Or Music means this land of ours
Some favour yet, to pity won
By Purcell from his Rosy Bowers, —
'Give me my so-long promised son,
Let Waring end what I begun!'
Then down he creeps and out he steals

Only when the night conceals
His face; in Kent 'tis cherry-time,
Or, hops are picking: or, at prime
Of March, he wanders as, too happy,
Years ago when he was young,
Some mild eve when woods grew sappy
And the early moths had sprung
To life from many a trembling sheath
Woven the warm boughs beneath;
While small birds said to themselves
What should soon be actual song,
And young gnats, by tens and twelves,
Made as if they were the throng
That crowd around and carry aloft
The sound they have nursed, so sweet and pure
Out of a myriad noises soft,
Into a tone that can endure
Amid the noise of a July noon
When all God's creatures crave their boon,
All at once and all in tune,
And get it, happy as Waring then,
Having first within his ken
What a man might do with men:
And far too glad, in the even-glow,
To mix with the world he meant to take
Into his hand, he told you, so —
And out of it his world to make,
To contract and to expand
As he shut or oped his hand.
Oh, Waring, what's to really be?
A clear stage and a crowd to see!
Some Garrick — say, — out shall not he
The heart of Hamlet's mystery pluck?
Or, where most unclean beasts are rife,
Some Junius — am I right? — shall tuck
His sleeve, and forth with flaying-knife!
Some Chatterton shall have the luck
Of calling Rowley into life!

Some one shall somehow run a muck
With this old world, for want of strife
Sound asleep. Contrive, contrive
To rouse us, Waring! Who's alive?
Our men scarce seem in earnest now.
Distinguished names! — but 'tis, somehow,
As if they played at being names
Still more distinguished, like the games
Of children. Turn our sport to earnest
With a visage of the sternest!
Bring the real times back, confessed
Still better than our very best!

II

I

'When I last saw Waring ... '
(How all turned to him who spoke —
You saw Waring? Truth or joke?
In land-travel, or sea-faring?)

II

'We were sailing by Triest,
Where a day or two we harboured:
A sunset was in the West,
When, looking over the vessel's side,
One of our company espied
A sudden speck to larboard.
And, as a sea-duck flies and swims
At once, so came the light craft up,
With its sole lateen sail that trims
And turns (the water round its rims
Dancing, as round a sinking cup)
And by us like a fish it curled,
And drew itself up close beside,
Its great sail on the instant furled,
And o'er its planks, a shrill voice cried,
(A neck as bronzed as a Lascar's)

"Buy wine of us, you English Brig?
Or fruit, tobacco and cigars?
A Pilot for you to Triest?
Without one, look you ne'er so big,
They'll never let you up the bay!
We natives should know best."
I turned, and "Just those fellows' way",
Our captain said, "The 'long-shore thieves
Are laughing at us in their sleeves."

III

'In truth, the boy leaned laughing back;
And one, half-hidden by his side
Under the furled sail, soon I spied,
With great grass hat and kerchief black,
Who looked up with his kingly throat,
Said somewhat, while the other shook
His hair back from his eyes to look
Their longest at us; then the boat,
I know not how, turned sharply round,
Laying her whole side on the sea
As a leaping fish does; from the lee,
Into the weather, cut somehow
Her sparkling path beneath our bow;
And so went off, as with a bound,
Into the rosy and golden half
Of the sky, to overtake the sun
And reach the shore, like the sea-calf
Its singing cave; yet I caught one
Glance ere away the boat quite passed,
And neither time nor toil could mar
Those features: so I saw the last
Of Waring!' — You? Oh, never star
Was lost here, but it rose afar!
Look East, where whole new thousands are!
In Vishnu-land what Avatar?

Note

Waring was Alfred Domett, a brilliant young friend of Browning who went to New Zealand, became Premier, and eventually returned to England.

The passage about the Kremlin has reference presumably to the murder of the half-crazy Czar Paul, the son of Catherine the Great. Readers of Kipling's *Stalky and Co.* may remember the use which Kipling makes of this passage to decide the fate of his enemy, King.   *A. P. W.*

CARGOES

JOHN MASEFIELD

QUINQUIREME of Nineveh from distant Ophir
Rowing home to haven in sunny Palestine,
With a cargo of ivory,
And apes and peacocks,
Sandalwood, cedarwood, and sweet white wine.

Stately Spanish galleon coming from the Isthmus,
Dipping through the Tropics by the palm-green shores,
With a cargo of diamonds,
Emeralds, amethysts,
Topazes, and cinnamon, and gold moidores.

Dirty British coaster with a salt-caked smoke-stack
Butting through the Channel in the mad March days,
With a cargo of Tyne coal,
Road-rails, pig-lead,
Firewood, iron-ware, and cheap tin trays.

THE SEA AND THE HILLS

RUDYARD KIPLING

WHO hath desired the Sea? — the sight of salt water unbounded —
The heave and the halt and the hurl and the crash of the comber
wind-hounded?
The sleek-barrelled swell before storm, grey, foamless, enormous,
and growing —
Stark calm on the lap of the Line or the crazy-eyed hurricane
blowing —
His Sea in no showing the same — his Sea and the same 'neath each
showing —
His Sea as she slackens or thrills?
So and no otherwise — so and no otherwise hillmen desire their Hills!

Who hath desired the Sea? — the immense and contemptuous surges?
The shudder, the stumble, the swerve, as the star-stabbing bowsprit
emerges?
The orderly clouds of the Trades, and the ridged, roaring sapphire
thereunder —
Unheralded cliff-haunting flaws and the headsail's low-volleying
thunder —
His Sea in no wonder the same — his Sea and the same through each
wonder:
His Sea as she rages or stills?
So and no otherwise — so and no otherwise hillmen desire their Hills.

Who hath desired the Sea? Her menaces swift as her mercies,
The in-rolling walls of the fog and the silver-winged breeze that
disperses?
The unstable mined berg going South and the calvings and groans
that declare it;
White water half-guessed overside and the moon breaking timely to
bare it;
His Sea as his fathers have dared — his Sea as his children shall dare it —
His Sea as she serves him or kills?
So and no otherwise — so and no otherwise hillmen desire their Hills.

Who hath desired the Sea? Her excellent loneliness rather
Than forecourts of kings, and her outermost pits than the streets
                                                    where men gather
Inland, among dust, under trees—inland where the slayer may slay him
Inland, out of reach of her arms, and the bosom whereon he must
                                                    lav him —
His Sea at the first that betrayed — at the last that shall never betray
                                                    him —
            His Sea that his being fulfils?
So and no otherwise — so and no otherwise hillmen desire their Hills.

SEA FEVER

JOHN MASEFIELD

I MUST go down to the seas again, to the lonely sea and the sky,
And all I ask is a tall ship and a star to steer her by;
And the wheel's kick and the wind's song and the white sail's shaking,
And a grey mist on the sea's face, and a grey dawn breaking.

I must go down to the seas again, for the call of the running tide
Is a wild call and a clear call that may not be denied;
And all I ask is a windy day with the white clouds flying,
And the flung spray and the blown spume, and the sea-gulls crying.

I must go down to the seas again, to the vagrant gypsy life,
To the gull's way and the whale's way where the wind's like a whetted
And all I ask is a merry yarn from a laughing fellow-rover,   [knife;
And quiet sleep and a sweet dream when the long trick's over.

SIR PATRICK SPENS

ANON

1. *The Sailing*

THE king sits in Dunfermline town
    Drinking the blude-red wine;
'O whare will I get a skeely skipper
    To sail this new ship o' mine?'

O up and spak an eldern knight,
  Sat at the king's right knee;
'Sir Patrick Spens is the best sailor
  That ever sail'd the sea.'

Our king has written a braid letter,
  And seal'd it with his hand,
And sent it to Sir Patrick Spens,
  Was walking on the strand.

'To Noroway, to Noroway,
  To Noroway o'er the faem;
The king's daughter o' Noroway,
  'Tis thou must bring her hame.'

The first word that Sir Patrick read
  So loud, loud laugh'd he;
The neist word that Sir Patrick read
  The tear blinded his e'e.

'O wha is this has done this deed
  And tauld the king o' me,
To send us out, at this time o' year,
  To sail upon the sea?

'Be it wind, be it weet, be it hail, be it sleet,
  Our ship must sail the faem;
The king's daughter o' Noroway,
  'Tis we must fetch her hame.'

They hoysed their sails on Monenday morn
  Wi' a' the speed they may;
They hae landed in Noroway
  Upon a Wodensday.

II. *The Return*

'Mak ready, mak ready, my merry men a'!
  Our gude ship sails the morn.'
'Now ever alack, my master dear,
  I fear a deadly storm.

'I saw the new moon late yestreen
  Wi' the auld moon in her arm;
And if we gang to sea, master,
  I fear we'll come to harm.'

They hadna sail'd a league, a league,
  A league but barely three,
When the lift grew dark, and the wind blew loud,
  And gurly grew the sea.

The ankers brak, and the topmast lap,
  It was sic a deadly storm:
And the waves cam owre the broken ship
  Till a' her sides were torn.

'Go fetch a web o' the silken claith,
  Another o' the twine,
And wap them into our ship's side,
  And let nae the sea come in.'

They fetch'd a web o' the silken claith,
  Another o' the twine,
And they wapp'd them round that gude ship's side
  But still the sea came in.

O laith, laith were our gude Scots lords
  To wet their cork-heel'd shoon;
But lang or a' the play was play'd
  They wat their hats aboon.

And mony was the feather bed
  That flatter'd on the faem;
And mony was the gude lord's son
  That never mair cam hame.

O lang, lang may the ladies sit,
　Wi' their fans into their hand,
Before they see Sir Patrick Spens
　Come sailing to the strand!

And lang, lang may the maidens sit
　Wi' their gowd kames in their hair,
A-waiting for their ain dear loves!
　For them they'll see nae mair.

Half-owre, half-owre to Aberdour,
　'Tis fifty fathoms deep;
And there lies gude Sir Patrick Spens,
　Wi' the Scots lords at his feet!

THE LONG TRAIL

Rudyard Kipling

There's a whisper down the field where the year has shot her yield
　And the ricks stand grey to the sun,
Singing: 'Over then, come over, for the bee has quit the clover,
　And your English summer's done.'
　　　　You have heard the beat of the off-shore wind,
　　　　And the thresh of the deep-sea rain;
　　　　You have heard the song — how long! how long!
　　　　Pull out on the trail again!
Ha' done with the Tents of Shem, dear lass,
We've seen the seasons through,
And it's time to turn on the old trail, our own trail, the out trail,
Pull out, pull out, on the Long Trail — the trail that is always new!

It's North you may run to the rime-ringed sun
　Or South to the blind Horn's hate;
Or East all the way into Mississippi Bay,
　Or West to the Golden Gate —

Where the blindest bluffs hold good, dear lass,
And the wildest tales are true,
And the men bulk big on the old trail, our own trail, the out
trail,
And life runs large on the Long Trail — the trail that is always
new.

The days are sick and cold, and the skies are grey and old,
    And the twice-breathed airs blow damp;
And I'd sell my tired soul for the bucking beam-sea roll
    Of a black Bilbao tramp,
        With her load-line over her hatch, dear lass,
        And a drunken Dago crew,
        And her nose held down on the old trail, our own trail, the
out trail,
        From Cadiz south on the Long Trail — the trail that is always
new.

There be triple ways to take, of the eagle or the snake,
    Or the ways of a man with a maid;
But the sweetest way to me is a ship's upon the sea
    In the heel of the North-East Trade.
        Can you hear the crash on her bows, dear lass,
        And the drum of the racing screw,
        As she ships it green on the old trail, our own trail, the out trail,
        As she lifts and 'scends on the Long Trail — the trail that is
always new?

See the shaking funnels roar, with the Peter at the fore,
    And the fenders grind and heave,
And the derricks clack and grate, as the tackle hooks the crate,
    And the fall-rope whines through the sheave;
        It's 'Gang-plank up and in,' dear lass,
        It's 'Hawsers warp her through!'
        And it's 'All clear aft' on the old trail, our own trail, the out
trail,
        We're backing down on the Long Trail — the trail that is always
new.

O the mutter overside, when the port-fog holds us tied,
  And the sirens hoot their dread,
When foot by foot we creep o'er the hueless, viewless deep
  To the sob of the questing lead!
      It's down by the Lower Hope, dear lass,
      With the Gunfleet Sands in view,
      Till the Mouse swings green on the old trail, our own trail, the
          out trail,
      And the Gull Light lifts on the Long Trail — the trail that is
          always new.

O the blazing tropic night, when the wake's a welt of light
  That holds the hot sky tame,
And the steady fore-foot snores through the planet-powdered floors
  Where the scared whale flukes in flame!
      Her plates are flaked by the sun, dear lass,
      And her ropes are taut with the dew,
      For we're booming down on the old trail, our own trail, the
          out trail,
      We're sagging south on the Long Trail — the trail that is always
          new.

Then home, get her home, where the drunken rollers comb,
  And the shouting seas drive by,
And the engines stamp and ring, and the wet bows reel and swing,
  And the Southern Cross rides high!
      Yes, the old lost stars wheel back, dear lass,
      That blaze in the velvet blue.
      They're all old friends on the old trail, our own trail, the out
          trail,
      They're God's own guides on the Long Trail — the trail that is
          always new.

Fly forward, O my heart, from the Foreland to the Start —
  We're steaming all too slow,
And it's twenty thousand mile to our little lazy isle
  Where the trumpet-orchids blow!

You have heard the call of the off-shore wind
And the voice of the deep-sea rain;
You have heard the song — how long! — how long!
Pull out on the trail again!
The Lord knows what we may find, dear lass,
And the deuce knows what we may do —
But we're back once more on the old trail, our own trail, the out
trail,
We're down, hull down, on the Long Trail — the trail that is always
new!

TARANTELLA

Hilaire Belloc

Do you remember an Inn,
Miranda?
Do you remember an Inn?
And the tedding and the spreading
Of the straw for a bedding,
And the fleas that tease in the High Pyrenees,
And the wine that tasted of the tar,
And the cheers and the jeers of the young muleteers
(Under the vine of the dark verandah)?
Do you remember an Inn, Miranda,
Do you remember an Inn?
And the cheers and the jeers of the young muleteers
Who hadn't got a penny,
And who weren't paying any,
And the hammer at the doors and the Din?
And the Hip! Hop! Hap!
Of the clap
Of the hands to the twirl and the swirl
Of the girl gone chancing,
Glancing,
Dancing,
Backing and advancing,

Snapping of the clapper to the spin
Out and in —
And the Ting, Tong, Tang of the Guitar!
Do you remember an Inn,
Miranda?
Do you remember an Inn?
Never more;
Miranda,
Never more.
Only the high peaks hoar:
And Aragon a torrent at the door.
No sound
In the walls of the Halls where falls
The tread
Of the feet of the dead to the ground.
No sound:
But the boom
Of the far Waterfall like Doom.

COULD MAN BE DRUNK FOR EVER

A. E. HOUSMAN

COULD man be drunk for ever
  With liquor, love, or fights,
Lief should I rouse at morning
  And lief lie down of nights.

But men at whiles are sober
  And think by fits and starts,
And if they think, they fasten
  Their hands upon their hearts.

THE FEET OF THE YOUNG MEN

RUDYARD KIPLING

Now the Four-way Lodge is opened, now the Hunting Winds are
                                      loose —
  Now the Smokes of Spring go up to clear the brain;
Now the Young Men's hearts are troubled for the whisper of the
                                     Trues,
  Now the Red Gods make their medicine again!
Who hath seen the beaver busied? Who hath watched the black-tail
                                     mating?
  Who hath lain alone to hear the wild-goose cry?
Who hath worked the chosen water where the ouananiche is waiting,
  Or the sea-trout's jumping-crazy for the fly?

> *He must go — go — go away from here!*
> *On the other side the world he's overdue.*
> *'Send your road is clear before you when the old*
> *Spring-fret comes o'er you*
> *And the Red Gods call for you!*

So for one the wet sail arching through the rainbow round the bow,
  And for one the creak of snow-shoes on the crust;
And for one the lakeside lilies where the bull-moose waits the cow,
  And for one the mule-train coughing in the dust.
Who hath smelt wood-smoke at midnight? Who hath heard the
                                 birch-log burning?
  Who is quick to read the noises of the night?
Let him follow with the others, for the Young Men's feet are turning
  To the camps of proved desire and known delight!

> *Let him go — go, etc.*

I

Do you know the blackened timber — do you know that racing stream
  With the raw, right-angled log-jam at the end;
And the bar of sun-warmed shingle where a man may bask and dream
  To the click of shod canoe-poles round the bend?

H

It is there that we are going with our rods and reels and traces,
  To a silent, smoky Indian that we know —
To a couch of new-pulled hemlock with the starlight on our faces,
  For the Red Gods call us out and we must go!

They must go — go, etc.

II

Do you know the shallow Baltic where the seas are steep and short,
  Where the bluff, lee-boarded fishing-luggers ride?
Do you know the joy of threshing leagues to leeward of your port
  On a coast you've lost the chart of overside?
It is there that I am going, with an extra hand to bale her —
  Just one able 'long-shore loafer that I know.
He can take his chance of drowning, while I sail and sail and sail her,
  For the Red Gods call me out and I must go!

He must go — go, etc.

III

Do you know the pile-built village where the sago-dealers trade —
  Do you know the reek of fish and wet bamboo?
Do you know the steaming stillness of the orchid-scented glade
  When the blazoned, bird-winged butterflies flap through?
It is there that I am going with my camphor, net, and boxes,
  To a gentle, yellow pirate that I know —
To my little waiting lemurs, to my palms and flying-foxes,
  For the Red Gods call me out and I must go!

He must go — go, etc.

IV

Do you know the world's white roof-tree — do you know that windy
                                                              rift
  Where the baffling mountain-eddies chop and change?
Do you know the long day's patience, belly-down on frozen drift,
  While the head of heads is feeding out of range?

It is there that I am going, where the boulders and the snow lie
　With a trusty, nimble tracker that I know,
I have sworn an oath, to keep it on the Horns of Ovis Poli,
　And the Red Gods call me out and I must go!

> *He must go — go, etc.*

Now the Four-way Lodge is opened — now the Smokes of Council
rise —
　Pleasant smokes, ere yet 'twixt trail and trail they choose —
Now the girths and ropes are tested: now they pack their last supplies:
　Now our Young Men go to dance before the Trues!
Who shall meet them at those altars — who shall light them to that
shrine?
　Velvet-footed, who shall guide them to their goal?
Unto each the voice and vision: unto each his spoor and sign —
Lonely mountain in the Northland, misty sweat-bath 'neath the
Line —

　And to each a man that knows his naked soul!
White or yellow, black or copper, he is waiting as a lover,
　Smoke of funnel, dust of hooves, or beat of train —
Where the high grass hides the horseman or the glaring flats discover —
Where the steamer hails the landing, or the surf-boat brings the
rover —
Where the rails run out in sand-drift ... Quick! ah, heave the camp-
kit over!

　For the Red Gods make their medicine again!

> *As we go — go — go away from here!*
> *On the other side the world we're overdue!*
> *'Send the road is clear before you when the old*
> *Spring-fret comes o'er you,*
> *And the Red Gods call for you!*

THE LAST CHANTEY

'And there was no more sea'

RUDYARD KIPLING

THUS said the Lord in the Vault above the Cherubim,
  Calling to the Angels and the Souls in their degree:
    'Lo! Earth has passed away
    On the smoke of Judgment Day.
  That Our word may be established shall We gather up the sea?'

Loud sang the souls of the jolly, jolly mariners:
  'Plague upon the hurricane that made us furl and flee!
    But the war is done between us,
    In the deep the Lord hath seen us —
  Our bones we'll leave the barracout', and God may sink the sea!'

Then said the soul of Judas that betrayèd Him:
  'Lord, hast Thou forgotten Thy covenant with me?
    How once a year I go
    To cool me on the floe?
  And Ye take my day of mercy if Ye take away the sea!'

Then said the soul of the Angel of the Off-shore Wind:
  (He that bits the thunder when the bull-mouthed breakers flee)
    'I have watch and ward to keep
    O'er Thy wonders on the deep,
  And Ye take mine honour from me if Ye take away the sea!'

Loud sang the souls of the jolly, jolly mariners:
  'Nay, but we were angry, and a hasty folk are we!
    If we worked the ship together
    Till she foundered in foul weather,
  Are we babes that we should clamour for a vengeance on the sea?'

Then said the souls of the slaves that men threw overboard:
  'Kennelled in the picaroon a weary band were we;
    But Thy arm was strong to save,
    And it touched us on the wave,
  And we drowsed the long tides idle till Thy Trumpets tore the sea.'

Then cried the soul of the stout Apostle Paul to God:
  'Once we frapped a ship, and she laboured woundily.
    There were fourteen score of these,
    And they blessed Thee on their knees,
  When they learned Thy Grace and Glory under Malta by the sea!'

Loud sang the souls of the jolly, jolly mariners,
  Plucking at their harps, and they plucked unhandily:
    'Our thumbs are rough and tarred,
    And the tune is something hard —
  May we lift a Deepsea Chantey such as seamen use at sea?'

Then said the souls of the gentlemen-adventurers —
  Fettered wrist to bar all for red iniquity:
    'Ho, we revel in our chains
    O'er the sorrow that was Spain's;
  Heave or sink it, leave or drink it, we were masters of the sea!'

Up spake the soul of a grey Gothavn 'speckshioner —
  (He that led the flinching in the fleets of fair Dundee):
    'Oh, the ice-blink white and near,
    And the bowhead breaching clear!
  Will Ye whelm them all for wantonness that wallow in the sea?'

Loud sang the souls of the jolly, jolly mariners,
  Crying: 'Under Heaven, here is neither lead nor lee!
    Must we sing for evermore
    On the windless, glassy floor?
  Take back your golden fiddles and we'll beat to open sea!'

Then stooped the Lord, and He called the good sea up to Him,
  And 'stablished his borders unto all eternity,
    That such as have no pleasure
    For to praise the Lord by measure,
  They may enter into galleons and serve Him on the sea.

Sun, wind, and cloud shall fail not from the face of it,
Stinging, ringing spindrift, nor the fulmar flying free;
  And the ships shall go abroad
  To the Glory of the Lord
Who heard the silly sailor-folk and gave them back their sea!

THE WISHING-CAPS

RUDYARD KIPLING

LIFE's all getting and giving,
I've only myself to give.
What shall I do for a living?
I've only one life to live.
End it? I'll not find another.
Spend it? But how shall I best?
Sure the wise plan is to live like a man
And Luck may look after the rest!
Largesse, largesse, Fortune!
Give or hold at your will.
If I've no care for Fortune,
Fortune must follow me still.

Bad Luck, she is never a lady
But the commonest wench on the street,
Shuffling, shabby and shady,
Shameless to pass or meet.
Walk with her once — it's a weakness!
Talk to her twice — it's a crime!
Thrust her away when she gives you 'good day'
And the besom won't board you next time.
Largesse, largesse, Fortune!
What is Your Ladyship's mood?
If I've no care for Fortune,
My Fortune is bound to be good!

Good Luck she is never a lady
But the cursedest quean alive!
Tricksey, wincing and jady,
Kittle to lead or drive.
Greet her — she's hailing a stranger!
Meet her — she's busking to leave.
Let her alone for a shrew to the bone,
And the hussy comes plucking your sleeve!
Largesse, largesse, Fortune!
I'll neither follow nor flee.
If I don't run after Fortune
Fortune must run after me!

THE DEATH AND LAST CONFESSION OF
WANDERING PETER

Hilaire Belloc

When Peter Wanderwide was young
    He wandered everywhere he would:
And all that he approved was sung,
    And most of what he saw was good.

When Peter Wanderwide was thrown
    By Death himself beyond Auxerre,
He chanted in heroic tone
    To priests and people gathered there:

'If all that I have loved and seen
    Be with me on the Judgment Day,
I shall be saved the crowd between
    From Satan and his foul array.

'Almighty God will surely cry,
    "St Michael! Who is this that stands
With Ireland in his dubious eye,
    And Perigord between his hands,

' "And on his arm the stirrup-thongs,
   And in his gait the narrow seas,
And in his mouth Burgundian songs,
   But in his heart the Pyrenees?"

'St Michael then will answer right
   (And not without angelic shame),
"I seem to know his face by sight:
   I cannot recollect his name ... "

'St Peter will befriend me then,
   Because my name is Peter too:
"I know him for the best of men
   That ever walloped barley brew.

' "And though I did not know him well
   And though his soul were clogged with sin,
I hold the keys of Heaven and Hell.
   Be welcome, noble Peterkin."

'Then shall I spread my native wings
   And tread secure the heavenly floor,
And tell the Blessed doubtful things
   Of Val d'Aran and Perigord.'

———

This was the last and solemn jest
   Of weary Peter Wanderwide.
He spoke it with a failing zest,
   And having spoken it, he died.

Note

One of my favourite characters in poetic fiction is Peter Wander-
wide. I hope he got to Heaven and cheered up the blessed in that
extremely dull abode with his dubious tales; but I fancy he would
soon have pawned his golden harp, mislaid his halo, and whistled
himself out on the road again — with the connivance, I hope, of
his namesake with the keys.   *A. P. W.*

From HASSAN

JAMES ELROY FLECKER

THY dawn, O Master of the world, thy dawn;
The hour the lilies open on the lawn,
The hour the grey wings pass beyond the mountains,
The hour of silence, when we hear the fountains,
The hour that dreams are brighter and winds colder,
The hour that young love wakes on a white shoulder,
O Master of the world, the Persian Dawn.
That hour, O Master, shall be bright for thee:
Thy merchants chase the morning down the sea,
The braves who fight thy war unsheathe the sabre,
The slaves who work thy mines are lashed to labour,
For thee the waggons of the world are drawn —
The ebony of night, the red of dawn!

Note

In the play these lines are spoken by the poet Ishak, who has
offended the Caliph Haroun al-Raschid, and is kneeling to await
his execution at Dawn. On the conclusion of these verses the
Caliph says to the expectant executioner: 'Sheathe your sword!
Would you kill my friend?'   *A. P. W.*

THREE FISHERS WENT SAILING

CHARLES KINGSLEY

THREE fishers went sailing out into the West,
   Away to the West as the sun went down;
Each thought on the woman who loved him the best,
   And the children stood watching them out of the town:
For men must work, and women must weep,
And there's little to earn, and many to keep,
   Though the harbour-bar be moaning.

Three wives sat up in the lighthouse tower,
  And they trimm'd the lamps as the sun went down;
And they looked at the squall, and they looked at the shower,
  And the night-rack came rolling up ragged and brown;
But men must work, and women must weep,
Though storms be sudden, and waters deep,
  And the harbour-bar be moaning.

Three corpses lay out on the shining sands,
  In the morning gleam, as the tide went down,
And the women are weeping and wringing their hands,
  For those who will never come home to the town.
For men must work, and women must weep,
And the sooner it's over, the sooner to sleep,
  And good-bye to the bar and its moaning.

Note

  I heard this song sung when I was very young and fell in love that night. It did not last, but the song and its memory have remained.   *A. P. W.*

THE SONG OF THE BANJO

RUDYARD KIPLING

You couldn't pack a Broadwood half a mile —
  You mustn't leave a fiddle in the damp —
You couldn't raft an organ up the Nile,
  And play it in an Equatorial swamp.
I travel with the cooking-pots and pails —
  I'm sandwiched 'tween the coffee and the pork —
And when the dusty column checks and tails,
  You should hear me spur the rearguard to a walk!

With my '*Pilly-willy-winky-winky popp!*'
  [Oh, it's any tune that comes into my head!]
So I keep 'em moving forward till they drop;
  So I play 'em up to water and to bed.

In the silence of the camp before the fight,
    When it's good to make your will and say your prayer,
You can hear my *strumpty-tumpty* overnight
    Explaining ten to one was always fair.
I'm the Prophet of the Utterly Absurd,
    Of the Patently Impossible and Vain —
And when the Thing that Couldn't has occurred,
    Give me time to change my leg and go again.

    With my '*Tumpa-tumpa-tumpa-tum-pa tump!*'
      In the desert where the dung-fed camp-smoke curled
    There was never voice before us till I led our lonely chorus.
      I — the war-drum of the White Man round the world!

By the bitter road the Younger Son must tread,
    Ere he win to hearth and saddle of his own, —
'Mid the riot of the shearers at the shed,
    In the silence of the herder's hut alone —
In the twilight, on a bucket upside down,
    Hear me babble what the weakest won't confess —
I am Memory and Torment — I am Town!
    I am all that ever went with evening dress!

    With my '*Tunk-a tunka-tunka-tunka-tunk!*'
      [So the lights — the London Lights — grow near and plain!]
    So I rowel 'em afresh towards the Devil and the Flesh,
      Till I bring my broken rankers home again.

In desire of many marvels over sea,
    Where the new-raised tropic city sweats and roars,
I have sailed with Young Ulysses from the quay
    Till the anchor rumbled down on stranger shores.
He is blooded to the open and the sky,
    He is taken in a snare that shall not fail,
He shall hear me singing strongly, till he die,
    Like the shouting of a backstay in a gale.

With my '*Hya! Heeya! Heeya! Hullah! Haul!*'
  [O the green that thunders aft along the deck!]
Are you sick o' towns and men? You must sign and sail again,
  For it's 'Johnny Bowlegs, pack your kit and trek!'

Through the gorge that gives the stars at noon-day clear —
  Up the pass that packs the scud beneath our wheel —
Round the bluff that sinks her thousand fathom sheer —
  Down the valley with our guttering brakes asqueal:
Where the trestle groans and quivers in the snow,
  Where the many-shedded levels loop and twine,
So I lead my reckless children from below
  Till we sing the Song of Roland to the pine.

  With my '*Tinka-tinka-tinka-tinka-tink!*'
    [And the axe has cleared the mountain, croup and crest!]
  So we ride the iron stallions down to drink,
    Through the cañons to the waters of the West!

And the tunes that mean so much to you alone —
  Common tunes that make you choke and blow your nose,
Vulgar tunes that bring the laugh that brings the groan —
  I can rip your very heartstrings out with those;
With the feasting, and the folly, and the fun —
  And the lying, and the lusting, and the drink,
And the merry play that drops you, when you're done,
  To the thoughts that burn like irons if you think.

  With my '*Plunka-lunka-lunka-lunka-lunk!*'
    Here's a trifle on account of pleasure past,
  Ere the wit that made you win gives you eyes to see your sin
    And the heavier repentance at the last!

Let the organ moan her sorrow to the roof —
  I have told the naked stars the Grief of Man!
Let the trumpets snare the foeman to the proof —
  I have known Defeat, and mocked it as we ran!

My bray ye may not alter nor mistake
　　When I stand to jeer the fatted Soul of Things,
But the Song of Lost Endeavour that I make,
　　Is it hidden in the twanging of the strings?

　　With my '*Ta-ra-rara-rara-ra-ra-rrrp!*'
　　[Is it naught to you that hear and pass me by?]
　　But the word — the word is mine, when the order moves the
　　　And the lean, locked ranks go roaring down to die.   [line

The grandam of my grandam was the Lyre —
　　[O the blue below the little fisher-huts!]
That the Stealer stooping beachward filled with fire,
　　Till she bore my iron head and ringing guts!
By the wisdom of the centuries I speak —
　　To the tune of yestermorn I set the truth —
I, the joy of life unquestioned — I, the Greek —
　　I, the everlasting Wonder Song of Youth!

　　With my '*Tinka-tinka-tinka-tinka-tink!*'
　　[What d'ye lack, my noble masters? What d'ye lack?]
　　So I draw the world together link by link:
　　　Yea, from Delos up to Limerick and back!

THE OUTLAW

Sir Walter Scott

O Brignall banks are wild and fair,
　　And Greta woods are green,
And you may gather garlands there,
　　Would grace a summer queen:
And as I rode by Dalton Hall,
　　Beneath the turrets high,
A Maiden on the castle wall
　　Was singing merrily: —

'O, Brignall banks are fresh and fair,
    And Greta woods are green!
I'd rather rove with Edmund there
    Than reign our English Queen.'

'If, Maiden, thou wouldst wend with me
    To leave both tower and town,
Thou first must guess what life lead we,
    That dwell by dale and down:
And if thou canst that riddle read,
    As read full well you may,
Then to the green-wood shalt thou speed
    As blithe as Queen of May.'

Yet sung she, 'Brignall banks are fair,
    And Greta woods are green!
I'd rather rove with Edmund there
    Than reign our English Queen.

'I read you by your bugle horn
    And by your palfrey good,
I read you for a Ranger sworn
    To keep the King's green-wood.'
'A Ranger, Lady, winds his horn,
    And 'tis at peep of light;
His blast is heard at merry morn,
    And mine at dead of night.'

Yet sung she, 'Brignall banks are fair,
    And Greta woods are gay!
I would I were with Edmund there,
    To reign his Queen of May!

'With burnish'd brand and musketoon
    So gallantly you come,
I read you for a bold Dragoon,
    That lists the tuck of drum.'

'I list no more the tuck of drum,
  No more the trumpet hear;
But when the beetle sounds his hum,
  My comrades take the spear.

'And O! though Brignall banks be fair
  And Greta woods be gay,
Yet mickle must the maiden dare,
  Would reign my Queen of May!

'Maiden! a nameless life I lead,
  A nameless death I'll die;
The fiend whose lantern lights the mead
  Were better mate than I!
And when I'm with my comrades met
  Beneath the green-wood bough,
What once we were we all forget,
  Nor think what we are now.'

Chorus.   Yet Brignall banks are fresh and fair,
  And Greta woods are green,
And you may gather flowers there
  Would grace a summer queen.

THE WRAGGLE TAGGLE GIPSIES

Anon

THREE gipsies stood at the Castle gate,
They sang so high, they sang so low,
The lady sate in her chamber late,
Her heart it melted away like snow.

They sang so sweet, they sang so shrill,
That fast her tears began to flow.
And she laid down her silken gown,
Her golden rings and all her show.

She plucked off her high-heeled shoes,
A-made of Spanish leather, O.
She would in the street, with her bare, bare feet;
All out in the wind and weather, O.

O saddle me my milk-white steed,
And go and fetch me my pony, O!
That I may ride and seek my bride,
Who is gone with the wraggle taggle gipsies, O!

O he rode high, and he rode low,
He rode through wood and copses too,
Until he came to an open field,
And there he espied his a-lady, O!

What makes you leave your house and land?
Your golden treasures for to go?
What makes you leave your new-wedded lord,
To follow the wraggle taggle gipsies, O?

What care I for my house and my land?
What care I for my treasure, O?
What care I for my new-wedded lord,
I'm off with the wraggle taggle gipsies, O!

Last night you slept on a goose-feather bed,
With the sheet turned down so bravely, O!
And to-night you'll sleep in a cold open field,
Along with the wraggle taggle gipsies, O!

What care I for a goose-feather bed,
With the sheet turned down so bravely, O!
For to-night I shall sleep in a cold open field,
Along with the wraggle taggle gipsies, O!

VAGABOND

John Masefield

Dunno a heap about the what an' why,
   Can't say's I ever knowed.
Heaven to me's a fair blue stretch of sky,
   Earth's jest a dusty road.

Dunno the name o' things, nor what they are,
   Can't say's I ever will.
Dunno about God — He's jest the noddin' star
   Atop the windy hill.

Dunno about Life — it's jest a tramp alone
   From wakin'-time to doss.
Dunno about Death — it's jest a quiet stone
   All over-grey wi' moss.

An' why I live, an' why the old world spins,
   Are things I never knowed;
My mark's the gipsy fires, the lonely inns,
   An' jest the dusty road.

Note

   This is a favourite of my wife's, learnt and included at her
request.   *A. P. W.*

LONDON TOWN

John Masefield

Oh London Town's a fine town, and London sights are rare,
And London ale is right ale, and brisk's the London air,
And busily goes the world there, but crafty grows the mind,
And London Town of all towns I'm glad to leave behind.
Then hey for croft and hop-yard, and hill, and field, and pond,
With Bredon Hill before me and Malvern Hill beyond,
The hawthorn white i' the hedgerow, and all the spring's attire,
In the comely land of Teme and Lugg, and Clent, and Clee, and
                                            Wyre.

Oh London girls are brave girls, in silk and cloth o' gold,
And London shops are rare shops, where gallant things are sold,
And bonnily clinks the gold there, but drowsily blinks the eye,
And London Town of all towns I'm glad to hurry by.

Then, hey for covert and woodland, and ash and elm and oak,
Tewkesbury inns, and Malvern roofs, and Worcester chimney smoke,
The apple trees in the orchard, the cattle in the byre,
And all the land from Ludlow town to Bredon church's spire.

Oh London tunes are new tunes, and London books are wise,
And London plays are rare plays, and fine to country eyes,
Wretchedly fare the most there, and happily fare the few,
And London Town of all towns I'm glad to hurry through.

So hey for the road, the west road, by mill and forge and fold,
Scent of the fern and song of the lark by brook, and field, and Wold,
To the comely folk at the hearth-stone and the talk beside the fire,
In the hearty land, where I was bred, my land of heart's desire.

THE ODYSSEY

ANDREW LANG

As one that for a weary space has lain
  Lull'd by the song of Circe and her wine
  In gardens near the pale of Proserpine,
Where that Ææan isle forgets the main,
And only the low lutes of love complain,
  And only shadows of wan lovers pine —
  As such an one were glad to know the brine
Salt on his lips, and the large air again —
So gladly from the songs of modern speech
  Men turn, and see the stars, and feel the free
    Shrill wind beyond the close of heavy flowers,
    And through the music of the languid hours
They hear like Ocean on a western beach
  The surge and thunder of the Odyssey.

Note

A contemporary of mine at Winchester, who has risen to great eminence and leadership in the youngest of the three Services, once told me that he adopted a military career simply because joining the Army Class was the only way in which he could escape having to learn Greek. Though this was not my reason for becoming a soldier, I too was thankful to give up the study of this language, which never appealed to me as Latin did. Perhaps I was unlucky in my teachers or the authors whom I had to study. I read the account of Xenophon and his ten thousand with intense boredom, partly because no one ever attempted to explain to me what Xenophon was doing or the great historical romance that lay behind the bald record of the number of 'parasangs' which marked his daily advance.

The plays of Sophocles also failed to interest me: their characters seemed unreal and the language stilted, and my teachers were apparently more interested in the niceties of grammar than in the dramatic or literary qualities of the writer.

The composition of a Greek task of prose or iambics was complicated by the fact that I never began to understand the system of accenting Greek, and was reduced to haphazard sprinkling, which one of my teachers called the 'pepperbox method'. Homer, 'to whom the Muses did carouse, a great deep cup with heavenly nectar filled', was the one exception to the distaste with which I regarded Greek. 'The surge and thunder of the Odyssey' attracted me deeply in the one term in which I read it, and I have always regretted my inability to read it in the original: for it will not easily bear translation, as T. E. Lawrence discovered.

I remember from my schooldays a pleasant little jingle about Homer, by A. D. Godley:

> Poluphloisboisterous Homer of old
> Threw all his augments into the sea
> Though he had often been courteously told
> 'Perfect imperfects begin with an e';
> But the poet replied with a dignified air,
> 'What the digamma does anyone care?'

A. P. W.

THE RISKS OF THE GAME

from YE WEARIE WAYFARER *by*

ADAM LINDSAY GORDON

I REMEMBER the lowering wintry morn,
  And the mist on the Cotswold hills,
Where I once heard the blast of the huntsman's horn
  Not far from the seven rills.
Jack Esdale was there, and Hugh St Clair,
  Bob Chapman and Andrew Kerr,
And big George Griffiths on Devil-May-Care,
  And — black Tom Oliver.
And one who rode on a dark-brown steed,
  Clean-jointed, sinewy, spare,
With the lean game head of the Blacklock breed,
And the resolute eye that loves the lead,
  And the quarters massive and square —
A tower of strength, with a promise of speed
  (There was Celtic blood in the pair).

I remember how merry a start we got,
  When the red fox broke from the gorse,
In a country so deep, with a scent so hot,
  That the hound could outpace the horse;
I remember how few in the front rank show'd,
  How endless appeared the tail,
On the brow hill side, where we cross'd the road,
  And headed towards the vale.

The dark-brown steed on the left was there,
  On the right was a dappled grey,
And between the pair, on a chestnut mare,
  The duffer who writes this lay.
What business had 'this child' there to ride?
  But little or none at all;
Yet I held my own for a while in 'the pride
  That goeth before a fall'.

Though rashness can hope for but one result,
  We are heedless when fate draws nigh us,
And the maxim holds good, '*Quem perdere vult*
  Deus, dementat prius'.

The right hand man to the left hand said
  As down in the vale we went,
'Harden your heart like a millstone, Ned,
  And set your face as a flint;
Solid and tall is the rasping wall
  That stretches before us yonder:
You must have it at speed or not at all,
  'Twere better to hold than to ponder,
For the stream runs wide on the take-off side,
  And washes the clay bank under;
Here goes for a pull, 'tis a madman's ride,
  And a broken neck if you blunder.'

No word in reply his comrade spoke,
  Nor waver'd, nor once look'd round,
But I saw him shorten his horse's stroke
  As we splash'd through the marshy ground;
I remember the laugh that all the while
  On his quiet features play'd: —
So he rode to his death, with that careless smile,
  In the van of the 'Light Brigade';
So stricken by Russian grape, the cheer
  Rang out while he toppled back,
From the shattered lungs as merry and clear
  As it did when it roused the pack.
Let never a tear his memory stain,
  Give his ashes never a sigh,
One of many who perished, NOT IN VAIN,
  AS A TYPE OF OUR CHIVALRY —

I remember one thrust he gave to his hat,
  And two to the flanks of the brown,
And still as a statue of old he sat,
  And he shot to the front, hands down;

I remember the snort and the stag-like bound
  Of the steed six lengths to the fore,
And the laugh of the rider while, landing sound,
He turned in the saddle and glanced around;
  I remember — but little more,
Save a bird's-eye gleam of the dashing stream,
  A jarring thud on the wall,
A shock and the blank of a nightmare's dream —
  I was down with a stunning fall.

HOW WE BEAT THE FAVOURITE

(A LAY OF THE LOAMSHIRE HUNT CUP)

Adam Lindsay Gordon

'Aye, squire,' said Stevens, 'they back him at evens!
  The race is all over, bar shouting, they say;
The Clown ought to beat her; Dick Neville is sweeter
  Than ever — he swears he can win all the way.

'A gentleman rider — well, I'm an outsider,
  But if he's a gent who the mischief's a jock?
You swells mostly blunder, Dick rides for the plunder,
  He rides, too, like thunder — he sits like a rock.

'He calls "hunted fairly" a horse that has barely
  Been stripp'd for a trot within sight of the hounds,
A horse that at Warwick beat Birdlime and Yorick,
  And gave Abdelkader at Aintree nine pounds.

'They say we have no test to warrant a protest;
  Dick rides for a lord and stands in with a steward;
The light of their faces they show him — his case is
  Prejudged and his verdict already secured.

'But none can outlast her, and few travel faster,
  She strides in her work clean away from The Drag,
You hold her and sit her, she couldn't be fitter,
  Whenever you hit her she'll spring like a stag.

'And p'rhaps the green jacket, at odds though they back it,
  May fall, or there's no knowing what may turn up.
The mare is quite ready, sit still and ride steady,
  Keep cool; and I think you may just win the Cup.'

Dark-brown with tan muzzle, just stripped for the tussle,
  Stood Iseult, arching her neck to the curb,
A lean head and fiery, strong quarters and wiry,
  A loin rather light, but a shoulder superb.

Some parting injunction, bestowed with great unction,
  I tried to recall, but forgot like a dunce,
When Reginald Murray, full tilt on White Surrey,
  Came down in a hurry to start us at once.

'Keep back in the yellow! Come up on Othello!
  Hold hard on the chestnut! Turn round on The Drag!
Keep back there on Spartan! Back you, sir, in tartan!
  So, steady there, easy,' and down went the flag.

We started, and Kerr made strong running on Mermaid,
  Through furrows that led to the first stake-and-bound,
The crack, half extended, look'd bloodlike and splendid,
  Held wide on the right where the headland was sound.

I pulled hard to baffle her rush with the snaffle,
  Before her two-thirds of the field got away,
All through the wet pasture where floods of the last year
  Still loitered, they clotted my crimson with clay.

The fourth fence, a wattle, floor'd Monk and Blue-bottle;
  The Drag came to grief at the blackthorn and ditch,
The rails toppled over Redoubt and Red Rover,
  The lane stopped Lycurgus and Leicestershire Witch.

She passed like an arrow Kildare and Cock Sparrow,
  And Mantrap and Mermaid refused the stone wall;
And Giles on The Greyling came down at the paling,
  And I was left sailing in front of them all.

I took them a burster, nor eased her nor nursed her
   Until the black bullfinch led into the plough,
And through the strong bramble we bored with a scramble —
   My cap was knock'd off by the hazel-tree bough.

Where furrows looked lighter I drew the rein tighter —
   Her dark chest all dappled with flakes of white foam,
Her flanks mud bespattered, a weak rail she shattered —
   We landed on turf with our heads turn'd for home.

Then crash'd a low binder, and then close behind her
   The sward to the strokes of the favourite shook;
His rush roused her mettle, yet ever so little
   She shorten'd her stride as we raced at the brook.

She rose when I hit her. I saw the stream glitter,
   A wide scarlet nostril flashed close to my knee,
Between sky and water The Clown came and caught her,
   The space that he cleared was a caution to see.

And forcing the running, discarding all cunning,
   A length to the front went the rider in green;
A long strip of stubble, and then the big double,
   Two stiff flights of rails with a quickset between.

She raced at the rasper, I felt my knees grasp her,
   I found my hands give to her strain on the bit,
She rose when The Clown did — our silks as we bounded
   Brush'd lightly, our stirrups clash'd loud as we lit.

A rise steeply sloping, a fence with stone coping —
   The last — we diverged round the base of the hill;
His path was the nearer, his leap was the clearer,
   I flogg'd up the straight, and he led sitting still.

She came to his quarter, and on still I brought her,
   And up to his girth, to his breast-plate she drew;
A short prayer from Neville just reach'd me, 'The devil',
   He mutter'd — lock'd level the hurdles we flew.

A hum of hoarse cheering, a dense crowd careering,
  All sights seen obscurely, all shouts vaguely heard;
'The green wins!' 'The crimson!' The multitude swims on,
  And figures are blended and features are blurr'd.

'The horse is her master!' 'The green forges past her!'
  'The Clown will outlast her!' 'The Clown wins!' 'The Clown!'
The white railing races with all the white faces,
  The chestnut outpaces, outstretches the brown.

On still past the gateway she strains in the straightway,
  Still struggles, 'The Clown by a short neck at most',
He swerves, the green scourges, the stand rocks and surges,
  And flashes, and verges, and flits the white post.

Aye! so ends the tussle, — I knew the tan muzzle
  Was first, though the ring-men were yelling 'Dead heat!'
A nose I could swear by, but Clarke said 'The mare by
  A short head.' And that's how the favourite was beat.

Note

I suppose that few of the present generation read the poems of
Adam Lindsay Gordon; he is still the best of those who wrote
from the saddle and should therefore be favoured of those who
read and ride. In Masefield's 'Reynard the Fox', Nob Manor sneers
at 'the poet-chap who thinks he rides'; Lindsay Gordon was a
rider-chap who tried his hand at poetry. He was conventionally
educated in England at Cheltenham, Woolwich, and Oxford but
was too restless for settled life and went to Australia in the
eighteen-fifties, where he was mounted policeman, horse-breaker,
steeplechase rider and politician. He ended his own life with a
bullet while still under forty.

The two items here are the best known of his riding verses.
Some examples of his philosophy of life will be found in Section 8.

Black Tom Oliver, of the first poem, was a famous steeplechase
rider and trainer near Cheltenham who won three Grand
Nationals. He was concerned in one of Lindsay Gordon's esca-

pades, when he broke open a stable and removed a horse, which
had been seized for debt, in order to ride it in a steeplechase. One
version of the story says that Tom Oliver got him out of the
trouble with the police which resulted, another version says that
Oliver aided and abetted him.   *A. P. W.*

REYNARD THE FOX

JOHN MASEFIELD

[*Extracts*]

I

HUNTER

TOM DANSEY was a famous whip,
Trained as a child in horsemanship,
Entered, as soon as he was able,
As boy at Caunter's racing-stable;
There, like the other boys, he slept
In stall beside the horse he kept,
Snug in the straw; and Caunter's stick
Brought morning to him all too quick.
He learned the high, quick gingery ways
Of thoroughbreds; his stable days
Made him a rider, groom and vet.
He promised to be too thick-set
For jockeying, so left it soon.
Now he was whip and rode Maroon.
He was a small, lean, wiry man,
With sunk cheeks weathered to a tan
Scarred by the spikes of hawthorn sprays
Dashed thro' head down, on going days,
In haste to see the line they took.
There was a beauty in his look,
It was intent. His speech was plain.
Maroon's head, reaching to the rein,
Had half his thought before he spoke.
His 'Gone away!' when foxes broke
Was like a bell. His chief delight
Was hunting fox from noon to night....

II

HOUNDS

They were a lovely pack for looks;
Their forelegs drumsticked without crooks,
Straight, without over-tread or bend,
Muscled to gallop to the end,
With neat feet round as any cat's.
Great-chested, muscled in the slats,
Bright, clean, short-coated, broad in shoulder,
With stag-like eyes that seemed to smoulder.
The heads well-cocked, the clean necks strong,
Brows broad, ears close, the muzzles long,
And all like racers in the thighs;
Their noses exquisitely wise,
Their minds being memories of smells;
Their voices like a ring of bells;
Their sterns all spirit; cock and feather;
Their colours like the English weather,
Magpie and hare, and badger-pye,
Like minglings in a double dye,
Some smutty-nosed, some tan, none bald;
Their manners were to come when called,
Their flesh was sinew knit to bone,
Their courage like a banner blown.
Their joy to push him out of cover,
And hunt him till they rolled him over.

III

HUNTED

The fox knew well that, before they tore him,
They should try their speed on the downs before him.
There were three more miles to the Wan Dyke Hill,
But his heart was high that he beat them still.
The wind of the downland charmed his bones,
So off he went for the Sarsen Stones.

*   *   *   *

The moan of the three great firs in the wind
And the 'Ai' of the foxhounds died behind;
Wind-dapples followed the hill-wind's breath
On the Kill Down Gorge where the Danes found death.
Larks scattered up; the peewits feeding
Rose in a flock from the Kill Down Steeding.
The hare leaped up from her form and swerved
Swift left for the Starveall, harebell-turved.
On the wind-bare thorn some longtails prinking
Cried sweet as though wind-blown glass were chinking.
Behind came thudding and loud halloo,
Or a cry from hounds as they came to view.

*   *   *   *

The pure clean air came sweet to his lungs,
Till he thought foul scorn of those crying tongues.
In a three mile more he would reach the haven
In the Wan Dyke croaked on by the raven.
In a three mile more he would make his berth
On the hard cool floor of a Wan Dyke earth,
Too deep for spade, too curved for terrier,
With the pride of the race to make rest the merrier.
In a three mile more he would reach his dream,
So his game heart gulped and he put on steam.

*   *   *   *

Like a rocket shot to a ship ashore
The lean red bolt of his body tore,
Like a ripple of wind running swift on grass;
Like a shadow on wheat when a cloud blows past,
Like a turn at the buoy in a cutter sailing
When the bright green gleam lips white at the railing,
Like the April snake whipping back to sheath,
Like the gannet's hurtle on fish beneath,
Like a kestrel chasing, like a sickle reaping,
Like all things swooping, like all things sweeping,
Like a hound for stay, like a stag for swift,
With his shadow beside like spinning drift....

On he went with a galloping rally
Past Maesbury Clump for Wan Brook Valley.
The blood in his veins went romping high,
'Get on, on, on, to the earth or die.'
The air of the downs went purely past
Till he felt the glory of going fast,
Till the terror of death, though there indeed,
Was lulled for a while by his pride of speed.
He was romping away from hounds and hunt,
He had Wan Dyke Hill and his earth in front,
In a one mile more when his point was made
He would rest in safety from dog or spade;
Nose between paws he would hear the shout
Of the 'Gone to earth!' to the hounds without,
The whine of the hounds, and their cat-feet gadding,
Scratching the earth, and their breath pad-padding;
He would hear the horn call hounds away,
And rest in peace till another day.

RIGHT ROYAL

John Masefield

[Extract]

In a race-course box behind the Stand
Right Royal shone from a strapper's hand.
A big dark bay with a restless tread,
Fetlock deep in a wheat-straw bed;
A noble horse of a nervy blood,
By O Mon Roi out of Rectitude.
Something quick in his eye and ear
Gave a hint that he might be queer.
In front, he was all to a horseman's mind;
Some thought him a trifle light behind.
By two good points might his rank be known,
A beautiful head and a jumping bone.

He had been the hope of Sir Button Budd,
Who bred him there at the Fletchings stud,
But the Fletchings jockey had flogged him cold
In a narrow thing as a two-year-old.
After that, with his sulks and swerves,
Dread of the crowd and fits of nerves,
Like a wastrel bee who makes no honey,
He had hardly earned his entry money.

Liking him still, though he failed at racing,
Sir Button trained him for steeple-chasing.
He jumped like a stag, but his heart was cowed;
Nothing would make him face the crowd.
When he reached the Straight where the crowds began
He would make no effort for any man.

Sir Button sold him, Charles Cothill bought him,
Rode him to hounds and soothed and taught him.
After two years' care Charles felt assured
That his horse's broken heart was cured,
And the jangled nerves in tune again.
And now, as proud as a King of Spain,
He moved in his box with a restless tread,
His eyes like sparks inhis lovely head,
Ready to run between the roar
Of the stands that face the Straight once more;
Ready to race, though blown, though beat,
As long as his will could lift his feet;
Ready to burst his heart to pass
Each gasping horse in that street of grass.

TO A BLACK GREYHOUND

JULIAN GRENFELL

SHINING black in the shining light,
 Inky black in the golden sun,

Graceful as the swallow's flight,
   Light as swallow, wingèd one,
Swift as driven hurricane —
   Double-sinewed stretch and spring,
Muffled thud of flying feet,
   See the black dog galloping,
   Hear his wild foot-beat.

See him lie when the day is dead,
   Black curves curled on the boarded floor.
Sleepy eyes, my sleepy-head —
   Eyes that were aflame before.
Gentle now, they burn no more;
   Gentle now and softly warm,
With the fire that made them bright
   Hidden — as when after storm
   Softly falls the night.

God of speed, who makes the fire —
   God of Peace, who lulls the same –
God who gives the fierce desire,
   Lust for blood as fierce as flame —
God who stands in Pity's name —
   Many may ye be or less,
Ye who rule the earth and sun:
   Gods of strength and gentleness,
   Ye are ever one.

Note

The dog, man's most intelligent and responsive friend in the animal world, has inspired little real poetry, while that foolish quadruped the horse has been the subject of much. Swift, in the last part of *Gulliver's Travels*, endowed his horses (Houyhnhnms) with superhuman wisdom and intelligence, the last thing that horses have ever had, in the view of their riders anyway. Beauty and speed have nearly always been preferred to solid worth — this is the reason for many divorces. When the dog is celebrated in verse, it is usually as the questing hound, the beast of the chase,

rather than as man's companion. Dogs bark, an unmusical
sound; hounds bay — 'a cry more tuneable'.

Kipling has written the best verse on the dog-about-the-house
(*The Power of the Dog*; *Dinah in Heaven*; *The Supplication of the Black
Aberdeen*); but most doggy verse is inclined to be doggerel. The
truth is that the dog-friend is too sensible, too homely to appeal
to the poet, by whom even the sleek, egotistical promiscuous cat
is better advertised. The dog has still to live down his Eastern and
biblical reputation as an unclean animal. Poor dog, his name is
ill-connected in our speech: a dog's life, sick as a dog, dog's-eared,
dog-tired, dogsbody, dog in the manger, dirty dog, 'grin like a
dog and run about the city'. And why should the name of the
dog's comparatively chaste female be such a term of opprobrium
while the cat's noisier and more frequent lapses from virtue
escape notice? Perhaps merely because the cat is a nocturnal
amorist, while the dog, sensibly, likes to see what he is making
love to — not that he seems to mind much.

Cats would never run after an electric mouse to amuse their
human friends, nor retrieve a sparrow. Never mind; 'Dogged
does it' is one of our best proverbs; and dogs have their Star and
cats have none.   *A. P. W.*

5. CONVERSATION PIECES

THE poem that tells a tale or propounds a philosophy is not usually regarded as a high form of poetic art, any more than the 'story picture' of the Royal Academy exhibition. Yet to tell a story was the duty of the original poet, the ballad-maker; and ballads and stories and philosophies in verse still have an appeal, at least for me. I like the old Border Ballads, though only one, *True Thomas*, seems to have stayed in my head in its entirety. Its meaning has sometimes intrigued me, as my note appended to the poem shows.

Two of my favourite makers of poetry, Browning and Kipling, have written conversation pieces, some of which are reproduced here. I like Browning's worldly bishops and rakish painter; they are human and credible, as Tennyson's smug Knights of the Round Table never are; Malory is so much truer and better reading unbowdlerized. I like too Kipling's unscrupulous old ship-owner of the *Mary Gloster*; he appeals to me more than the companion portrait of the puritanical mechanized M'Andrew; the contrast of both with the effete Tomlinson, who has not even the spirit to sin sufficiently to satisfy the Devil, is in accordance with Kipling's gospel of action, which is also mine. I feel fairly confident that I could satisfy the Devil — if I believed in Hell.

The philosophy of the Rubáiyát may be shallow and pagan but the verses have stayed in my head since I first read them; so has most of the theatrical and insincere *Ballad of Reading Gaol*. The other pieces here have appealed to me for various reasons, and seemed to fall into this section better than into any other.   *A. P. W.*

BISHOP BLOUGRAM'S APOLOGY

ROBERT BROWNING

[*Extracts*]

No more wine? then we'll push back chairs and talk.
A final glass for me, though: cool, i' faith!
We ought to have our Abbey back, you see.
It's different, preaching in basilicas,
And doing duty in some masterpiece
Like this of brother Pugin's, bless his heart!

I

I doubt if they're half baked, those chalk rosettes,
Ciphers and stucco-twiddlings everywhere;
It's just like breathing in a lime-kiln: eh?
These hot long ceremonies of our church
Cost us a little — oh, they pay the price,
You take me — amply pay it! Now, we'll talk.

So, you despise me, Mr Gigadibs.

        *   *   *   *

An unbelieving Pope won't do, you say.
It's like those eerie stories nurses tell,
Of how some actor played Death on a stage
With pasteboard crown, sham orb and tinselled dart,
And called himself the monarch of the world,
Then, going in the tire-room afterward
Because the play was done, to shift himself,
Got touched upon the sleeve familiarly
The moment he had shut the closet door
By Death himself. Thus God might touch a Pope
At unawares, ask what his baubles mean,
And whose part he presumed to play just now?
Best be yourself, imperial, plain and true!

        *   *   *   *

The common problem, yours, mine, every one's,
Is not to fancy what were fair in life
Provided it could be, — but, finding first
What may be, then find how to make it fair
Up to our means — a very different thing!
No abstract intellectual plan of life
Quite irrespective of life's plainest laws,
But one, a man, who is man and nothing more,
May lead within a world which (by your leave)
Is Rome or London — not Fool's-paradise.
Embellish Rome, idealize away,
Make Paradise of London if you can,
You're welcome, nay, you're wise.
          A simile!

We mortals cross the ocean of this world
Each in his average cabin of a life —
The best's not big, the worst yields elbow-room.
Now for our six months' voyage — how prepare?
You come on shipboard with a landsman's list
Of things he calls convenient — so they are!
An India screen is pretty furniture,
A piano-forte is a fine resource,
All Balzac's novels occupy one shelf,
The new edition fifty volumes long;
And little Greek books, with the funny type
They get up well at Leipsic, fill the next —
Go on! slabbed marble, what a bath it makes!
And Parma's pride, the Jerome, let us add!
'Twere pleasant could Correggio's fleeting glow
Hang full in face of one where'er one roams,
Since he more than the others brings with him
Italy's self, — the marvellous Modenese!
Yet 'twas not on your list before, perhaps.
— Alas! friend, here's the agent ... is't the name?
The captain, or whoever's master here —
You see him screw his face up; what's his cry
Ere you set foot on shipboard? 'Six feet square!'
If you won't understand what six feet mean,
Compute and purchase stores accordingly —
And if in pique because he overhauls
Your Jerome, piano and bath, you come on board
Bare — why, you cut a figure at the first
While sympathetic landsmen see you off;
Not afterwards, when, long ere half seas over,
You peep up from your utterly naked boards
Into some snug and well-appointed berth,
Like mine, for instance (try the cooler jug —
Put back the other, but don't jog the ice)
And mortified you mutter 'Well and good —
He sits enjoying his sea-furniture —
'Tis stout and proper, and there's store of it,
Though I've the better notion, all agree,

Of fitting rooms up! hang the carpenter,
Neat ship-shape fixings and contrivances —
I would have brought my Jerome, frame and all!'
And meantime you bring nothing: never mind —
You've proved your artist-nature: what you don't,
You might bring, so despise me, as I say.

*   *   *   *

Just when we are safest, there's a sunset-touch,
A fancy from a flower-bell, some one's death,
A chorus-ending from Euripides, —
And that's enough for fifty hopes and fears
As old and new at once as Nature's self,
To rap and knock and enter in our soul,
Take hands and dance there, a fantastic ring,
Round the ancient idol, on his base again, —
The grand Perhaps! we look on helplessly, —
There the old misgivings, crooked questions are —
This good God, — what He could do, if He would,
Would, if He could — then must have done long since:
If so, when, where, and how? some way must be, —
Once feel about, and soon or late you hit
Some sense, in which it might be, after all.
Why not, 'The Way, the Truth, the Life?'
                              — That way
Over the mountain, which who stands upon
Is apt to doubt if it be indeed a road;
While if he views it from the waste itself,
Up goes the line there, plain from base to brow,
Not vague, mistakeable! what's a break or two
Seen from the unbroken desert either side?
And then (to bring in fresh philosophy)
What if the breaks themselves should prove at last
The most consummate of contrivances
To train a man's eye, teach him what is faith?
And so we stumble at truth's very test!
All we have gained then by our unbelief

Is a life of doubt diversified by faith,
For one of faith diversified by doubt:
We called the chess-board white, — we call it black.

*   *   *   *

You see one lad o'erstride a chimney-stack;
Him you must watch — he's sure to fall, yet stands!
Our interest's on the dangerous edge of things.
The honest thief, the tender murderer.
The superstitious atheist, demireps
That love and save their souls in new French books —
We watch while these in equilibrium keep
The giddy line midway: one step aside,
They're classed and done with. I, then, keep the line
Before your sages, — just the men to shrink
From the gross weights, coarse scales, and labels broad
You offer their refinement. Fool or knave?
Why needs a bishop be a fool or knave
When there's a thousand diamond weights between?

*   *   *   *

What matter though I doubt at every pore,
Head-doubts, heart-doubts, doubts at my fingers' ends,
Doubts in the trivial work of every day,
Doubts at the very bases of my soul
In the grand moments when she probes herself —
If finally I have a life to show,
The thing I did, brought out in evidence
Against the thing done to me underground
By Hell and all its brood, for aught I know?
I say, whence sprang this? shows it faith or doubt?
All's doubt in me; where's break of faith in this?
It is the idea, the feeling and the love
God means mankind should strive for and show forth,
Whatever be the process to that end, —
And not historic knowledge, logic sound,
And metaphysical acumen, sure!
'What think ye of Christ,' friend? when all's done and said,
Like you this Christianity or not?

It may be false, but will you wish it true?
Has it your vote to be so if it can?
Trust you an instinct silenced long ago
That will break silence and enjoin you love
What mortified philosophy is hoarse,
And all in vain, with bidding you despise?
If you desire faith — then you've faith enough:
What else seeks God — nay, what else seek ourselves?

       *   *   *   *

    You'll say, once all believed, man, woman, child,
In that dear middle-age these noodles praise.
How you'd exult if I could put you back
Six hundred years, blot out cosmogony,
Geology, ethnology, what not,
(Greek endings with the little passing-bell
That signifies some faith's about to die)
And set you square with Genesis again, —
When such a traveller told you his last news,
He saw the ark a-top of Ararat
But did not climb there since 'twas getting dusk
And robber-bands infest the mountain's foot!
How should you feel, I ask, in such an age,
How act? As other people felt and did;
With soul more blank than this decanter's knob,
Believe — and yet lie, kill, rob, fornicate
Full in belief's face, like the beast you'd be!

    No, when the fight begins within himself,
A man's worth something. God stoops o'er his head,
Satan looks up between his feet — both tug —
He's left, himself, in the middle: the soul wakes
And grows. Prolong that battle through his life!
Never leave growing till the life to come!

       *   *   *   *

    Do you know, I have often had a dream
(Work it up in your next month's article)
Of man's poor spirit in its progress still

Losing true life for ever and a day
Through ever trying to be and ever being
In the evolution of successive spheres,
Before its actual sphere and place of life,
Halfway into the next, which having reached,
It shoots with corresponding foolery
Halfway into the next still, on and off!
As when a traveller, bound from North to South,
Scouts fur in Russia — what's its use in France?
In France spurns flannel — where's its need in Spain?
In Spain drops cloth — too cumbrous for Algiers!
Linen goes next, and last the skin itself,
A superfluity at Timbuctoo.
When, through his journey, was the fool at ease?

   * * * *

'*Pastor est tui Dominus.*' You find
In these the pleasant pastures of this life
Much you may eat without the least offence,
Much you don't eat because your maw objects,
Much you would eat but that your fellow-flock
Open great eyes at you and even butt,
And thereupon you like your mates so well
You cannot please yourself, offending them —
Though when they seem exorbitantly sheep,
You weigh your pleasure with their butts and bleats
And strike the balance. Sometimes certain fears
Restrain you — real checks since you find them so —
Sometimes you please yourself and nothing checks;
And thus you graze through life with not one lie,
And like it best.

     But do you, in truth's name?
If so, you beat — which means, you are not I —
Who needs must make earth mine and feed my fill
Not simply unbutted at, unbickered with,
But motioned to the velvet of the sward
By those obsequious wethers' very selves.

Look at me, sir; my age is double yours:
At yours, I knew beforehand, so enjoyed,
What now I should be — as, permit the word,
I pretty well imagine your whole range
And stretch of tether twenty years to come.
We both have minds and bodies much alike,
In truth's name, don't you want my bishopric,
My daily bread, my influence and my state?
You're young, I'm old, you must be old one day;
Will you find then, as I do hour by hour,
Women their lovers kneel to, that cut curls
From your fat lap-dog's ears to grace a brooch —
Dukes, that petition just to kiss your ring —
With much beside you know or may conceive?

                    *   *   *   *

What's your reward, self-abnegating friend?
Stood you confessed of those exceptional
And privileged great natures that dwarf mine —
A zealot with a mad ideal in reach,
A poet just about to print his ode,
A statesman with a scheme to stop this war,
An artist whose religion is his art,
I should have nothing to object! such men
Carry the fire, all things grow warm to them,
Their drugget's worth my purple, they beat me.
But you — you're just as little those as I —
You, Gigadibs, who, thirty years of age,
Write stately for Blackwood's magazine,
Believe you see two points in Hamlet's soul
Unseized by the Germans yet — which view you'll print —
Meantime the best you have to show being still
That lively lightsome article we took
Almost for the true Dickens, — what's its name?
'The Slum and Cellar — or Whitechapel life
Limned after dark!' it made me laugh, I know,
And pleased a month and brought you in ten pounds.

Over his wine so smiled and talked his hour
Sylvester Blougram, styled *in partibus*
Episcopus, nec non — (the deuce knows what
It's changed to by our novel hierarchy)
With Gigadibs the literary man,
Who played with spoons, explored his plate's design,
And ranged the olive-stones about its edge,
While the great bishop rolled him out his mind.

* * * *

TRUE THOMAS

ANON

TRUE Thomas lay on Huntlie bank;
   A ferlie he spied wi' his e'e;
And there he saw a ladye bright
   Come riding down by the Eildon Tree.

Her skirt was o' the grass-green silk,
   Her mantle o' the velvet fyne;
At ilka tett o' her horse's mane,
   Hung fifty siller bells and nine.

True Thomas he pu'd aff his cap,
   And louted low down on his knee:
'Hail to thee, Mary, Queen of Heaven!
   For thy peer on earth could never be.'

'O no, O no, Thomas,' she said,
   'That name does not belang to me;
I'm but the Queen o' fair Elfland,
   That am hither come to visit thee.

'Harp and carp, Thomas,' she said;
   'Harp and carp along wi' me;
And if ye dare to kiss my lips,
   Sure of your bodie I will be.'

'Betide me weal, betide me woe,
   That weird shall never daunten me.'
Syne he has kiss'd her rosy lips,
   All underneath the Eildon Tree.

'Now ye maun go wi' me,' she said,
   'True Thomas, ye maun go wi' me;
And ye maun serve me seven years,
   Thro' weal or woe as may chance to be.'

She's mounted on her milk-white steed,
   She's ta'en true Thomas up behind;
And aye, whene'er her bridle rang,
   The steed gaed swifter than the wind.

O they rade on, and farther on,
   The steed gaed swifter than the wind;
Until they reach'd a desert wide,
   And living land was left behind.

'Light down, light down now, true Thomas,
   And lean your head upon my knee;
Abide ye there a little space,
   And I will show you ferlies three.

'O see ye not yon narrow road,
   So thick beset wi' thorns and briers?
That is the Path of Righteousness,
   Though after it but few inquires.

'And see ye not yon braid, braid road,
   That lies across the lily leven?
That is the Path of Wickedness,
   Though some call it the Road to Heaven.

'And see ye not yon bonny road
   That winds about the fernie brae?
That is the Road to fair Elfland,
   Where thou and I this night maun gae.

'But, Thomas, ye sall haud your tongue,
  Whatever ye may hear or see;
For speak ye word in Elfyn-land,
  Ye'll ne'er win back to your ain countrie.'

O they rade on, and farther on,
  And they waded rivers abune the knee;
And they saw neither sun nor moon,
  But they heard the roaring of the sea.

It was mirk, mirk night, there was nae starlight,
  They waded thro' red blude to the knee;
For a' the blude that's shed on the earth
  Rins through the springs o' that countrie.

Syne they came to a garden green,
  And she pu'd an apple frae a tree:
'Take this for thy wages, true Thomas;
  It will give thee the tongue that can never lee.'

'My tongue is my ain,' true Thomas he said;
  'A gudely gift ye wad gie to me!
I neither dought to buy or sell
  At fair or tryst where I might be.

'I dought neither speak to prince or peer,
  Nor ask of grace from fair ladye!'
'Now haud thy peace, Thomas,' she said,
  'For as I say, so must it be.'

He has gotten a coat of the even cloth,
  And a pair o' shoon of the velvet green;
And till seven years were gane and past,
  True Thomas on earth was never seen.

Note

This is my favourite ballad. I have sometimes speculated idly whether the writer had an allegory in his mind — the allegory of marriage. True Thomas begins as all men in love by regarding his lady as one sent from Heaven; to find that what she wants is to be kissed on earth. He accepts, as all men would, a challenge from a charming lady, and finds himself bound to her service — for weal or woe, for better for worse. Thomas got off with seven years, many men receive a life sentence. Mark how the lady gives Thomas no choice of the three roads; she is not in the least concerned with Heaven or Hell, with righteousness or wickedness, only with the road that leads to the country where she is Queen — the country of men's hearts. How comes all the blood that is shed on earth to flow through her land, is it the heart's blood of unsuccessful lovers? I have puzzled over the prohibition to Thomas to utter word in Elfinland (except surely to the Queen herself) and the gift of a tongue that can never lie to take back to his own country. It is all a part of woman's guile; to make sure that Thomas cannot flirt with any other elves in Elfinland; nor — as he himself perceives at once — 'ask of grace from fair ladye', when he returns to his own country with a tongue that can speak naught but the perfect truth. An artful Elfin Queen — was she worth it, True Thomas?

Kipling's ballad is a sequel which shows that Thomas overcame his handicap of 'a tongue that never can lie' so far as speaking to prince or peer was concerned; but Kipling is rightly silent on the matter of asking grace from 'fair ladye' with the same handicap. *A. P. W.*

THE LAST RHYME OF TRUE THOMAS

Rudyard Kipling

THE King has called for priest and cup,
　　The King has taken spur and blade
To dub True Thomas a belted knight,
　　And all for the sake o' the songs he made.

They have sought him high, they have sought him low,
　　They have sought him over down and lea;
They have found him by the milk-white thorn
　　That guards the gates o' Faerie.

'Twas bent beneath and blue above,
   Their eyes were held that they might not see
The kine that grazed beneath the knowes,
   Oh, they were the Queens o' Faerie!

'Now cease your song,' the King he said,
   'Oh, cease your song and get you dight
To vow your vow and watch your arms,
   For I will dub you a belted knight.

'For I will give you a horse o' pride,
   Wi' blazon and spur and page and squire;
Wi' keep and tail and seizin and law,
   And land to hold at your desire.'

True Thomas smiled above his harp,
   And turned his face to the naked sky,
Where, blown before the wastrel wind,
   The thistle-down she floated by.

'I ha' vowed my vow in another place,
   And bitter oath it was on me,
I ha' watched my arms the lee-long night,
   Where five-score fighting men would flee.

'My lance is tipped o' the hammered flame,
   My shield is beat o' the moonlight cold;
And I won my spurs in the Middle World,
   A thousand fathom beneath the mould.

'And what should I make wi' a horse o' pride,
   And what should I make wi' a sword so brown,
But spill the rings o' the Gentle Folk
   And flyte my kin in the Fairy Town?

'And what should I make wi' blazon and belt,
   Wi' keep and tail and seizin and fee,
And what should I do wi' page and squire
   That am a king in my own countrie?

'For I send east and I send west,
  And I send far as my will may flee,
By dawn and dusk and the drinking rain,
  And syne my Sendings return to me.

'They come wi' news of the groanin' earth,
  They come wi' news o' the roarin' sea,
Wi' word of Spirit and Ghost and Flesh,
  And man, that's mazed among the three.'

The King he bit his nether lip,
  And smote his hand upon his knee:
'By the faith o' my soul, True Thomas,' he said,
  'Ye waste no wit in courtesie!

'As I desire, unto my pride,
  Can I make Earls by three and three,
To run before and ride behind
  And serve the sons o' my body.'

'And what care I for your row-foot earls,
  Or all the sons o' your body?
Before they win to the Pride o' Name,
  I trow they all ask leave o' me.

'For I make Honour wi' muckle mouth,
  As I make Shame wi' mincin' feet,
To sing wi' the priests at the market-cross,
  Or run wi' the dogs in the naked street.

'And some they give me the good red gold,
  And some they give me the white money,
And some they give me a clout o' meal,
  For they be people o' low degree.

'And the song I sing for the counted gold
  The same I sing for the white money,
But best I sing for the clout o' meal
  That simple people given me.'

The King cast down a silver groat,
   A silver groat o' Scots money:
'If I come wi' a poor man's dole,' he said,
   'True Thomas, will ye harp to me?'

'Whenas I harp to the children small,
   They press me close on either hand.
And who are you,' True Thomas said,
   'That you should ride while they must stand?

'Light down, light down from your horse o' pride,
   I trow ye talk too loud and hie,
And I will make you a triple word,
   And syne, if ye dare, ye shall 'noble me.'

He has lighted down from his horse o' pride,
   And set his back against the stone.
'Now guard you well,' True Thomas said,
   'Ere I rax your heart from your breast-bone!'

True Thomas played upon his harp,
   The fairy harp that couldna lee,
And the first least word the proud King heard,
   It harpit the salt tear out o' his e'e.

'Oh, I see the love that I lost long syne,
   I touch the hope that I may not see,
And all that I did o' hidden shame,
   Like little snakes they hiss at me.

'The sun is lost at noon — at noon!
   The dread o' doom has grippit me.
True Thomas, hide me under your cloak,
   God wot, I'm little fit to dee!'

'Twas bent beneath and blue above —
   'Twas open field and running flood —
Where, hot on heath and dyke and wall,
   The high sun warmed the adder's brood.

'Lie down, lie down,' True Thomas said.
　'The God shall judge when all is done.
But I will bring you a better word
　And lift the cloud that I laid on.'

True Thomas played upon his harp,
　That birled and brattled to his hand,
And the next least word True Thomas made,
　It garred the King take horse and brand.

'Oh, I hear the tread o' the fighting-men,
　I see the sun on splent and spear.
I mark the arrow outen the fern
　That flies so low and sings so clear!

'Advance my standards to that war,
　And bid my good knights prick and ride;
The gled shall watch as fierce a fight
　As e'er was fought on the Border side!'

'Twas bent beneath and blue above,
　'Twas nodding grass and naked sky,
Where, ringing up the wastrel wind,
　The eyass stooped upon the pye.

True Thomas sighed above his harp,
　And turned the song on the midmost string;
And the last least word True Thomas made,
　He harpit his dead youth back to the King.

'Now I am prince, and I do well
　To love my love withouten fear;
To walk wi' man in fellowship,
　And breathe my horse behind the deer.

'My hounds they bay unto the death,
　The buck has couched beyond the burn,
My love she waits at her window
　To wash my hands when I return.

'For that I live am I content
   (Oh! I have seen my true love's eyes)
To stand wi' Adam in Eden-glade,
   And run in the woods o' Paradise!'

'Twas naked sky and nodding grass,
   'Twas running flood and wastrel wind,
Where, checked against the open pass,
   The red deer turned to wait the hind.

True Thomas laid his harp away,
   And louted low at the saddle-side;
He has taken stirrup and hauden rein,
   And set the King on his horse o' pride.

'Sleep ye or wake,' True Thomas said,
   'That sit so still, that muse so long;
Sleep ye or wake? — till the latter sleep
   I trow ye'll not forget my song.

'I ha' harpit a shadow out o' the sun
   To stand before your face and cry;
I ha' armed the earth beneath your heel,
   And over your head I ha' dusked the sky.

'I ha' harpit ye up to the throne o' God,
   I ha' harpit your midmost soul in three;
I ha' harpit ye down to the Hinges o' Hell,
   And — ye — would — make — a Knight o' me!'

THE MARY GLOSTER

RUDYARD KIPLING

I'VE paid for your sickest fancies; I've humoured your crackedest
                                                           whim —
Dick, it's your daddy, dying; you've got to listen to him!
Good for a fortnight, am I? The doctor told you? He lied.
I shall go under by morning, and — Put that nurse outside.
'Never seen death yet, Dickie? Well, now is your time to learn,
And you'll wish you held my record before it comes to your turn.

Not counting the Line and the Foundry, the yards and the village, too,
I've made myself and a million; but I'm damned if I made you.
Master at two-and-twenty, and married at twenty-three —
Ten thousand men on the pay-roll, and forty freighters at sea!
Fifty years between 'em, and every year of it fight,
And now I'm Sir Anthony Gloster, dying, a baronite:
For I lunched with his Royal 'Ighness — what was it the papers a-had?
'Not least of our merchant-princes.' Dickie, that's me, your dad!
I didn't begin with askings. *I* took my job and I stuck;
And I took the chances they wouldn't, an' now they're calling it luck.
Lord, what boats I've handled — rotten and leaky and old!
Ran 'em, or — opened the bilge-cock, precisely as I was told.
Grub that 'ud bind you crazy, and crews that 'ud turn you grey,
And a big fat lump of insurance to cover the risk on the way.
The others they dursn't do it; they said they valued their life
(They've served me since as skippers). *I* went, and I took my wife.
Over the world I drove 'em, married at twenty-three,
And your mother saving the money and making a man of me,
I was content to be master, but she said there was better behind;
She took the chances I wouldn't, and I followed your mother blind.
She egged me to borrow the money, an' she helped me to clear the
                                                              loan,
When we bought half shares in a cheap 'un and hoisted a flag of our
                                                              own.
Patching and coaling on credit, and living the Lord knew how,
We started the Red Ox freighters — we've eight-and-thirty now.
And those were the days of clippers, and the freights were clipper-
                                                           freights,
And we knew we were making our fortune, but she died in Macassar
                                                           Straits —
By the Little Paternosters, as you come to the Union Bank —
And we dropped her in fourteen fathom; I pricked it off where she
                                                           sank.
Owners we were, full owners, and the boat was christened for her,
And she died in the Mary Gloster. My heart, how young we were!
So I went on a spree round Java and well-nigh ran her ashore,
But your mother came and warned me and I wouldn't liquor no
                                                           more:

Strict I stuck to my business, afraid to stop or I'd think,
Saving the money (she warned me), and letting the other men drink.
And I met M'Cullough in London (I'd turned five 'undred then),
And 'tween us we started the Foundry — three forges and twenty
men:
Cheap repairs for the cheap 'uns. It paid, and the business grew,
For I bought me a steam-lathe patent, and that was a gold mine too.
'Cheaper to build 'em than buy 'em,' I said, but M'Cullough he shied,
And we wasted a year in talking before we moved to the Clyde.
And the Lines were all beginning, and we all of us started fair,
Building our engines like houses and staying the boilers square.
But M'Cullough 'e wanted cabins with marble and maple and all,
And Brussels an' Utrecht velvet, and baths and a Social Hall,
And pipes for closets all over, and cutting the frames too light,
But M'Cullough he died in the Sixties, and — Well, I'm dying to-
night ...
I knew — I knew what was coming, when we bid on the *Byfleet's* keel —
They piddled and piffled with iron: I'd given my orders for steel!
Steel and the first expansions. It paid, I tell you, it paid,
When we came with our nine-knot freighters and collared the long-
run trade!
And they asked me how I did it, and I gave 'em the Scripture text,
'You keep your light so shining a little in front o' the next!'
They copied all they could follow, but they couldn't copy my mind,
And I left 'em sweating and stealing a year and a half behind.
Then came the armour-contracts, but that was M'Cullough's side;
He was always best in the Foundry, but better, perhaps, he died.
I went through his private papers; the notes was plainer than print;
And I'm no fool to finish if a man'll give me a hint.
(I remember his widow was angry.) So I saw what the drawings meant,
And I started the six-inch rollers, and it paid me sixty per cent —
Sixty per cent *with* failures, and more than twice we could do,
And a quarter-million to credit, and I saved it all for you!
I thought — it doesn't matter — you seemed to favour your ma,
But you're nearer forty than thirty, and I know the kind you are.
Harrer an' Trinity College! I ought to ha' sent you to sea —
But I stood you an education, an' what have you done for me?
The things I knew was proper you wouldn't thank me to give,

And the things I knew was rotten you said was the way to live.
For you muddled with books and pictures, an' china an' etchin's an'
fans,
And your rooms at college was beastly — more like a whore's than a
man's —
Till you married that thin-flanked woman, as white and as stale as a
bone,
An' she gave you your social nonsense; but where's that kid o' your
own?
I've seen your carriages blocking the half o' the Cromwell Road,
But never the doctor's brougham to help the missus unload.
(So there isn't even a grandchild, an' the Gloster family's done.)
Not like your mother, she isn't. *She* carried her freight each run.
But they died, the pore little beggars! At sea she had 'em — they died.
Only you, an' you stood it; you haven't stood much beside.
Weak, a liar, and idle, and mean as a collier's whelp
Nosing for scraps in the galley. No help — my son was no help!
So he gets three 'undred thousand, in trust and the interest paid.
I wouldn't give it you, Dickie — you see, I made it in trade.
You're saved from soiling your fingers, and if you have no child,
It all comes back to the business. Gad, won't your wife be wild!
'Calls and calls in her carriage, her 'andkerchief up to 'er eye:
'Daddy! dear daddy's dyin'!' and doing her best to cry.
Grateful? Oh, yes, I'm grateful, but keep her away from here.
Your mother 'ud never ha' stood 'er, and, anyhow, women are
queer ...
There's women will say I've married a second time. Not quite!
But give pore Aggie a hundred, and tell her your lawyers'll fight.
She was the best o' the boiling — you'll meet her before it ends;
I'm in for a row with the mother — I'll leave you settle my friends:
For a man he must go with a woman, which women don't under-
stand —
Or the sort that say they can see it they aren't the marrying brand.
But I wanted to speak o' your mother that's Lady Gloster still —
I'm going to up and see her, without it's hurting the will.
Here! Take your hand off the bell-pull. Five thousand's waiting for
you,
If you'll only listen a minute, and do as I bid you do.

They'll try to prove me crazy, and, if you bungle, they can;
And I've only you to trust to! (O God, why ain't he a man?)
There's some waste money on marbles, the same as M'Cullough
                                                         tried —
Marbles and mausoleums — but I call that sinful pride.
There's some ship bodies for burial — we've carried 'em, soldered and
                                                         packed;
Down in their wills they wrote it, and nobody called *them* cracked.
But me — I've too much money, and people might ... All my fault:
It come o' hoping for grandsons and buying that Wokin' vault.
I'm sick o' the 'ole dam' business; I'm going back where I came.
Dick, you're the son o' my body, and you'll take charge o' the same!
I want to lie by your mother, ten thousand mile away,
And they'll want to send me to Woking; and that's where you'll earn
                                                         your pay.
I've thought it out on the quiet, the same as it ought to be done —
Quiet, and decent, and proper — an' here's your orders, my son.
You know the Line? You don't, though. You write to the Board, and
                                                         tell
Your father's death has upset you an' you're goin' to cruise for a spell,
An' you'd like the Mary Gloster — I've held her ready for this —
They'll put her in working order and you'll take her out as she is.
Yes, it was money idle when I patched her and put her aside
(Thank God, I can pay for my fancies!) — the boat where your mother
                                                         died,
By the Little Paternosters, as you come to the Union Bank,
We dropped her — I think I told you — and I pricked it off where she
                                                         sank —
['Tiny she looked on the grating — that oily, treacly sea —]
'Hundred and eighteen East, remember, and South just three.
Easy bearings to carry — three South — three to the dot;
But I gave M'Andrew a copy in case of dying — or not.
And so you'll write to M'Andrew, he's Chief of the Maori Line;
They'll give him leave, if you ask 'em and say it's business o' mine.
I built three boats for the Maoris, an' very well pleased they were,
An' I've known Mac since the Fifties, and Mac knew me — and her.
After the first stroke warned me I sent him the money to keep
Against the time you'd claim it, committin' your dad to the deep;

For you are the son o' my body, and Mac was my oldest friend,
I've never asked 'im to dinner, but he'll see it out to the end.
Stiff-necked Glasgow beggar, I've heard he's prayed for my soul,
But he couldn't lie if you paid him, and he'd starve before he stole!
He'll take the Mary in ballast — you'll find her a lively ship;
And you'll take Sir Anthony Gloster, that goes on 'is wedding-trip,
Lashed in our old deck-cabin with all three port-holes wide,
The kick o' the screw beneath him and the round blue seas outside!
Sir Anthony Gloster's carriage — our 'ouse-flag flyin' free —
Ten thousand men on the pay-roll and forty freighters at sea!
He made himself and a million, but this world is a fleetin' show,
And he'll go to the wife of 'is bosom the same as he ought to go —
By the heel of the Paternosters — there isn't a chance to mistake —
And Mac'll pay you the money as soon as the bubbles break!
Five thousand for six weeks' cruising, the staunchest freighter afloat,
And Mac he'll give you your bonus the minute I'm out o' the boat!
He'll take you round to Macassar, and you'll come back alone;
He knows what I want o' the Mary ... I'll do what I please with my
own
Your mother 'ud call it wasteful, but I've seven-and-thirty more;
I'll come in my private carriage and bid it wait at the door ...
For my son 'e was never a credit: 'e muddled with books and art,
And 'e lived on Sir Anthony's money and 'e broke Sir Anthony's
heart.

There isn't even a grandchild, and the Gloster family's done —
The only one you left me, O mother, the only one!
Harrer and Trinity College — me slavin' early an' late —
An' he thinks I'm dying crazy, and you're in Macassar Strait!
Flesh o' my flesh, my dearie, for ever an' ever amen,
That first stroke come for a warning; I ought to ha' gone to you then.
But — cheap repairs for a cheap 'un — the doctors said I'd do:
Mary, why didn't *you* warn me? I've allus heeded to you,
Excep' — I know — about women; but you are a spirit now;
An', wife, they was only women, and I was a man. That's how.
An' a man 'e must go with a woman, as you could not understand;
But I never talked 'em secrets. I paid 'em out o' hand.
Thank Gawd, I can pay for my fancies! Now what's five thousand to
me,

For a berth off the Paternosters in the haven where I would be?
I believe in the Resurrection, if I read my Bible plain,
But I wouldn't trust 'em at Wokin'; we're safer at sea again.
For the heart it shall go with the treasure — go down to the sea in
 & nbsp;   ships.

I'm sick of the hired women — I'll kiss my girl on her lips!
I'll be content with my fountain, I'll drink from my own well,
And the wife of my youth shall charm me — an' the rest can go to
& nbsp;   Hell!

(Dickie, *he* will, that's certain.) I'll lie in our standin'-bed,
An' Mac'll take her in ballast — an' she trims best by the head ...
Down by the head an' sinkin', her fires are drawn and cold,
And the water's splashin' hollow on the skin of the empty hold —
Churning an' choking and chuckling, quiet and scummy and dark—
Full to her lower hatches and risin' steady. Hark!
That was the after-bulkhead ... She's flooded from stem to stern ...
Never seen death yet, Dickie? ... Well, now is your time to learn!

THE BISHOP ORDERS HIS TOMB AT
SAINT PRAXED'S CHURCH
[ROME, 15 —]
ROBERT BROWNING

VANITY, saith the preacher, vanity!
Draw round my bed: is Anselm keeping back?
Nephews — sons mine ... ah God, I know not! Well —
She, men would have to be your mother once,
Old Gandolf envied me, so fair she was!
What's done is done, and she is dead beside,
Dead long ago, and I am Bishop since,
And as she died so must we die ourselves,
And thence ye may perceive the world's a dream.
Life, how and what is it? As here I lie
In this state-chamber, dying by degrees,
Hours and long hours in the dead night, I ask
'Do I live, am I dead?' Peace, peace seems all.

Saint Praxed's ever was the church for peace;
And so, about this tomb of mine. I fought
With tooth and nail to save my niche, ye know:
— Old Gandolf cozened me, despite my care;
Shrewd was that snatch from out the corner South
He graced his carrion with, God curse the same!
Yet still my niche is not so cramped but thence
One sees the pulpit o' the epistle-side,
And somewhat of the choir, those silent seats,
And up into the aery dome where live
The angels, and a sunbeam's sure to lurk:
And I shall fill my slab of basalt there,
And 'neath my tabernacle take my rest,
With those nine columns round me, two and two,
The odd one at my feet where Anselm stands:
Peach-blossom marble all, the rare, the ripe
As fresh-poured red wine of a mighty pulse
— Old Gandolf with his paltry onion-stone,
Put me where I may look at him! True peach,
Rosy and flawless: how I earned the prize!
Draw close: that conflagration of my church
— What then? So much was saved if aught were missed!
My sons, ye would not be my death? Go dig
The white-grape vineyard where the oil-press stood,
Drop water gently till the surface sinks,
And if ye find ... Ah, God I know not, I! ...
Bedded in store of rotten figleaves soft,
And corded up in a tight olive-frail,
Some lump, ah God, of *lapis lazuli*,
Big as a Jew's head cut off at the nape,
Blue as a vein o'er the Madonna's breast ...
Sons, all have I bequeathed you, villas, all,
That brave Frascati villa with its bath,
So, let the blue lump poise between my knees,
Like God the Father's globe on both His hands
Ye worship in the Jesu Church so gay,
For Gandolf shall not choose but see and burst!
Swift as a weaver's shuttle fleet our years:

Man goeth to the grave, and where is he?
Did I say basalt for my slab, sons? Black —
'Twas ever antique-black I meant! How else
Shall ye contrast my frieze to come beneath?
The bas-relief in bronze ye promised me,
Those Pans and Nymphs ye wot of, and perchance
Some tripod, thyrsus, with a vase or so,
The Saviour at his sermon on the mount,
Saint Praxed in a glory, and one Pan
Ready to twitch the Nymph's last garment off,
And Moses with the tables ... but I know
Ye mark me not! What do they whisper thee,
Child of my bowels, Anselm? Ah, ye hope
To revel down my villas while I gasp
Bricked o'er with beggar's mouldy travertine
Which Gandolf from his tomb-top chuckles at!
Nay, boys, ye love me — all of jasper, then!
'Tis jasper ye stand pledged to, lest I grieve.
My bath must needs be left behind, alas!
One block, pure green as a pistachio-nut,
There's plenty jasper somewhere in the world —
And have I not Saint Praxed's ear to pray
Horses for ye, and brown Greek manuscripts,
And mistresses with great smooth marbly limbs?
— That's if ye carve my epitaph aright,
Choice Latin, picked phrase, Tully's every word,
No gaudy ware like Gandolf's second line —
Tully, my masters? Ulpian serves his need!
And then how I shall lie through centuries,
And hear the blessed mutter of the mass,
And see God made and eaten all day long,
And feel the steady candle-flame, and taste
Good strong thick stupefying incense-smoke!
For as I lie here, hours of the dead night,
Dying in state and by such slow degrees,
I fold my arms as if they clasped a crook,
And stretch my feet forth straight as stone can point,
And let the bedclothes for a mortcloth drop

Into great laps and folds of sculptor's-work:
And as yon tapers dwindle, and strange thoughts
Grow, with a certain humming in my ears,
About the life before I lived this life,
And this life too, Popes, Cardinals and Priests,
Saint Praxed at his sermon on the mount,
Your tall pale mother with her talking eyes,
And new-found agate urns as fresh as day,
And marble's language, Latin pure, discreet,
— Aha, ELUCESCEBAT quoth our friend?
No Tully, said I, Ulpian at the best!
Evil and brief hath been my pilgrimage.
All *lapis*, all, sons! Else I give the Pope
My villas: will ye ever eat my heart?
Ever your eyes were as a lizard's quick,
They glitter like your mother's for my soul,
Or ye would heighten my impoverished frieze,
Piece out its starved design, and fill my vase
With grapes, and add a vizor and a Term,
And to the tripod ye would tie a lynx
That in his struggle throws the thyrsus down,
To comfort me on my entablature
Whereon I am to lie till I must ask
'Do I live, am I dead?' There, leave me, there!
For ye have stabbed me with ingratitude
To death — ye wish it — God, ye wish it! Stone —
Gritstone, a-crumble! Clammy squares which sweat
As if the corpse they keep were oozing through —
And no more *lapis* to delight the world!
Well, go! I bless ye. Fewer tapers there,
But in a row: and, going, turn your backs
— Ay, like departing altar-ministrants,
And leave me in my church, the church for peace,
That I may watch at leisure if he leers —
Old Gandolf, at me, from his onion-stone,
As still he envied me, so fair she was!

M'ANDREW'S HYMN

Rudyard Kipling

Lord, Thou hast made this world below the shadow of a dream,
An', taught by time, I tak' it so — exceptin' always Steam.
From coupler-flange to spindle-guide I see Thy Hand, O God —
Predestination in the stride o' yon connectin'-rod.
John Calvin might ha' forged the same — enormous, certain, slow —
Ay, wrought it in the furnace-flame — *my* 'Institutio'.
I cannot get my sleep to-night; old bones are hard to please;
I'll stand the middle watch up here — alone wi' God an' these
My engines, after ninety days o' race an' rack an' strain
Through all the seas of all Thy world, slam-bangin' home again.
Slam-bang too much — they knock a wee — the crosshead-gibs are
loose;
But thirty thousand mile o' sea has gied them fair excuse ...
Fine, clear an' dark — a dull-draught breeze, wi' Ushant out o' sight,
An' Ferguson relievin' Hay. Old girl, ye'll walk to-night!
His wife's at Plymouth ... Seventy — One — Two — Three since he
began —
Three turns for Mistress Ferguson ... and who's to blame the man?
There's none at any port for me, by drivin' fast or slow,
Since Elsie Campbell went to Thee, Lord, thirty years ago.
(The year the *Sarah Sands* was burned. Oh roads we used to tread,
Fra' Maryhill to Pollokshaws — fra' Govan to Parkhead!)
Not but they're ceevil on the Board. Ye'll hear Sir Kenneth say:
'Good morrn, M'Andrew! Back again? An' how's your bilge to-day?'
Miscallin' technicalities but handin' me my chair
To drink Madeira wi' three Earls — the auld Fleet Engineer,
That started as a boiler-whelp — when steam and he were low.
I mind the time we used to serve a broken pipe wi' tow.
Ten pound was all the pressure then — Eh! Eh! — a man wad drive;
An' here, our workin' gauges give one hunder fifty-five!
We're creepin' on wi' each new rig — less weight an' larger power:
There'll be the loco-boiler next an' thirty knots an hour!
Thirty an' more. What I ha' seen since ocean-steam began
Leaves me no doot for the machine: but what about the man?
The man that counts, wi' all his runs, one million mile o' sea:

Four time the span from earth to moon ... How far, O Lord, from
Thee?
That wast beside him night an' day. Ye mind my first typhoon?
It scoughed the skipper on his way to jock wi' the saloon.
Three feet were on the stokehold-floor — just slappin' to an' fro —
An' cast me on a furnace-door. I have the marks to show.
Marks! I ha' marks o' more than burns — deep in my soul an' black,
An' times like this, when things go smooth, my wickudness comes
back.

The sins o' four and forty years, all up an' down the seas,
Clack an' repeat like valves half-fed ... Forgie's our trespasses.
Nights when I'd come on deck to mark, wi' envy in my gaze,
The couples kittlin' in the dark between the funnel stays;
Years when I raked the ports wi' pride to fill my cup o' wrong —
Judge not, O Lord, my steps aside at Gay Street in Hong-Kong!
Blot out the wastrel hours of mine in sin when I abode —
Jane Harrigan's an' Number Nine, The Reddick an' Grant Road!
An' waur than all — my crownin' sin — rank blasphemy an' wild.
I was not four and twenty then — Ye wadna judge a child?
I'd seen the Tropics first that run — new fruit, new smells, new air —
How could I tell — blind-fou wi' sun — the Deil was lurkin' there?
By day like playhouse-scenes the shore slid past our sleepy eyes;
By night those soft, lasceevious stars leered from those velvet skies,
In port (we used no cargo-steam) I'd daunder down the streets —
An ijjit grinnin' in a dream — for shells an' parrakeets,
An' walkin'-sticks o' carved bamboo an' blowfish stuffed an' dried —
Fillin' my bunk wi' rubbishry the Chief put overside.
Till, off Sambawa Head, Ye mind, I heard a land-breeze ca',
Milk-warm wi' breath o' spice an' bloom: 'M'Andrew, come awa'!'
Firm, clear an' low — no haste, no hate — the ghostly whisper went,
Just statin' eevidential facts beyon' all argument:
'Your mither's God's a graspin' deil, the shadow o' yoursel',
Got out o' books by meenisters clean daft on Heaven an' Hell.
They mak' him in the Broomielaw, o' Glasgie cold an' dirt,
A jealous, pridefu' fetich, lad, that's only strong to hurt,
Ye'll not go back to Him again an' kiss His red-hot rod,
But come wi' Us' (Now, who were *They*?) 'an' know the Leevin' God,
That does not kipper souls for sport or break a life in jest,

But swells the ripenin' cocoanuts an' ripes the woman's breast.'
An' there it stopped: cut off: no more; that quiet, certain voice —
For me, six months o' twenty-four, to leave or take at choice.
'Twas on me like a thunderclap — it racked me through an' through —
Temptation past the show o' speech, unnameable an' new —
The Sin against the Holy Ghost? ... An' under all, our screw.
That storm blew by but left behind her anchor-shiftin' swell,
Thou knowest all my heart an' mind, Thou knowest, Lord, I fell.
Third on the *Mary Gloster* then, and first that night in Hell!
Yet was Thy hand beneath my head, about my feet Thy care —
Fra' Deli clear to Torres Strait, the trial o' despair,
But when we touched the Barrier Reef Thy answer to my prayer!
We dared not run that sea by night but lay an' held our fire,
An' I was drowsin' on the hatch — sick — sick wi' doubt an' tire:
'*Better the sight of eyes that see than wanderin' o' desire!*'
Ye mind that word? Clear as our gongs — again, an' once again,
When rippin' down through coral-trash ran out our moorin'-chain;
An' by Thy Grace I had the Light to see my duty plain.
Light on the engine-room — no more — bright as our carbons burn.
I've lost it since a thousand times, but never past return.

.   .   .   .   .

Obsairve. Per annum we'll have here two thousand souls aboard —
Think not I dare to justify myself before the Lord,
But — average fifteen hunder souls safe-borne fra' port to port —
I *am* o' service to my kind. Ye wadna blame the thought?
Maybe they steam from grace to wrath — to sin by folly led, —
It isna mine to judge their path — their lives are on my head.
Mine at the last — when all is done it all comes back to me,
The fault that leaves six thousand ton a log upon the sea.
We'll tak' one stretch — three weeks an' odd by any road ye steer —
Fra' Cape Town east to Wellington — ye need an engineer.
Fail there — ye've time to weld your shaft — ay, eat it, ere ye're spoke;
Or make Kerguelen under sail — three jiggers burned wi' smoke!
An' home again, the Rio run: it's no child's play to go
Steamin' to bell for fourteen days o' snow an' floe an' blow —
The bergs like kelpies overside that girn an' turn an' shift
Whaur, grindin' like the Mills o' God, goes by the big South drift.

(Hail, snow an' ice that praise the Lord: I've met them at their work,
An' wished we had anither route or they anither kirk.)
Yon's strain, hard strain, o' head an' hand, for though Thy Power brings
All skill to naught, Ye'll understand a man must think o' things.
Then, at the last, we'll get to port an' hoist their baggage clear —
The passengers, wi' gloves an' canes — an' this is what I'll hear:
'Well, thank ye for a pleasant voyage. The tender's comin' now.'
While I go testin' follower-bolts an' watch the skipper bow.
They've words for every one but me — shake hands wi' half the crew,
Except the dour Scots engineer, the man they never knew.
An' yet I like the wark for all we've dam' few pickin's here —
No pension, an' the most we earn's four hunder pound a year.
Better myself abroad? Maybe. *I'd* sooner starve than sail
Wi' such as call a snifter-rod *ross* ... French for nightingale.
Commeesion on my stores? Some do; but I can not afford
To lie like stewards wi' patty-pans — . I'm older than the Board.
A bonus on the coal I save? Ou ay, the Scots are close,
But when I grudge the strength Ye gave I'll grudge their food to *those*.

(There's bricks that I might recommend — an' clink the fire-bars cruel.
No! Welsh — Wangarti at the worst — an' damn all patent fuel!)
Inventions? Ye must stay in port to mak' a patent pay.
My Deeferential Valve-Gear taught me how that business lay,
I blame no chaps wi' clearer head for aught they make or sell.
I found that I could not invent an' look to these — as well.
So, wrestled wi' Apollyon — Nah! — fretted like a bairn —
But burned the workin'-plans last run wi' all I hoped to earn.
Ye know how hard an Idol dies, an' what that meant to me —
E'en tak' it for a sacrifice acceptable to Thee ...
Below there! Oiler! What's your wark? Ye find it runnin' hard?
Ye needn't swill the cap wi' oil — this isn't the Cunard!
Ye thought? Ye are not paid to think. Go, sweat that off again!
Tck! Tck! It's deeficult to sweer nor tak' The Name in vain!
Men, ay an' women, call me stern. Wi' these to oversee
Ye'll note I've little time to burn on social repartee.
The bairns see what their elders miss; they'll hunt me to an' fro,

Till for the sake of — well, a kiss — I tak' em down below.
That minds me of our Viscount loon — Sir Kenneth's kin — the chap
Wi' Russia leather tennis-shoon an' spar-decked yachtin'-cap.
I showed him round last week, o'er all — an' at the last says he:
'Mister M'Andrew, don't you think steam spoils romance at sea?'
Damned ijjit! I'd been doon that morn to see what ailed the throws,
Manholin', on my back — the cranks three inches off my nose.
Romance! Those first-class passengers they like it very well,
Printed an' bound in little books; but why don't poets tell?
I'm sick of all their quirks an' turns — the loves an' doves they dream—
Lord, send a man like Robbie Burns to sing the Song o' Steam!
To match wi' Scotia's noblest speech yon orchestra sublime
Whaurto — uplifted like the Just — the tail-rods mark the time.
The crank-throws give the double-bass, the feed-pump sobs an'
           heaves,
An' now the main eccentrics start their quarrel on the sheaves:
Her time, her own appointed time, the rocking link-head bides,
Till — hear that note? — the rod's return whings glimmerin' through
           the guides.
They're all awa! True beat, full power, the clangin' chorus goes
Clear to the tunnel where they sit, my purrin' dynamoes.
Interdependence absolute, foreseen, ordained, decreed,
To work, Ye'll note, at any tilt an' every rate o' speed.
Fra' skylight-lift to furnace-bars, backed, bolted, braced an' stayed,
An' singin' like the Mornin' Stars for joy that they are made;
While, out o' touch o' vanity, the sweatin' thrust-block says:
'Not unto us the praise, or man — not unto us the praise!'
Now, a' together, hear them lift their lesson — theirs an' mine:
'Law, Orrder, Duty an' Restraint, Obedience, Discipline!'
Mill, forge an' try-pit taught them that when roarin' they arose,
An' whiles I wonder if a soul was gi'en them wi' the blows.
Oh for a man to weld it then, in one trip-hammer strain,
Till even first-class passengers could tell the meanin' plain!
But no one cares except mysel' that serve an' understand
My seven thousand horse-power here. Eh, Lord! They're grand —
           they're grand!
Uplift am I? When first in store the new-made beasties stood,
Were Ye cast down that breathed the Word declarin' all things good?

Not so! O', that warld-liftin' joy no after-fall could vex,
Ye've left a glimmer still to cheer the Man — the Arrtifex!
That holds, in spite o' knock and scale, o' friction, waste, an' slip,
An' by that light — now, mark my word — we'll build the Perfect
Ship.

I'll never last to judge her lines or take her curve — not I.
But I ha' lived an' I ha' worked. 'Be thanks to Thee, Most High!
An' I ha' done what I ha' done — judge Thou if ill or well —
Always Thy Grace preventin' me ...

Losh! Yon's the 'Stand by' bell.
Pilot so soon? His flare it is. The mornin'-watch is set.
Well, God be thanked, as I was sayin', I'm no Pelagian yet.
Now I'll tak' on ...

'Morrn, Ferguson. Man, have ye ever thought
What your good leddy costs in coal? ... I'll burn 'em down to port.

FRA LIPPO LIPPI

ROBERT BROWNING

I AM poor brother Lippo, by your leave!
You need not clap your torches to my face.
Zooks, what's to blame? you think you see a monk!
What, it's past midnight, and you go the rounds,
And here you catch me at an alley's end
Where sportive ladies leave their doors ajar?
The Carmine's my cloister: hunt it up,
Do, — harry out, if you must show your zeal,
Whatever rat, there, haps on his wrong hole,
And nip each softling of a wee white mouse,
Weke, weke, that's crept to keep him company!
Aha, you know your betters? Then, you'll take
Your hand away that's fiddling on my throat,
And please to know me likewise. Who am I?
Why, one, sir, who is lodging with a friend
Three streets off — he's a certain ... how d'ye call?
Master — a ... Cosimo of the Medici,

In the house that caps the corner. Boh! you were best
Remember and tell me, the day you're hanged,
How you affected such a gullet's-gripe!
But you, sir, it concerns you that your knaves
Pick up a manner nor discredit you.
Zooks, are we pilchards, that they sweep the streets
And count fair prize what comes into their net?
He's Judas to a tittle, that man is!
Just such a face! why, sir, you make amends.
Lord, I'm not angry! Bid your hang-dogs go
Drink out this quarter-florin to the health
Of the munificent House that harbours me
(And many more beside, lads! more beside!)
And all's come square again. I'd like his face —
His, elbowing on his comrade in the door
With pike and lantern, — for the slave that holds
John Baptist's head a-dangle by the hair
With one hand ('look you, now,' as who should say)
And his weapon in the other, yet unwiped!
It's not your chance to have a bit of chalk,
A wood-coal or the like? or you should see!
Yes, I'm the painter, since you style me so.
What, brother Lippo's doings, up and down,
You know them and they take you? like enough!
I saw the proper twinkle in your eye —
'Tell you, I liked your looks at very first.
Let's sit and set things straight now, hip to haunch.
Here's spring come, and the nights one makes up bands
To roam the town and sing out carnival,
And I've been three weeks shut within my mew,
A-painting for the great man, saints and saints
And saints again. I could not paint all night —
Ouf! I leaned out of window for fresh air.
There came a hurry of feet and little feet,
A sweep of lute-strings, laughs, and whiffs of song, —
Flower o' the broom,
Take away love, and our earth is a tomb!
Flower o' the quince,

I let Lisa go, and what good's in life since?
Flower o' the thyme — and so on. Round they went.
Scarce had they turned the corner when a titter
Like the skipping of rabbits by moonlight, — three slim shapes —
And a face that looked up ... zooks, sir, flesh and blood,
That's all I'm made of! Into shreds it went,
Curtain and counterpane and coverlet,
All the bed-furniture — a dozen knots,
There was a ladder! down I let myself,
Hands and feet, scrambling somehow, and so dropped,
And after them. I came up with the fun
Hard by Saint Laurence, hail fellow, well met, —
Flower o' the rose,
If I've been merry, what matter who knows?
And so as I was stealing back again
To get to bed and have a bit of sleep
Ere I rise up to-morrow and go work
On Jerome knocking at his poor old breast
With his great round stone to subdue the flesh,
You snap me of the sudden. Ah, I see!
Though your eye twinkles still, you shake your head —
Mine's shaved, — a monk, you say — the sting's in that!
If Master Cosimo announced himself,
Mum's the word naturally; but a monk!
Come, what am I a beast for? tell us, now!
I was a baby when my mother died
And father died and left me in the street
I starved there, God knows how, a year or two
On fig skins, melon-parings, rinds and shucks,
Refuse and rubbish. One fine frosty day
My stomach being empty as your hat,
The wind doubled me up and down I went.
Old Aunt Lapaccia trussed me with one hand,
(Its fellow was a stinger as I knew)
And so along the wall, over the bridge,
By the straight cut to the convent. Six words, there,
While I stood munching my first bread that month:
'So, boy, you're minded,' quoth the good fat father

Wiping his own mouth, 'twas refection-time —
'To quit this very miserable world?
Will you renounce' ... The mouthful of bread? thought I;
By no means! Brief, they made a monk of me;
I did renounce the world, its pride and greed,
Palace, farm, villa, shop and banking-house,
Trash, such as these poor devils of Medici
Have given their hearts to — all at eight years old.
Well, sir, I found in time, you may be sure,
'Twas not for nothing — the good bellyful,
The warm serge and the rope that goes all round,
And day-long blessed idleness beside!
'Let's see what the urchin's fit for' — that came next.
Not overmuch their way, I must confess.
Such a to-do! they tried me with their books.
Lord, they'd have taught me Latin in pure waste!
Flower o' the clove,
All the Latin I construe is, 'amo' I love!
But, mind you, when a boy starves in the streets
Eight years together, as my fortune was,
Watching folk's faces to know who will fling
The bit of half-stripped grape-bunch he desires,
And who will curse or kick him for his pains —
Which gentleman processional and fine,
Holding a candle to the Sacrament
Will wink and let him lift a plate and catch
The droppings of the wax to sell again,
Or holla for the Eight and have him whipped, —
How say I? — nay, which dog bites, which lets drop
His bone from the heap of offal in the street, —
Why, soul and sense of him grow sharp alike,
He learns the look of things, and none the less
For admonitions from the hunger-pinch.
I had a store of such remarks, be sure,
Which, after I found leisure, turned to use:
I drew men's faces on my copy-books,
Scrawled them within the antiphonary's marge,
Joined legs and arms to the long music-notes,

Found nose and eyes and chin for A.s and B.s,
And made a string of pictures of the world
Betwixt the ins and outs of verb and noun,
On the wall, the bench, the door. The monks looked black.
'Nay,' quoth the Prior, 'turn him out, d'ye say?
In no wise. Lose a crow and catch a lark.
What if at last we get our man of parts,
We Carmelites, like those Camaldolese
And Preaching Friars, to do our church up fine
And put the front on it that ought to be!'
And hereupon they bade me daub away.
Thank you! my head being crammed, their walls a blank,
Never was such prompt disemburdening.
First, every sort of monk, the black and white,
I drew them, fat and lean: then, folks at church,
From good old gossips waiting to confess
Their cribs of barrel-droppings, candle-ends, —
To the breathless fellow at the altar-foot,
Fresh from his murder, safe and sitting there
With the little children round him in a row
Of admiration, half for his beard and half
For that white anger of his victim's son
Shaking a fist at him with one fierce arm,
Signing himself with the other because of Christ
(Whose sad face on the cross sees only this
After the passion of a thousand years)
Till some poor girl, her apron o'er her head
Which the intense eyes looked through, came at eve
On tip-toe, said a word, dropped in a loaf,
Her pair of earrings and a bunch of flowers
The brute took growling, prayed, and then was gone.
I painted all, then cried "tis ask and have —
Choose, for more's ready!' — laid the ladder flat,
And showed my covered bit of cloister-wall.
The monks closed in a circle and praised loud
Till checked, — taught what to see and not to see,
Being simple bodies, — 'that's the very man!
Look at the boy who stoops to pat the dog!

That woman's like the Prior's niece who comes
To care about his asthma: it's the life!'
But there my triumph's straw-fire flared and funked —
Their betters took their turn to see and say:
The Prior and the learned pulled a face
And stopped all that in no time. 'How? what's here?
Quite from the mark of painting, bless us all!
Faces, arms, legs and bodies like the true
As much as pea and pea! it's devil's-game!
Your business is not to catch men with show,
With homage to the perishable clay,
But lift them over it, ignore it all,
Make them forget there's such a thing as flesh.
Your business is to paint the souls of men —
Man's soul, and it's a fire, smoke ... no it's not ...
It's vapour done up like a new-born babe —
(In that shape when you die it leaves your mouth)
It's ... well, what matters talking, it's the soul!
Give us no more of body than shows soul!
Here's Giotto, with his Saint a-praising God,
That sets you praising, — why not stop with him?
Why put all thoughts of praise out of our heads
With wonder at lines, colours, and what not?
Paint the soul, never mind the legs and arms!
Rub all out, try at it a second time.
Oh, that white smallish female with the breasts,
She's just my niece ... Herodias, I would say, —
Who went and danced and got men's heads cut off —
Have it all out!' Now, is this sense, I ask?
A fine way to paint soul, by painting body
So ill, the eye can't stop there, must go further
And can't fare worse! Thus, yellow does for white
When what you put for yellow's simply black,
And any sort of meaning looks intense
When all beside itself means and looks nought.
Why can't a painter lift each foot in turn,
Left foot and right foot, go a double step,
Make his flesh liker and his soul more like,

Both in their order? Take the prettiest face,
The Prior's niece ... patron-saint — is it so pretty
You can't discover if it means hope, fear,
Sorrow or joy? won't beauty go with these?
Suppose I've made her eyes all right and blue,
Can't I take breath and try to add life's flash,
And then add soul and heighten them threefold?
Or say there's beauty with no soul at all —
(I never saw it — put the case the same —)
If you get simple beauty and nought else,
You get about the best thing God invents, —
That's somewhat. And you'll find the soul you have missed,
Within yourself when you return Him thanks,
'Rub all out!' Well, well, there's my life, in short.
And so the thing has gone on ever since.
I'm grown a man no doubt, I've broken bounds —
You should not take a fellow eight years old
And make him swear to never kiss the girls.
I'm my own master, paint now as I please —
Having a friend, you see, in the Corner-house!
Lord, it's fast holding by the rings in front —
Those great rings serve more purposes than just
To plant a flag in, or tie up a horse!
And yet the old schooling sticks, the old grave eyes
Are peeping o'er my shoulder as I work,
The heads shake still — 'It's Art's decline, my son!
You're not of the true painters, great and old;
Brother Angelico's the man, you'll find;
Brother Lorenzo stands his single peer:
Fag on at flesh, you'll never make the third!'
Flower o' the pine,
You keep your mistr ... manners, and I'll stick to mine!
I'm not the third, then: bless us, they must know!
Don't you think they're the likeliest to know,
They with their Latin? so, I swallow my rage,
Clench my teeth, suck my lips in tight, and paint
To please them — sometimes do, and sometimes don't,
For, doing most, there's pretty sure to come

A turn, some warm eve finds me at my saints —
A laugh, a cry, the business of the world —
(*Flower o' the peach,*
Death for us all, and his own life for each!)
And my whole soul revolves, the cup runs over,
The world and life's too big to pass for a dream,
And I do these wild things in sheer despite,
And play the fooleries you catch me at,
In pure rage! the old mill-horse, out at grass
After hard years, throws up his stiff heels so,
Although the miller does not preach to him
The only good of grass is to make chaff.
What would men have? Do they like grass or no —
May they or mayn't they? all I want's the thing
Settled for ever one way: as it is,
You tell too many lies and hurt yourself.
You don't like what you only like too much,
You do like what, if given you at your word,
You find abundantly detestable.
For me, I think I speak as I was taught —
I always see the Garden and God there
A-making man's wife — and, my lesson learned,
The value and significance of flesh,
I can't unlearn ten minutes afterwards.

You understand me: I'm a beast, I know.
But see, now — why, I see as certainly
As that the morning-star's about to shine,
What will hap some day. We've a youngster here
Comes to our convent, studies what I do,
Slouches and stares and lets no atom drop —
His name is Guidi — he'll not mind the monks —
They call him Hulking Tom, he lets them talk —
He picks my practice up — he'll paint apace,
I hope so — though I never live so long,
I know what's sure to follow. You be judge!
You speak no Latin more than I, belike —
However, you're my man, you've seen the world

— The beauty and the wonder and the power,
The shapes of things, their colours, lights and shades,
Changes, surprises, — and God made it all!
— For what? do you feel thankful, ay or no,
For this fair town's face, yonder river's line,
The mountain round it and the sky above,
Much more the figures of man, woman, child,
These are the frame to? What's it all about?
To be passed over, despised? or dwelt upon,
Wondered at? oh, this last of course! — you say,
But why not do as well as say, — paint these
Just as they are, careless what comes of it?
God's works — paint anyone, and count it crime
To let a truth slip. Don't object, 'His works
Are here already — nature is complete:
Suppose you reproduce her — (which you can't)
There's no advantage! you must beat her, then.'
For, don't you mark, we're made so that we love
First when we see them painted, things we have passed
Perhaps a hundred times nor cared to see;
And so they are better, painted — better to us,
Which is the same thing. Art was given for that —
God uses us to help each other so,
Lending our minds out. Have you noticed, now,
Your cullion's hanging face? A bit of chalk,
And trust me but you should, though! How much more,
If I drew higher things with the same truth!
That were to take the Prior's pulpit-place,
Interpret God to all of you! oh, oh,
It makes me mad to see what men shall do
And we in our graves! This world's no blot for us,
Nor blank — it means intensely, and means good:
To find its meaning is my meat and drink.
'Ay, but you don't so instigate to prayer!'
Strikes in the Prior: 'when your meaning's plain
It does not say to folks — remember matins,
Or, mind you fast next Friday.' Why, for this
What need of art at all? A skull and bones,

Two bits of stick nailed cross-wise, or, what's best,
A bell to chime the hour with, does as well.
I painted a Saint Laurence six months since
At Prato, splashed the fresco in fine style:
'How looks my painting, now the scaffold's down?'
I ask a brother: 'Hugely,' he returns —
'Already not one phiz of your three slaves
That turn the Deacon off his toasted side,
But's scratched and prodded to our hearts' content,
The pious people have so eased their own
When coming to say prayers there in a rage:
We get on fast to see the bricks beneath.
Expect another job this time next year,
For pity and religion grow i' the crowd —
Your painting serves its purpose!'
              Hang the fools!

      — That is — you'll not mistake an idle word
Spoke in a huff by a poor monk, God wot,
Tasting the air this spicy night which turns
The unaccustomed head like Chianti wine!
Oh, the church knows! don't misreport me, now!
It's natural a poor monk out of bounds
Should have his apt word to excuse himself:
And hearken how I plot to make amends.
I have bethought me: I shall paint a piece
... There's for you! Give me six months, then go, see
Something in Sant' Ambrogio's! Bless the nuns!
They want a cast of my office. I shall paint
God in the midst, Madonna and her babe,
Ringed by a bowery, flowery angel-brood,
Lilies and vestments and white faces, sweet
As puff on puff of grated orris-root
When ladies crowd to church at mid-summer.
And then in the front, of course a saint or two —
Saint John, because he saves the Florentines,
Saint Ambrose, who puts down in black and white
The convent's friends and gives them a long day,

And Job, I must have him there past mistake,
The man of Uz, (an Us without the z,
Painters who need his patience.) Well, all these
Secured at their devotions, up shall come
Out of a corner when you least expect,
As one by a dark stair into a great light,
Music and talking, who but Lippo! I! —
Mazed, motionless and moon-strick — I'm the man!
Back I shrink — what is this I see and hear?
I, caught up with my monk's things by mistake,
My old serge gown and rope that goes all round,
I, in this presence, this pure company!
Where's a hole, where's a corner for escape?
Then steps a sweet angelic slip of thing
Forward, puts out a soft palm — 'Not so fast!'
— Addresses the celestial presence, 'nay —
He made you and devised you, after all,
Though he's none of you! Could Saint John there, draw —
His camel-hair make up a painting-brush?
We come to brother Lippo for all that,
Iste perfecit opus!' So, all smile —
I shuffle sideways with my blushing face
Under the cover of a hundred wings
Thrown like a spread of kirtles when you're gay
And play hot cockles, all the doors being shut,
Till, wholly unexpected, in there pops
The hothead husband! Thus I scuttle off
To some safe bench behind, not letting go
The palm of her, the little lily thing
That spoke the good word for me in the nick,
Like the Prior's niece ... Saint Lucy, I would say.
And so all's saved for me, and for the church
A pretty picture gained. Go, six months hence!
Your hand, sir, and good-bye: no lights, no lights!
The street's hushed, and I know my own way back,
Don't fear me! There's the grey beginning. Zooks!

TOMLINSON

RUDYARD KIPLING

[Extracts]

Now Tomlinson gave up the ghost in his house in Berkeley Square,
And a Spirit came to his bedside and gripped him by the hair —
A Spirit gripped him by the hair and carried him far away,
Till he heard as the roar of a rain-fed ford the roar of the Milky Way;
Till he heard the roar of the Milky Way die down and drone and
cease,
And they came to the Gate within the Wall where Peter holds the
keys.
'Stand up, stand up now, Tomlinson, and answer loud and high
'The good that ye did for the sake of men or ever ye came to die —
'The good that ye did for the sake of men in little earth so lone!'
And the naked soul of Tomlinson grew white as a rain-washed bone.
'O I have a friend on earth,' he said, 'that was my priest and guide,
'And well would he answer all for me if he were by my side.'
— 'For that ye strove in neighbour-love it shall be written fair,
'But now ye wait at Heaven's Gate and not in Berkeley Square:
'Though we called your friend from his bed this night, he could not
speak for you,
'For the race is run by one and one and never by two and two.'

.   .   .   .   .

'O none may reach by hired speech of neighbour, priest, and kin
'Through borrowed deed to God's good meed that lies so fair within;
'Get hence, get hence to the Lord of Wrong, for doom has yet to run,
'And ... the faith that ye share with Berkeley Square uphold you,
Tomlinson!'

.   .   .   .   .

The Devil he sat behind the bars, where the desperate legions drew,
But he caught the hasting Tomlinson and would not let him through.
'Wot ye the price of good pit-coal that I must pay?' said he,
'That ye rank yoursel' so fit for Hell and ask no leave of me?
'I am all o'er-sib to Adam's breed that ye should give me scorn,
'For I strove with God for your First Father the day that he was born.

'Sit down, sit down upon the slag, and answer loud and high
'The harm that ye did to the Sons of Men or ever you came to die.'

.   .   .   .   .

'O I had a love on earth,' said he, 'that kissed me to my fall,
'And if ye would call my love to me I know she would answer all.'
— 'All that ye did in love forbid it shall be written fair,
'But now ye wait at Hell-Mouth Gate and not in Berkeley Square:
'Though we whistled your love from her bed to-night, I trow she
would not run,
'For the sin ye do by two and two ye must pay for one by one!'

.   .   .   .   .

Then Tomlinson he gripped the bars and yammered, 'Let me in —
'For I mind that I borrowed my neighbour's wife to sin the deadly sin.'
The Devil he grinned behind the bars, and banked the fires high:
'Did ye read of that sin in a book,' said he; and Tomlinson said, 'Ay!'

.   .   .   .   .

The Devil he bowed his head on his breast and rumbled deep and
low: —
'I'm all o'er-sib to Adam's breed that I should bid him go.
'Yet close we lie, and deep we lie, and if I gave him place,
'My gentlemen that are so proud would flout me to my face;
'They'd call my house a common stews and me a careless host,
'And — I would not anger my gentlemen for the sake of a shiftless
ghost.'
The Devil he looked at the mangled Soul that prayed to feel the
flame,
And he thought of Holy Charity but he thought of his own good
name: —
'Now ye could haste my coal to waste, and sit ye down to fry:
'Did ye think of that theft for yourself?' said he; and Tomlinson said
'Ay!'
The Devil he blew an outward breath, for his heart was free from
care: —
'Ye have scarce the soul of a louse,' he said, 'but the roots of sin are
there,
'And for that sin should ye come in were I the lord alone.

'But sinful pride has rule inside — and mightier than my own.
'Honour and Wit, fore-damned they sit, to each his priest and whore:
'Nay, scarce I dare myself go there, and you they'd torture sore.
'Ye are neither spirit nor spirk,' he said; 'ye are neither book nor
brute —
'Go, get ye back to the flesh again for the sake of Man's repute.
'I'm all o'er-sib to Adam's breed that I should mock your pain,
'But look that ye win to worthier sin ere ye come back again.
'Get hence, the hearse is at your door — the grim black stallions wait —
'They bear your clay to place to-day. Speed, lest ye come too late!
'Go back to Earth with a lip unsealed — go back with an open eye,
'And carry my word to the Sons of Men or ever ye come to die:
'That the sin they do by two and two they must pay for one by one —
'And ... the God that you took from a printed book be with you,
Tomlinson!'

A TOCCATA OF GALUPPI'S

Robert Browning

I

Oh, Galuppi, Baldassaro, this is very sad to find!
I can hardly misconceive you; it would prove me deaf and blind;
But although I take your meaning, 'tis with such a heavy mind!

II

Here you come with your old music, and here's all the good it brings.
What, they lived once thus at Venice where the merchants were the
kings,
Where St Mark's is, where the Doges used to wed the sea with rings?

III

Ay, because the sea's the street there; and 'tis arched by ... what you
call
... Shylock's bridge with houses on it, where they kept the carnival:
I was never out of England — it's as if I saw it all!

IV

Did young people take their pleasure when the sea was warm in May?
Balls and masks begun at midnight, burning ever to mid-day
When they made up fresh adventures for the morrow, do you say?

V

Was a lady such a lady, cheeks so round and lips so red, —
On her neck the small face buoyant, like a bell-flower on its bed,
O'er the breast's superb abundance where a man might base his head?

VI

Well, (and it was graceful of them) they'd break talk off and afford
— She, to bite her mask's black velvet, he, to finger on his sword,
While you sat and played Toccatas, stately at the clavichord?

VII

What? Those lesser thirds so plaintive, sixths diminished, sigh on
                                                                sigh,
Told them something? Those suspensions, those solutions — 'Must
                                                              we die?'
Those commiserating sevenths — 'Life might last! we can but try!'

VIII

'Were you happy?' — 'Yes.' — 'And are you still as happy?' — 'Yes.
                                                        And you?'
— 'Then, more kisses!' — 'Did I stop them, when a million seemed so
                                                              few?'
Hark! the dominant's persistence, till it must be answered to!

IX

So an octave struck the answer. Oh, they praised you, I dare say!
'Brave Galuppi! that was music! good alike at grave and gay!
I can always leave off talking, when I hear a master play.'

X

Then they left you for their pleasure: till in due time, one by one,
Some with lives that came to nothing, some with deeds as well
                                                        undone,
Death came tacitly and took them where they never see the sun.

XI

But when I sit down to reason, think to take my stand nor swerve,
While I triumph o'er a secret wrung from nature's close reserve,
In you come with your cold music, till I creep thro' every nerve.

XII

Yes, you, like a ghostly cricket, creaking where a house was burned —
'Dust and ashes', dead and done with, Venice spent what Venice
                                                        earned!
The soul, doubtless, is immortal — where a soul can be discerned.

XIII

Yours for instance, you know physics, something of geology,
Mathematics are your pastime; souls shall rise in their degree;
Butterflies may dread extinction, — you'll not die, it cannot be!

XIV

As for Venice and its people, merely born to bloom and drop,
Here on earth they bore their fruitage, mirth and folly were the crop:
What of soul was left, I wonder, when the kissing had to stop?

XV

'Dust and ashes!' So you creak it, and I want the heart to scold.
Dear dead women, with such hair too — what's become of all the
                                                        gold
Used to hang and brush their bosoms? I feel chilly and grown old.

RUBÁIYÁT OF OMAR KHAYYÁM

Edward FitzGerald

I

Wake! For the Sun, who scatter'd into flight
The Stars before him from the Field of Night,
  Drives Night along with them from Heav'n, and strikes
The Sultan's Turret with a Shaft of Light.

II

Before the phantom of False morning died,
Methought a Voice within the Tavern cried,
  'When all the Temple is prepared within,
Why nods the drowsy Worshipper outside?'

III

And, as the Cock crew, those who stood before
The Tavern shouted — 'Open then the Door!
  You know how little while we have to stay,
And, once departed, may return no more.'

IV

Now the New Year reviving old Desires,
The thoughtful Soul to Solitude retires,
  Where the White Hand of Moses on the Bough
Puts out, and Jesus from the Ground suspires.

V

Iram indeed is gone with all his Rose,
And Jamshýd's Sev'n-ring'd Cup where no one knows;
  But still a Ruby kindles in the Vine,
And many a Garden by the Water blows.

VI

And David's lips are lockt; but in divine
High-piping Pehleví, with 'Wine! Wine! Wine!
  Red Wine!' — the Nightingale cries to the Rose
That shallow cheek of hers t' incarnadine.

VII

Come, fill the Cup, and in the fire of Spring
Your Winter-garment of Repentance fling:
  The Bird of Time has but a little way
To flutter — and the Bird is on the Wing.

VIII

Whether at Naishápúr or Babylon,
Whether the Cup with sweet or bitter run,
  The Wine of Life keeps oozing drop by drop,
The Leaves of Life keep falling one by one.

IX

Each Morn a thousand Roses brings, you say;
Yes, but where leaves the Rose of Yesterday?
  And this first Summer month that brings the Rose
Shall take Jamshýd and Kaikobád away.

X

Well, let it take them! What have we to do
With Kaikobád the Great, or Kaikhosrú?
  Let Zál and Rustum bluster as they will,
Or Hátim call to Supper — heed not you.

XI

With me along the strip of Herbage strown
That just divides the desert from the sown,
  Where name of Slave and Sultán is forgot —
And Peace to Mahmud on his golden Throne!

XII

A Book of Verses underneath the Bough,
A Jug of Wine, a Loaf of Bread — and Thou
  Beside me singing in the Wilderness —
Oh, Wilderness were Paradise enow!

XIII

Some for the Glories of This World; and some
Sigh for the Prophet's Paradise to come;
   Ah, take the Cash, and let the Credit go,
Nor heed the rumble of a distant Drum!

XIV

Look to the blowing Rose about us — 'Lo,
Laughing,' she says, 'into the world I blow,
   At once the silken tassel of my Purse
Tear, and its Treasure on the Garden throw.'

XV

And those who husbanded the Golden grain,
And those who flung it to the winds like Rain,
   Alike to no such aureate Earth are turn'd
As, buried once, Men want dug up again.

XVI

The Worldly Hope men set their Hearts upon
Turns Ashes — or it prospers; and anon,
   Like Snow upon the Desert's dusty Face,
Lighting a little hour or two — is gone.

XVII

Think, in this batter'd Caravanserai
Whose Portals are alternate Night and Day,
   How Sultán after Sultán with his Pomp
Abode his destined Hour, and went his way.

XVIII

They say the Lion and the Lizard keep
The Courts where Jamshýd gloried and drank deep:
   And Bahrám, that great Hunter — the Wild Ass
Stamps o'er his Head, but cannot break his Sleep.

XIX

I sometimes think that never blows so red
The Rose as where some buried Caesar bled;
    That every Hyacinth the Garden wears
Dropt in her Lap from some once lovely Head.

XX

And this reviving Herb whose tender Green
Fledges the River-Lip on which we lean —
    Ah, lean upon it lightly! for who knows
From what once lovely Lip it springs unseen!

XXI

Ah, my Belovèd, fill the Cup that clears
TO-DAY of past Regrets and future Fears:
    To-morrow! — Why, To-morrow I may be
Myself with Yesterday's Sev'n Thousand Years.

XXII

For some we loved, the loveliest and the best
That from his Vintage rolling Time hath prest,
    Have drunk their Cup a Round or two before,
And one by one crept silently to rest.

XXIII

And we, that now make merry in the Room
They left, and Summer dresses in new bloom,
    Ourselves must we beneath the Couch of Earth
Descend — ourselves to make a Couch — for whom?

XXIV

Ah, make the most of what we yet may spend,
Before we too into the Dust descend;
    Dust into Dust, and under Dust to lie
Sans Wine, sans Song, sans Singer, and — sans End!

XXV

Alike for those who for To-DAY prepare,
And those that after some To-MORROW stare,
   A Muezzín from the Tower of Darkness cries,
'Fools! your Reward is neither Here nor There.'

XXVI

Why, all the Saints and Sages who discuss'd
Of the Two Worlds so wisely — they are thrust
   Like foolish Prophets forth; their Words to Scorn
Are scatter'd, and their Mouths are stopt with Dust.

XXVII

Myself when young did eagerly frequent
Doctor and Saint, and heard great argument
   About it and about: but evermore
Came out by the same door where in I went.

XXVIII

With them the seed of Wisdom did I sow,
And with mine own hand wrought to make it grow,
   And this was all the Harvest that I reap'd —
'I came like Water, and like Wind I go.'

XXIX

Into this Universe, and *Why* not knowing
Nor *Whence*, like Water willy-nilly flowing;
   And out of it, as Wind along the Waste,
I know not *Whither*, willy-nilly blowing.

XXX

What, without asking, hither hurried *Whence?*
And, without asking, *Whither* hurried hence!
   Oh, many a Cup of this forbidden Wine
Must drown the memory of that insolence!

XXXI

Up from Earth's Centre through the Seventh Gate
I rose, and on the Throne of Saturn sate;
   And many a Knot unravel'd by the Road;
But not the Master-knot of Human Fate.

XXXII

There was the Door to which I found no Key;
There was the Veil through which I might not see:
   Some little talk awhile of ME and THEE
There was — and then no more of THEE and ME.

XXXIII

Earth could not answer; nor the Seas that mourn
In flowing Purple, of their Lord forlorn;
   Nor rolling Heaven, with all his Signs reveal'd
And hidden by the sleeve of Night and Morn.

XXXIV

Then of the THEE IN ME who works behind
The Veil, I lifted up my hands to find
   A Lamp amid the Darkness; and I heard,
As from Without — 'THE ME WITHIN THEE blind!'

XXXV

Then to the lip of this poor earthen Urn
I lean'd, the Secret of my Life to learn:
   And Lip to Lip it murmur'd — 'While you live,
Drink! — for, once dead, you never shall return.'

XXXVI

I think the Vessel, that with fugitive
Articulation answer'd, once did live,
   And drink; and Ah! the passive Lip I kiss'd,
How many Kisses might it take — and give!

XXXVII

For I remember stopping by the way
To watch a Potter thumping his wet Clay:
    And with its all-obliterated Tongue
It murmur'd — 'Gently, Brother, gently, pray!'

XXXVIII

And has not such a Story from of Old
Down Man's successive generations roll'd
    Of such a clod of saturated Earth
Cast by the Maker into Human mould?

XXXIX

And not a drop that from our Cups we throw
For Earth to drink of, but may steal below
    To quench the fire of Anguish in some Eye
There hidden — far beneath, and long ago.

XL

As then the Tulip for her morning sup
Of Heav'nly Vintage from the soil looks up,
    Do you devoutly do the like, till Heav'n
To Earth invert you — like an empty Cup.

XLI

Perplext no more with Human or Divine,
To-morrow's tangle to the winds resign,
    And lose your fingers in the tresses of
The Cypress-slender Minister of Wine.

XLII

And if the Wine you drink, the Lip you press,
End in what All begins and ends in — Yes;
    Think then you are TO-DAY what YESTERDAY
You were — TO-MORROW you shall not be less.

XLIII

So when that Angel of the darker Drink
At last shall find you by the river-brink,
   And, offering his Cup, invite your Soul
Forth to your Lips to quaff — you shall not shrink.

XLIV

Why, if the Soul can fling the Dust aside,
And naked on the Air of Heaven ride,
   Were't not a Shame — were't not a Shame for him
In this clay carcase crippled to abide?

XLV

'Tis but a Tent where takes his one day's rest
A Sultán to the realm of Death addrest;
   The Sultán rises, and the dark Ferrásh
Strikes, and prepares it for another Guest.

XLVI

And fear not lest Existence closing your
Account, and mine, should know the like no more;
   The Eternal Sákí from that Bowl has pour'd
Millions of Bubbles like us, and will pour.

XLVII

When You and I behind the Veil are past,
Oh, but the long, long while the World shall last,
   Which of our Coming and Departure heeds
As the Sea's self should heed a pebble-cast.

XLVIII

A Moment's Halt — a momentary taste
Of BEING from the Well amid the Waste —
   And Lo! — the phantom Caravan has reach'd
The NOTHING it set out from — Oh, make haste!

XLIX

Would you that spangle of Existence spend
About THE SECRET — quick about it, Friend!
   A Hair perhaps divides the False and True —
And upon what, prithee, may life depend?

L

A Hair perhaps divides the False and True;
Yes; and a single Alif were the clue —
   Could you but find it — to the Treasure-house,
And peradventure to THE MASTER too;

LI

Whose secret Presence, through Creation's veins
Running Quicksilver-like eludes your pains;
   Taking all shapes from Máh to Máhi; and
They change and perish all — but He remains;

LII

A moment guess'd — then back behind the Fold
Immerst of Darkness round the Drama roll'd
   Which, for the Pastime of Eternity,
He doth Himself contrive, enact, behold.

LIII

But if in vain, down on the stubborn floor
Of Earth, and up to Heav'n's unopening Door,
   You gaze TO-DAY, while You are You — how then
TO-MORROW, when You shall be You no more?

LIV

Waste not your Hour, nor in the vain pursuit
Of This and That endeavour and dispute;
   Better be jocund with the fruitful Grape
Than sadden after none, or bitter, Fruit.

LV

You know, my Friends, with what a brave Carouse
I made a Second Marriage in my house;
    Divorced old barren Reason from my Bed,
And took the Daughter of the Vine to Spouse.

LVI

For 'Is' and 'Is-NOT' though with Rule and Line
And 'Up-AND-DOWN' by logic I define,
    Of all that one should care to fathom, I
Was never deep in anything but — Wine.

LVII

Ah, but my Computations, People say,
Reduced the Year to better reckoning? — Nay,
    'Twas only striking from the Calendar
Unborn To-morrow, and dead Yesterday.

LVIII

And lately, by the Tavern Door agape,
Came shining through the Dusk an Angel Shape
    Bearing a Vessel on his Shoulder; and
He bid me taste of it; and 'twas — the Grape!

LIX

The Grape that can with Logic absolute
The Two-and-Seventy jarring Sects confute:
    The Sovereign Alchemist that in a trice
Life's leaden metal into Gold transmute:

LX

The mighty Mahmúd, Allah-breathing Lord,
That all the misbelieving and black Horde
    Of Fears and Sorrows that infest the Soul
Scatters before him with his whirlwind Sword.

LXI

Why, be this Juice the growth of God, who dare
Blaspheme the twisted tendril as a Snare?
  A Blessing, we should use it, should we not?
And if a Curse — why, then, Who set it there?

LXII

I must abjure the Balm of Life, I must,
Scared by some After-reckoning ta'en on trust,
  Or lured with Hope of some Diviner Drink,
To fill the Cup — when crumbled into Dust!

LXIII

Oh threats of Hell and Hopes of Paradise!
One thing at least is certain — *This* Life flies;
  One thing is certain and the rest is Lies;
The Flower that once has blown for ever dies.

LXIV

Strange, is it not? that of the myriads who
Before us pass'd the door of Darkness through,
  Not one returns to tell us of the Road,
Which to discover we must travel too.

LXV

The Revelations of Devout and Learn'd
Who rose before us, and as Prophets burn'd,
  Are all but Stories, which, awoke from Sleep,
They told their comrades, and to Sleep return'd.

LXVI

I sent my Soul through the Invisible,
Some letter of that After-life to spell:
  And by and by my Soul return'd to me,
And answered 'I Myself am Heav'n and Hell':

LXVII

Heav'n but the Vision of fulfill'd Desire,
And Hell the Shadow from a Soul on fire,
   Cast on the Darkness into which Ourselves,
So late emerged from, shall so soon expire.

LXVIII

We are no other than a moving row
Of Magic Shadow-shapes that come and go
   Round with the Sun-illumined Lantern held
In Midnight by the Master of the Show;

XIX

But helpless Pieces of the Game He plays
Upon this Chequer-board of Nights and Days;
   Hither and thither moves, and checks, and slays,
And one by one back in the Closet lays.

LXX

The Ball no question makes of Ayes and Noes,
But Here or There as strikes the Player goes;
   And He that toss'd you down into the Field,
He knows about it all — HE knows — HE knows!

LXXI

The Moving Finger writes; and, having writ,
Moves on: nor all your Piety nor Wit
   Shall lure it back to cancel half a Line,
Nor all your Tears wash out a Word of it.

LXXII

And that inverted Bowl they call the Sky,
Whereunder crawling coop'd we live and die,
   Lift not your hands to *It* for help — for It
As impotently moves as you or I.

LXXIII

With Earth's first Clay They did the Last Man knead,
And there of the Last Harvest sow'd the Seed:
    And the first Morning of Creation wrote
What the Last Dawn of Reckoning shall read.

LXXIV

YESTERDAY *This* Day's Madness did prepare;
TO-MORROW's Silence, Triumph, or Despair:
    Drink! for you know not whence you came, nor why:
Drink! for you know not why you go, nor where.

LXXV

I tell you this — When, started from the Goal,
Over the flaming shoulders of the Foal
    Of Heav'n Parwín and Mushtarí they flung,
In my predestined Plot of Dust and Soul

LXXVI

The Vine had struck a fibre: which about
If clings my being — let the Dervish flout;
    Of my Base metal may be filed a Key,
That shall unlock the Door he howls without.

LXXVII

And this I know: whether the one True Light
Kindle to Love, or Wrath — consume me quite,
    One Flash of It within the Tavern caught
Better than in the Temple lost outright.

LXXVIII

What! out of senseless Nothing to provoke
A conscious Something to resent the yoke
    Of unpermitted Pleasure, under pain
Of Everlasting Penalties, if broke!

LXXIX

What! from his helpless Creature be repaid
Pure Gold for what he lent him dross-allay'd,
    Sue for a Debt he never did contract,
And cannot answer — Oh the sorry trade!

LXXX

Oh Thou, who didst with pitfall and with gin
Beset the Road I was to wander in,
    Thou wilt not with Predestined Evil round
Enmesh, and then impute my Fall to Sin!

LXXXI

Oh Thou, who Man of baser Earth didst make,
And ev'n with Paradise devise the Snake:
    For all the Sin wherewith the Face of Man
Is blacken'd — Man's forgiveness give — and take!

*   *   *   *

LXXXII

As under cover of departing Day
Slunk hunger-stricken Ramazán away,
    Once more within the Potter's house alone
I stood, surrounded by the Shapes of Clay.

LXXXIII

Shapes of all Sorts and Sizes, great and small,
That stood along the floor and by the wall;
    And some loquacious Vessels were; and some
Listen'd perhaps, but never talk'd at all.

LXXXIV

Said one among them — 'Surely not in vain
My substance of the common Earth was ta'en
    And to this Figure moulded, to be broke,
Or trampled back to shapeless Earth again.'

LXXXV

Then said a Second — 'Ne'er a peevish Boy
Would break the Bowl from which he drank in joy;
   And He that with his hand the Vessel made
Will surely not in after Wrath destroy.'

LXXXVI

After a momentary silence spake
Some Vessel of a more ungainly Make;
   'They sneer at me for leaning all awry:
What! did the Hand then of the Potter shake?'

LXXXVII

Whereat some one of the loquacious Lot —
I think a Súfi pipkin — waxing hot —
   'All this of Pot and Potter — Tell me then,
Who is the Potter, pray, and who the Pot?'

LXXXVIII

'Why,' said another, 'Some there are who tell
Of one who threatens he will toss to Hell
   The luckless Pots he marr'd in making — Pish!
He's a Good Fellow, and 't will all be well.'

LXXXIX

'Well,' murmur'd one, 'Let whoso make or buy,
My Clay with long Oblivion is gone dry:
   But fill me with the old familiar Juice,
Methinks I might recover by and by.'

XC

So while the Vessels one by one were speaking,
The little Moon look'd in that all were seeking:
   And then they jogg'd each other, 'Brother! Brother!
Now for the Porter's shoulder-knot a-creaking!'

*   *   *   *

XCI

Ah, with the Grape my fading Life provide,
And wash the Body whence the Life has died,
   And lay me, shrouded in the living Leaf,
By some not unfrequented Garden-side.

XCII

That ev'n my buried Ashes such a snare
Of Vintage shall fling up into the Air
   As not a True-believer passing by
But shall be overtaken unaware.

XCIII

Indeed the Idols I have loved so long
Have done my credit in this World much wrong:
   Have drown'd my Glory in a shallow Cup
And sold my Reputation for a Song.

XCIV

Indeed, indeed, Repentance oft before
I swore — but was I sober when I swore?
   And then and then came Spring, and Rose-in-hand
My thread-bare Penitence apieces tore.

XCV

And much as Wine has play'd the Infidel,
And robb'd me of my Robe of Honour — Well,
   I wonder often what the Vintners buy
One half so precious as the stuff they sell.

XCVI

Yet Ah, that Spring should vanish with the Rose!
That Youth's sweet-scented manuscript should close!
   The Nightingale that in the branches sang,
Ah whence, and whither flown again, who knows!

XCVII

Would but the Desert of the Fountain yield
One glimpse — if dimly, yet indeed, reveal'd,
    To which the fainting Traveller might spring,
As springs the trampled herbage of the field!

XCVIII

Would but some wingéd Angel ere too late
Arrest the yet unfolded Roll of Fate,
    And make the Stern Recorder otherwise
Enregister, or quite obliterate!

XCIX

Ah Love! could you and I with Him conspire
To grasp this sorry Scheme of Things entire,
    Would not we shatter it to bits — and then
Re-mould it nearer to the Heart's Desire!

*   *   *   *

C

Yon rising Moon that looks for us again —
How oft hereafter will she wax and wane;
    How oft hereafter rising look for us
Through this same Garden — and for *one* in vain!

CI

And when like her, oh Sákí, you shall pass
Among the Guests Star-scatter'd on the Grass,
    And in your joyous errand reach the spot
Where I made One — turn down an empty Glass!

TAMÁM

THE BALLAD OF READING GAOL
Oscar Wilde
[*Extracts*]
I

HE did not wear his scarlet coat,
   For blood and wine are red,
And blood and wine were on his hands
   When they found him with the dead,
The poor dead woman whom he loved,
   And murdered in her bed.

He walked amongst the Trial Men
   In a suit of shabby gray;
A cricket cap was on his head,
   And his step seemed light and gay;
But I never saw a man who looked
   So wistfully at the day.

I never saw a man who looked
   With such a wistful eye
Upon that little tent of blue
   Which prisoners call the sky,
And at every drifting cloud that went
   With sails of silver by.

I walked, with other souls in pain,
   Within another ring,
And was wondering if the man had done
   A great or little thing,
When a voice behind me whispered low,
   '*That fellow's got to swing.*'

Dear Christ! the very prison walls
   Suddenly seemed to reel,
And the sky above my head became
   Like a casque of scorching steel;
And, though I was a soul in pain,
   My pain I could not feel.

L

I only knew what hunted thought
   Quickened his step, and why
He looked upon the garish day
   With such a wistful eye;
The man had killed the thing he loved,
   And so he had to die.

Yet each man kills the thing he loves,
   By each let this be heard,
Some do it with a bitter look,
   Some with a flattering word,
The coward does it with a kiss,
   The brave man with a sword!

Some kill their love when they are young,
   And some when they are old;
Some strangle with the hands of Lust,
   Some with the hands of Gold:
The kindest use a knife, because
   The dead so soon grow cold.

Some love too little, some too long,
   Some sell, and others buy;
Some do the deed with many tears,
   And some without a sigh:
For each man kills the thing he loves,
   Yet each man does not die.

He does not die a death of shame
   On a day of dark disgrace,
Nor have a noose about his neck,
   Nor a cloth upon his face,
Nor drop feet foremost through the floor
   Into an empty place.

He does not sit with silent men
   Who watch him night and day;
Who watch him when he tries to weep,

And when he tries to pray;
Who watch him lest himself should rob
   The prison of its prey.

He does not wake at dawn to see
   Dread figures throng his room,
The shivering Chaplain robed in white,
   The Sheriff stern with gloom,
And the Governor all in shiny black,
   With the yellow face of Doom.

He does not rise in piteous haste
   To put on convict-clothes,
While some coarse-mouthed Doctor gloats, and notes
   Each new and nerve-twitched pose,
Fingering a watch whose little ticks
   Are like horrible hammer-blows.

He does not know that sickening thirst
   That sands one's throat, before
The hangman with his gardener's gloves
   Slips through the padded door,
And binds one with three leathern thongs,
   That the throat may thirst no more.

He does not bend his head to hear
   The Burial Office read,
Nor, while the terror of his soul
   Tells him he is not dead,
Cross his own coffin, as he moves
   Into the hideous shed.

He does not stare upon the air
   Through a little roof of glass:
He does not pray with lips of clay
   For his agony to pass;
Nor feel upon his shuddering cheek
   The kiss of Caiaphas.

II

Six weeks our guardsman walked the yard,
    In the suit of shabby gray:
His cricket cap was on his head,
    And his step seemed light and gay,
But I never saw a man who looked
    So wistfully at the day.

I never saw a man who looked
    With such a wistful eye
Upon that little tent of blue
    Which prisoners call the sky,
And at every wandering cloud that trailed
    Its ravelled fleeces by.

He did not wring his hands, as do
    Those witless men who dare
To try to rear the changeling Hope
    In the cave of black Despair:
He only looked upon the sun,
    And drank the morning air.

He did not wring his hands nor weep,
    Nor did he peek or pine,
But he drank the air as though it held
    Some healthful anodyne;
With open mouth he drank the sun
    As though it had been wine!

And I and all the souls in pain,
    Who tramped the other ring,
Forgot if we ourselves had done
    A great or little thing,
And watched with gaze of dull amaze
    The man who had to swing.

And strange it was to see him pass
    With a step so light and gay,

And strange it was to see him look
    So wistfully at the day,
And strange it was to think that he
    Had such a debt to pay.

For oak and elm have pleasant leaves
    That in the spring-time shoot:
But grim to see is the gallows-tree,
    With its adder-bitten root,
And, green or dry, a man must die
    Before it bears its fruit!

The loftiest place is that seat of grace
    For which all worldlings try:
But who would stand in hempen band
    Upon a scaffold high,
And through a murderer's collar take
    His last look at the sky?

It is sweet to dance to violins
    When Love and Life are fair:
To dance to flutes, to dance to lutes
    Is delicate and rare:
But it is not sweet with nimble feet
    To dance upon the air!

So with curious eyes and sick surmise
    We watched him day by day,
And wondered if each one of us
    Would end the self-same way,
For none can tell to what red Hell
    His sightless soul may stray.

At last the dead man walked no more
    Amongst the Trial Men,
And I knew that he was standing up
    In the black dock's dreadful pen,
And that never would I see his face
    In God's sweet world again.

Like two doomed ships that pass in storm
  We had crossed each other's way:
But we made no sign, we said no word,
  We had no word to say;
For we did not meet in the holy night,
  But in the shameful day.

A prison wall was round us both,
  Two outcast men we were:
The world had thrust us from its heart,
  And God from out His care:
And the iron gin that waits for Sin
  Had caught us in its snare.

     .   .   .   .   .

VI

In Reading gaol by Reading town
  There is a pit of shame,
And in it lies a wretched man
  Eaten by teeth of flame,
In a burning winding-sheet he lies,
  And his grave has got no name.

And there, till Christ call forth the dead,
  In silence let him lie:
No need to waste the foolish tear,
  Or heave the windy sigh:
The man had killed the thing he loved,
  And so he had to die.

And all men kill the thing they love,
  By all let this be heard,
Some do it with a bitter look,
  Some with a flattering word,
The coward does it with a kiss,
  The brave man with a sword!

MY LAST DUCHESS

FERRARA

ROBERT BROWNING

THAT's my last Duchess painted on the wall,
Looking as if she were alive; I call
That piece a wonder, now: Frà Pandolf's hands
Worked busily a day, and there she stands.
Will't please you sit and look at her? I said
'Frà Pandolf' by design, for never read
Strangers like you that pictured countenance,
The depth and passion of its earnest glance,
But to myself they turned (since none puts by
The curtain I have drawn for you, but I)
And seemed as they would ask me, if they durst,
How such a glance came there; so, not the first
Are you to turn and ask thus. Sir, 'twas not
Her husband's presence only, called that spot
Of joy into the Duchess' cheek: perhaps
Frà Pandolf chanced to say 'Her mantle laps
Over my Lady's wrist too much,' or 'Paint
Must never hope to reproduce the faint
Half-flush that dies along her throat;' such stuff
Was courtesy, she thought, and cause enough
For calling up that spot of joy. She had
A heart ... how shall I say? ... too soon made glad,
Too easily impressed; she liked whate'er
She looked on, and her looks went everywhere,
Sir, 't was all one! My favour at her breast,
The dropping of the daylight in the West,
The bough of cherries some officious fool
Broke in the orchard for her, the white mule
She rode with round the terrace — all and each
Would draw from her alike the approving speech,
Or blush, at least. She thanked men, — good; but thanked
Somehow ... I know not how ... as if she ranked
My gift of a nine-hundred-years-old name
With anybody's gift. Who'd stoop to blame

This sort of trifling? Even had you skill
In speech — (which I have not) — to make your will
Quite clear to such an one, and say 'Just this
Or that in you disgusts me; here you miss,
Or there exceed the mark' — and if she let
Herself be lessoned so, nor plainly set
Her wits to yours, forsooth, and made excuse,
— E'en then would be some stooping, and I chuse
Never to stoop. Oh, Sir, she smiled, no doubt,
Whene'er I passed her; but who passed without
Much the same smile? This grew; I gave commands;
Then all smiles stopped together. There she stands
As if alive. Will't please you rise? We'll meet
The company below, then. I repeat,
The Count your Master's known munificence
Is ample warrant that no just pretence
Of mine for dowry will be disallowed;
Though his fair daughter's self, as I avowed
At starting, is my object. Nay, we'll go
Together down, Sir! Notice Neptune, though,
Taming a sea-horse, thought a rarity,
Which Claus of Innsbruck cast in bronze for me.

THE SECRET PEOPLE

G. K. CHESTERTON

SMILE at us, pay us, pass us; but do not quite forget;
For we are the people of England, that never have spoken yet.
There is many a fat farmer that drinks less cheerfully,
There is many a free French peasant who is richer and sadder than we.
There are no folk in the whole world so helpless or so wise.
There is hunger in our bellies, there is laughter in our eyes;
You laugh at us and love us, both mugs and eyes are wet:
Only you do not know us. For we have not spoken yet.

The fine French kings came over in a flutter of flags and dames.
We liked their smiles and battles, but we never could say their names.

The blood ran red to Bosworth and the high French lords went down;
There was naught but a naked people under a naked crown.
And the eyes of the King's Servants turned terribly every way,
And the gold of the King's Servants rose higher every day.
They burnt the homes of the shaven men, that had been quaint and
                                                              kind,
Till there was no bed in a monk's house, nor food that man could
                                                              find.
The inns of God where no man paid, that were the wall of the weak,
The King's Servants ate them all. And still we did not speak.

And the face of the King's Servants grew greater than the King:
He tricked them, and they trapped him, and stood round him in a
                                                              ring.
The new grave lords closed round him, that had eaten the abbey's
                                                            fruits,
And the men of the new religion, with their bibles in their boots,
We saw their shoulders moving, to menace or discuss,
And some were pure and some were vile; but none took heed of us.
We saw the King as they killed him, and his face was proud and pale;
And a few men talked of freedom, while England talked of ale.

A war that we understood not came over the world and woke
Americans, Frenchmen, Irish; but we knew not the things they spoke.
They talked about rights and nature and peace and the people's
                                                            reign:
And the squires, our masters, bade us fight; and scorned us never
                                                            again.
Weak if we be for ever, could none condemn us then;
Men called us serfs and drudges; men knew that we were men.
In foam and flame at Trafalgar, on Albuera plains,
We did and died like lions, to keep ourselves in chains,
We lay in living ruins; firing and fearing not
The strange fierce face of the Frenchmen who knew for what they
                                                            fought,
And the man who seemed to be more than man we strained against
                                                        and broke;
And we broke our own rights with him. And still we never spoke.

Our patch of glory ended; we never heard guns again.
But the squire seemed struck in the saddle; he was foolish, as if in
pain,
He leaned on a staggering lawyer, he clutched a cringing Jew,
He was stricken; it may be, after all, he was stricken at Waterloo.
Or perhaps the shades of the shaven men, whose spoil is in his house,
Come back in shining shapes at last to spoil his last carouse:
We only know the last sad squires ride slowly towards the sea,
And a new people takes the land: and still it is not we.

They have given us into the hand of new unhappy lords,
Lords without anger and honour, who dare not carry their swords.
They fight by shuffling papers; they have bright dead alien eyes;
They look at our labour and laughter as a tired man looks at flies.
And the load of their loveless pity is worse than the ancient wrongs,
Their doors are shut in the evening; and they know no songs.

We hear men speaking for us of new laws strong and sweet,
Yet is there no man speaketh as we speak in the street.
It may be we shall rise the last as Frenchmen rose the first,
Our wrath come after Russia's wrath and our wrath be the worst.
It may be we are meant to mark with our riot and our rest
God's scorn for all men governing. It may be beer is best.
But we are the people of England; and we have not spoken yet.
Smile at us, pay us, pass us. But do not quite forget.

THE HIGH TIDE ON THE COAST OF
LINCOLNSHIRE (1571)

JEAN INGELOW

THE old mayor climbed the belfry tower,
  The ringers ran by two, by three;
'Pull, if ye never pulled before;
  Good ringers, pull your best,' quoth he.
'Play up, play up, O Boston bells!
Ply all your changes, all your swells,
  Play up *The Brides of Enderby*.'

Men say it was a stolen tide —
   The Lord that sent it, He knows all;
But in mine ears doth still abide
   The message that the bells let fall:
And there was naught of strange, beside
The flights of mews and peewits pied
   By millions crouched on the old sea wall.

I sat and spun within the door,
   My thread brake off, I raised mine eyes;
The level sun, like ruddy ore,
   Lay sinking in the barren skies;
And dark against day's golden death
She moved where Lindis wandereth,
My son's fair wife, Elizabeth.

'Cusha! Cusha! Cusha!' calling,
Ere the early dews were falling,
Far away I heard her song.
'Cusha! Cusha!' all along;
Where the reedy Lindis floweth,
    Floweth, floweth,
From the meads where melick groweth
Faintly came her milking song. —

'Cusha! Cusha! Cusha!' calling,
'For the dews will soon be falling;
Leave your meadow grasses mellow,
    Mellow, mellow;
Quit your cowslips, cowslips yellow;
Come up Whitefoot, come up Lightfoot;
Quit the stalks of parsley hollow,
    Hollow, hollow;
Come up Jetty, rise and follow,
From the clovers lift your head;
Come up Whitefoot, come up Lightfoot,
Come up Jetty, rise and follow,
Jetty, to the milking shed.'

If it be long, aye, long ago,
   When I begin to think how long,
Again I hear the Lindis flow,
   Swift as an arrow, sharp and strong;
And all the air, it seemeth me,
Bin full of floating bells (saith she),
That ring the tune of Enderby.

All fresh the level pasture lay,
   And not a shadow mote be seen,
Save where full five good miles away
   The steeple towered from out the green;
And lo! the great bell far and wide
Was heard in all the country side
That Saturday at eventide.

The swanherds where their sedges are
   Moved on in sunset's golden breath,
The shepherd lads I heard afar,
   And my son's wife, Elizabeth;
Till floating o'er the grassy sea
Came down that kindly message free,
The Brides of Mavis Enderby.

Then some looked up into the sky,
   And all along where Lindis flows
To where the goodly vessels lie,
   And where the lordly steeple shows.
They said 'And why should this thing be?
What danger lowers by land or sea?
They ring the tune of Enderby!

'For evil news from Mablethorpe,
   Of pirate galleys warping down;
For ships ashore beyond the scorpe,
   They have not spared to wake the town:
But while the west bin red to see,
And storms be none, and pirates flee,
Why ring *The Brides of Enderby?*'

I looked without, and lo! my son
  Came riding down with might and main:
He raised a shout as he drew on,
  Till all the welkin rang again,
'Elizabeth! Elizabeth!'
(A sweeter woman ne'er drew breath
Than my son's wife, Elizabeth.)

'The old sea wall (he cried) is down,
  The rising tide comes on apace,
And boats adrift in yonder town
  Go sailing up the market-place.'
He shook as one that looks on death:
'God save you, mother!' straight he saith;
'Where is my wife, Elizabeth?'

'Good son, where Lindis winds away
  With her two bairns I marked her long;
And ere yon bells began to play
  Afar I heard her milking song.'
He looked across the grassy lea,
To right, to left, 'Ho Enderby!'
They rang *The Brides of Enderby*!

With that he cried and beat his breast;
  For, lo!, along the river's bed
A mighty eagre reared his crest,
  And up the Lindis raging sped.
It swept with thunderous noises loud;
Shaped like a curling snow-white cloud,
Or like a demon in a shroud.

And rearing Lindis backward pressed,
  Shook all her trembling banks amain;
Then madly at the eagre's breast
  Flung up her weltering walls again.
Then banks came down with ruin and rout —
Then beaten foam flew round about —
Then all the mighty floods were out.

So far, so fast the eagre drave,
  The heart had hardly time to beat,
Before a shallow seething wave
  Sobbed in the grasses at our feet:
The feet had hardly time to flee
Before it brake against the knee,
And all the world was in the sea.

Upon the roof we sat that night,
  The noise of bells went sweeping by:
I marked the lofty beacon light
  Stream from the church tower, red and high —
A lurid mark and dread to see;
And awesome bells they were to me,
That in the dark rang *Enderby*.

They rang the sailor lads to guide
  From roof to roof who fearless rowed;
And I — my son was at my side,
  And yet the ruddy beacon glowed:
And yet he moaned beneath his breath,
'O come in life, or come in death!
O lost! my love, Elizabeth.'

And didst thou visit him no more?
  Thou didst, thou didst, my daughter dear;
The waters laid thee at his door,
  Ere yet the early dawn was clear.
Thy pretty bairns in fast embrace,
The lifted sun shone on thy face,
Down drifted to thy dwelling place.

That flow strewed wrecks about the grass,
  That ebb swept out the flocks to sea;
A fatal ebb and flow, alas!
  To many more than mine and me:
But each will mourn his own (she saith).
And sweeter woman ne'er drew breath
Than my son's wife, Elizabeth.

I shall never hear her more
By the reedy Lindis shore,
'Cusha! Cusha! Cusha!' calling,
Ere the early dews be falling;
I shall never hear her song,
'Cusha! Cusha!' all along,
Where the sunny Lindis floweth,
    Goeth, floweth;
From the meads where melick groweth,
When the water winding down,
Onward floweth to the town.

I shall never see her more
Where the reeds and rushes quiver,
    Shiver, quiver;
Stand beside the sobbing river,
Sobbing, throbbing, in its falling,
To the sandy lonesome shore;
I shall never hear her calling,
'Leave your meadow grasses mellow,
    Mellow, mellow;
Quit your cowslips, cowslips yellow;
Come up Whitefoot, come up Lightfoot;
Quit your pipes of parsley hollow,
    Hollow, hollow;
Come up Lightfoot, rise and follow;
    Lightfoot, Whitefoot,
From your clovers lift the head;
Come up Jetty, follow, follow,
Jetty, to the milking shed.'

IF

RUDYARD KIPLING

IF you can keep your head when all about you
    Are losing theirs and blaming it on you;
If you can trust yourself when all men doubt you,
    But make allowance for their doubting too;

If you can wait and not be tired by waiting,
  Or being lied about, don't deal in lies,
Or being hated don't give way to hating,
  And yet don't look too good, nor talk too wise.

If you can dream — and not make dreams your master;
  If you can think — and not make thoughts your aim;
If you can meet with Triumph and Disaster
  And treat those two impostors just the same;
If you can bear to hear the truth you've spoken
  Twisted by knaves to make a trap for fools,
Or watch the things you gave your life to broken,
  And stoop and build 'em up with worn-out tools.

If you can make one heap of all your winnings
  And risk it on one turn of pitch-and-toss,
And lose, and start again at your beginnings
  And never breathe a word about your loss;
If you can force your heart and nerve and sinew
  To serve your turn long after they are gone,
And so hold on when there is nothing in you
  Except the Will which says to them: 'Hold on!'

If you can talk with crowds and keep your virtue
  Or walk with Kings — nor lose the common touch,
If neither foes nor loving friends can hurt you,
  If all men count with you, but none too much;
If you can fill the unforgiving minute
  With sixty seconds' worth of distance run,
Yours is the Earth and everything that's in it,
  And — which is more — you'll be a Man, my son!

Note

    This and RECESSIONAL are the two most hackneyed of Kipling's poems. He had George Washington in mind when he wrote *If*. It has been much parodied. One of the most intriguing versions begins:

      'If you can keep your girl, when all around you,
        Are losing theirs and blaming it on you'

But I have never heard the continuation.   *A. P. W.*

MENDING WALL

Robert Frost

Something there is that doesn't love a wall,
That sends the frozen-ground-swell under it,
And spills the upper boulders in the sun;
And makes gaps even two can pass abreast.
The work of hunters is another thing:
I have come after them and made repair
Where they have left not one stone on a stone,
But they would have the rabbit out of hiding,
To please the yelping dogs. The gaps I mean,
No one has seen them made or heard them made,
But at spring mending-time we find them there.
I let my neighbour know beyond the hill;
And on a day we meet to walk the line
And set the wall between us once again.
We keep the wall between us as we go.
To each the boulders that have fallen to each.
And some are loaves and some so nearly balls
We have to use a spell to make them balance:
'Stand where you are until our backs are turned!'
We wear our fingers rough with handling them.
Oh, just another kind of outdoor game,
One on a side. It comes to little more:
He is all pine and I am apple-orchard.
My apple-trees will never get across
And eat the cones under his pines, I tell him.
He only says, 'Good fences make good neighbours,'
Spring is the mischief in me, and I wonder
If I could put a notion in his head:
'Why do they make good neighbours? Isn't it
Where there are cows? But here there are no cows.
Before I built a wall I'd ask to know
What I was walling in or walling out,
And to whom I was like to give offence.
Something there is that doesn't love a wall
That wants it down!' I could say 'Elves' to him,

But it's not elves exactly, and I'd rather
He said it for himself. I see him there,
Bringing a stone grasped firmly by the top
In each hand, like an old-stone savage armed.
He moves in darkness as it seems to me,
Not of woods only and the shade of trees.
He will not go behind his father's saying,
And he likes having thought of it so well
He says again, 'Good fences make good neighbours.'

THE FEMALE OF THE SPECIES

RUDYARD KIPLING

WHEN the Himalayan peasant meets the he-bear in his pride,
He shouts to scare the monster, who will often turn aside,
But the she-bear thus accosted rends the peasant tooth and nail.
For the female of the species is more deadly than the male.

When Nag the basking cobra hears the careless foot of man,
He will sometimes wriggle sideways and avoid it if he can.
But his mate makes no such motion where she camps beside the trail.
For the female of the species is more deadly than the male.

When the early Jesuit fathers preached to Hurons and Choctaws,
They prayed to be delivered from the vengeance of the squaws.
'Twas the women, not the warriors, turned those stark enthusiasts
For the female of the species is more deadly than the male.   [pale.

Man's timid heart is bursting with the things he must not say,
For the Woman that God gave him isn't his to give away;
But when hunter meets with husband, each confirms the other's
The female of the species is more deadly than the male.   [tale —

Man, a bear in most relations — worm and savage otherwise, —
Man propounds negotiations, Man accepts the compromise.
Very rarely will he squarely push the logic of a fact
To its ultimate conclusion in unmitigated act.

Fear, or foolishness, impels him, ere he lay the wicked low,
To concede some form of trial even to his fiercest foe.
Mirth obscene diverts his anger — Doubt and Pity oft perplex
Him in dealing with an issue — to the scandal of The Sex!

But the Woman that God gave him, every fibre of her frame
Proves her launched for one sole issue, armed and engined for the
And to serve that single issue, lest the generations fail,   [same;
The female of the species must be deadlier than the male.

She who faces Death by torture for each life beneath her breast
May not deal in doubt or pity — must not swerve for fact or jest.
These be purely male diversions — not in these her honour dwells.
She the Other Law we live by, is that Law and nothing else.

She can bring no more to living than the powers that make her great
As the Mother of the Infant and the Mistress of the Mate.
And when Babe and Man are lacking and she strides unclaimed to
Her right as femme (and baron), her equipment is the same.   [claim

She is wedded to convictions — in default of grosser ties;
Her contentions are her children, Heaven help him who denies! —
He will meet no suave discussion, but the instant, white-hot, wild,
Wakened female of the species warring as for spouse and child.

Unprovoked and awful charges — even so the she-bear fights,
Speech that drips, corrodes, and poisons — even so the cobra bites,
Scientific vivisection of one nerve till it is raw
And the victim writhes in anguish — like the Jesuit with the squaw.

So it comes that Man, the coward, when he gathers to confer
With his fellow-braves in council, dare not leave a place for her
Where, at war with Life and Conscience, he uplifts his erring hands
To some God of Abstract Justice — which no woman understands.

And Man knows it! Knows, moreover, that the Woman that God gave
him
Must command but may not govern — shall enthral but not enslave
him.
And *She* knows, because She warns him, and Her instincts never fail,
That the Female of Her Species is more deadly than the Male.

LUCY ASHTON'S SONG

from THE BRIDE OF LAMMERMOOR *by*

SIR WALTER SCOTT

LOOK not thou on beauty's charming;
Sit thou still when kings are arming;
Taste not when the wine-cup glistens;
Speak not when the people listens;
Stop thine ear against the singer;
From the red gold keep thy finger;
Vacant heart and hand and eye,
Easy live and quiet die.

Note

This is perhaps hardly a Conversation Piece, except that it does
in some sort propound a philosophy of life. I have known the
jingle for many years, and could not disagree more heartily with
every precept in it, except perhaps the fourth line. I have found
few things in life more satisfactory to look on than beauty's
charming. My profession, and inclination, have forbidden that I
should sit still when kings, or dictators, are arming. I enjoy the
wine that maketh glad the heart of man, and, like Jurgen, am
willing to taste of any cup once. I have no wish to speak in public,
but am occasionally obliged to do so. Though quite unmusical, I
have never gone so far as to stop my ear against the singer. The
only thing which has kept my fingers from red gold is a lack of
financial ability — and since the last war, a lack of red gold. As
for a vacant heart, easy life or quiet death, I desire none of them.
The slogan 'Safety First' nearly ruined an Empire.   *A. P. W.*

6. THE LIGHTER SIDE

IT is no use arguing about tastes in humour, and I do not propose to do so. The recently published *Oxford Book of Light Verse* shows what curious views may be held on what constitutes light verse (the grim *Danny Deever*, for example).

English verse is rich in humorous writers: Edward Lear, Barham of the *Ingoldsby Legends*, Lewis Carroll, Calverley, A. D. Godley, J. K. Stephen, Harry Graham, Owen Seaman, Hilaire Belloc, A. P. Herbert, and that prolific writer Anon, to name only a few. And many of our serious poets have had their lighter moments.

The poems in this section have amused me enough to be remembered; others may prefer to forget them.   *A. .P W.*

THE PIED PIPER OF HAMELIN
ROBERT BROWNING

HAMELIN Town's in Brunswick,
By famous Hanover city;
    The river Weser, deep and wide,
    Washes its wall on the southern side;
    A pleasanter spot you never spied;
But, when begins my ditty,
    Almost five hundred years ago,
    To see the townsfolk suffer so
From vermin, was a pity.

    Rats!
They fought the dogs, and killed the cats,
    And bit the babies in the cradles,
And ate the cheeses out of the vats,
    And licked the soup from the cooks' own ladles,
Split open the kegs of salted sprats,
Made nests inside men's Sunday hats,
And even spoiled the women's chats,
    By drowning their speaking
    With shrieking and squeaking
In fifty different sharps and flats

At last the people in a body
 To the Town Hall came flocking:
''Tis clear,' cried they, 'our Mayor's a noddy;
 And as for our Corporation — shocking
To think we buy gowns lined with ermine
For dolts that can't or won't determine
What's best to rid us of our vermin!
You hope, because you're old and obese,
To find in the furry civic robe ease?
Rouse up, Sirs! Give your brains a racking
To find the remedy we're lacking,
Or, sure as fate, we'll send you packing!'
At this the Mayor and Corporation
Quaked with a mighty consternation.

An hour they sate in council,
 At length the Mayor broke silence:
'For a guilder I'd my ermine gown sell;
 I wish I were a mile hence!
It's easy to bid one rack one's brain —
I'm sure my poor head aches again,
I've scratched it so, and all in vain.
Oh for a trap, a trap, a trap!'
Just as he said this, what should hap
At the chamber door but a gentle tap?
'Bless us,' cried the Mayor, 'what's that?'
(With the Corporation as he sat,
Looking little though wondrous fat;
Nor brighter was his eye, nor moister
Than a too-long-opened oyster,
Save when at noon his paunch grew mutinous
For a plate of turtle green and glutinous)
'Only a scraping of shoes on the mat?
Anything like the sound of a rat
Makes my heart go pit-a-pat!'

'Come in!' — the Mayor cried, looking bigger:
And in did come the strangest figure!

His queer long coat from heel to head
Was half of yellow and half of red;
And he himself was tall and thin,
With sharp blue eyes, each like a pin,
And light loose hair, yet swarthy skin,
No tuft on cheek nor beard on chin,
But lips where smiles went out and in —
There was no guessing his kith and kin!
And nobody could enough admire
The tall man and his quaint attire:
Quoth one: 'It's as my great-grandsire,
Starting up at the Trump of Doom's tone,
Had walked this way from his painted tomb-stone!'

He advanced to the council-table:
And, 'Please your honours,' said he, 'I'm able
By means of a secret charm to draw
All creatures living beneath the sun,
That creep or swim or fly or run,
After me so as you never saw!
And I chiefly use my charm
On creatures that do people harm,
The mole and toad and newt and viper;
And people call me the Pied Piper.'
(And here they noticed round his neck
A scarf of red and yellow stripe,
To match with his coat of the self-same cheque,
And at the scarf's end hung a pipe;
And his fingers, they noticed, were ever straying
As if impatient to be playing
Upon this pipe, as low it dangled
Over his vesture so old-fangled.)
'Yet,' said he, 'poor piper as I am,
In Tartary I freed the Cham,
Last June, from his huge swarms of gnats;
I eased in Asia the Nizam
Of a monstrous brood of vampyre-bats:
And as for what your brain bewilders,

If I can rid your town of rats
Will you give me a thousand guilders?'
'One? fifty thousand!' — was the exclamation
Of the astonished Mayor and Corporation.

Into the streets the Piper stept,
    Smiling first a little smile,
As if he knew what magic slept
    In his quiet pipe the while;
Then, like a musical adept,
To blow the pipe his lips he wrinkled,
And green and blue his sharp eyes twinkled
Like a candle-flame where salt is sprinkled;
And ere three shrill notes the pipe uttered,
You heard as if an army muttered;
And the muttering grew to a grumbling;
And the grumbling grew to a mighty rumbling;
And out of the houses the rats came tumbling.
Great rats, small rats, lean rats, brawny rats,
Brown rats, black rats, grey rats, tawny rats,
Grave old plodders, gay young friskers,
    Fathers, mothers, uncles, cousins,
Cocking tails and pricking whiskers,
    Families by tens and dozens,
Brothers, sisters, husbands, wives —
Followed the Piper for their lives.
From street to street he piped advancing,
And step for step they followed dancing,
Until they came to the river Weser
Wherein all plunged and perished!
Save one who, stout as Julius Caesar,
Swam across and lived to carry
(As he, the manuscript he cherished)
To Rat-land home his commentary:
Which was, 'At the first shrill notes of the pipe,
I heard a sound as of scraping tripe,
And putting apples, wondrous ripe,
Into a cider-press's gripe:

And a moving away of pickle-tub-boards,
And a leaving ajar of conserve-cupboards,
And a drawing the corks of train-oil-flasks,
And a breaking the hoops of butter-casks;
And it seemed as if a voice
(Sweeter far than by harp or by psaltery
Is breathed) called out, Oh rats, rejoice!
The world is grown to one vast dry-saltery!
So, munch on, crunch on, take your nuncheon,
Breakfast, supper, dinner, luncheon!
And just as a bulky sugar-puncheon,
All ready staved, like a great sun shone
Glorious scarce an inch before me,
Just as methought it said, Come, bore me!
— I found the Weser rolling o'er me.'

You should have heard the Hamelin people
Ringing the bells till they rocked the steeple.
'Go,' cried the Mayor, 'and get long poles!
Poke out the nests and block up the holes!
Consult with carpenters and builders,
And leave in our town not even a trace
Of the rats!' — when suddenly, up the face
Of the Piper perked in the market-place,
With a, 'First, if you please, my thousand guilders!'

A thousand guilders! The Mayor looked blue;
So did the Corporation too.
For council dinners made rare havoc
With Claret, Moselle, Vin-de-Grave, Hock;
And half the money would replenish
Their cellar's biggest butt with Rhenish.
To pay this sum to a wandering fellow
With a gipsy coat of red and yellow!
'Beside', quoth the Mayor with a knowing wink,
'Our business was done at the river's brink;
We saw with our eyes the vermin sink,
And what's dead can't come to life, I think.

So, friend, we're not the folks to shrink
From the duty of giving you something for drink,
And a matter of money to put in your poke;
But as for the guilders, what we spoke
Of them, as you very well know, was in joke.
Beside, our losses have made us thrifty.
A thousand guilders! Come, take fifty!'

The Piper's face fell, and he cried,
'No trifling! I can't wait, beside!
I've promised to visit by dinner time
Bagdat, and accept the prime
Of the Head-Cook's pottage, all he's rich in,
For having left, in the Caliph's kitchen,
Of a nest of scorpions no survivor —
With him I proved no bargain driver,
With you, don't think I'll bate a stiver!
And folks who put me in a passion
May find me pipe to another fashion.'

'How?' cried the Mayor, 'd'ye think I'll brook
Being worse treated than a Cook?
Insulted by a lazy ribald
With idle pipe and vesture piebald?
You threaten us, fellow? Do your worst,
Blow your pipe there till you burst!'

Once more he stept into the street;
    And to his lips again
Laid his long pipe of smooth straight cane;
    And ere he blew three notes (such sweet
Soft notes as yet musicians' cunning
    Never gave the enraptured air)
There was a rustling, that seemed like a bustling
Of merry crowds justling at pitching and hustling,
Small feet were pattering, wooden shoes clattering,
Little hands clapping and little tongues chattering,
And, like fowls in a farm-yard when barley is scattering,

Out came the children running.
All the little boys and girls,
With rosy cheeks and flaxen curls,
And sparkling eyes and teeth like pearls,
Tripping and skipping, ran merrily after
The wonderful music with shouting and laughter.

The Mayor was dumb, and the Council stood
As if they were changed into blocks of wood,
Unable to move a step, or cry
To the children merrily skipping by —
And could only follow with the eye
That joyous crowd at the Piper's back.
But how the Mayor was on the rack,
And the wretched Council's bosoms beat,
As the Piper turned from the High Street
To where the Weser rolled its waters
Right in the way of their sons and daughters!
However he turned from South to West,
And to Koppelberg Hill his steps addressed,
And after him the children pressed;
Great was the joy in every breast.
'He never can cross that mighty top!
He's forced to let the piping drop,
And we shall see our children stop!'
When, lo, as they reached the mountain's side,
A wondrous portal opened wide,
As if a cavern was suddenly hollowed;
And the Piper advanced and the children followed,
And when all were in to the very last,
The door in the mountain-side shut fast.
Did I say, all? No! One was lame,
And could not dance the whole of the way;
And in after years, if you would blame
His sadness, he was used to say, —
'It's dull in our town since my playmates left!
I can't forget that I'm bereft
Of all the pleasant sights they see,

Which the Piper also promised me.
For he led us, he said, to a joyous land,
Joining the town and just at hand,
Where waters gushed and fruit-trees grew,
And flowers put forth a fairer hue,
And everything was strange and new;
The sparrows were brighter than peacocks here,
And their dogs outran our fallow deer,
And honey-bees had lost their stings,
And horses were born with eagles' wings:
And just as I became assured,
My lame foot would be speedily cured,
The music stopped and I stood still,
And found myself outside the Hill,
Left alone against my will,
To go now limping as before,
And never hear of that country more!'

Alas, alas for Hamelin!
   There came into many a burgher's pate
   A text which says that Heaven's Gate
   Opes to the Rich at as easy rate
As the needle's eye takes a camel in!
The Mayor sent East, West, North and South,
To offer the Piper, by word of mouth,
   Wherever it was men's lot to find him,
Silver and gold to his heart's content,
If he'd only return the way he went,
   And bring the children behind him.
But when they saw 'twas a lost endeavour,
And Piper and dancers were gone for ever,
They made a decree that lawyers never
   Should think their records dated duly
If, after the day of the month and year,
These words did not as well appear,
'And so long after what happened here
   On the Twenty-second of July,
Thirteen hundred and seventy-six':

And the better in memory to fix
The place of the children's last retreat,
They called it, the Pied Piper's Street —
Where any one playing on pipe or tabor
Was sure for the future to lose his labour.
Nor suffered they hostelry or tavern
    To shock with mirth a street so solemn;
But opposite the place of the cavern
    They wrote the story on a column,
And on the great Church-Window painted
The same, to make the world acquainted
How their children were stolen away;
And there it stands to this very day.
And I must not omit to say
That in Transylvania there's a tribe
Of alien people that ascribe
The outlandish ways and dress
On which their neighbours lay such stress,
To their fathers and mothers having risen
Out of some subterraneous prison
Into which they were trepanned
Long time ago in a mighty band
Out of Hamelin town in Brunswick land,
But how or why, they don't understand.

So, Willy, let me and you be wipers
Of scores out with all men — especially pipers:
And, whether they pipe us free, from rats or from mice,
If we've promised them aught, let us keep our promise.

THE LAY OF ST CUTHBERT

R. H. Barham

It's in Bolton Hall, and the clock strikes One,
    And the roast meat's brown and the boil'd meat's done,
And the barbecu'd sucking-pig's crisp'd to a turn,
And the pancakes are fried, and beginning to burn;

The fat stubble-goose Swims in gravy and juice,
With the mustard and apple-sauce ready for use;
Fish, flesh, and fowl, and all of the best,
Want nothing but eating — they're all ready drest,
But where is the Host, and where is the Guest?

Pantler and serving-man, henchman and page,
Stand sniffing the duck-stuffing (onion and sage),
    And the scullions and cooks, With fidgety looks,
Are grumbling and mutt'ring, and scowling as black
As cooks always do when the dinner's put back;
For though the board's deckt, and the napery, fair
As the unsunn'd snow-flake, is spread out with care,
And the Dais is furnish'd with stool and with chair,
And plate of *orfèvrerie* costly and rare,
Apostle-spoons, salt-cellar, all are there,
    And Mess John in his place, With his rubicund face,
And his hands ready folded, prepared to say Grace,
Yet where is the Host? — and his convives — where?

The Scroope sits lonely in Bolton Hall,
And he watches the dial that hangs by the wall,
He watches the large hand, he watches the small,
    And he fidgets, and looks As cross as the cooks,
And he utters — a word which we'll soften to 'Zooks!'
And he cries, 'What on earth has become of them all?
    What can delay De Vaux and De Saye?
What makes Sir Gilbert de Umfraville stay?
What's gone with Poyntz, and Sir Reginald Braye?

Why are Ralph Ufford and Marny away?
And De Nokes, and De Styles, and Lord Marmaduke Grey?
    And De Roe? And De Doe? —
Poynings, and Vavasour — where be they?
Fitz-Walter, Fitz-Osbert, Fitz-Hugh, and Fitz-John,
And the Mandevilles, *père et filz* (father and son)?
Their cards said "Dinner precisely at One"!
    There's nothing I hate, in the world, like waiting!

It's a monstrous great bore, when a Gentleman feels
A good appetite, thus to be kept from his meals!'

It's in Bolton Hall, and the clock strikes Two!
And the scullions and cooks are themselves in 'a stew',
And the kitchen-maids stand, and don't know what to do,
For the rich plum-puddings are bursting their bags,
And the mutton and turnips are boiling to rags,
    And the fish is all spoil'd, And the butter's all oil'd,
And the soup's got cold in the silver tureen,
And there's nothing, in short, that is fit to be seen!
While Sir Guy Le Scroope continues to fume,
And to fret by himself in the tapestried room,
    And still fidgets, and looks More cross than the cooks,
And repeats that bad word, which we've soften'd to 'Zooks!'

Two o'clock's come, and Two o'clock's gone,
And the large and the small hands move steadily on,
    Still nobody's there, No De Roos, or De Clare,
To taste of the Scroope's most delicate fare,
Or to quaff off a health unto Bolton's Heir,
That nice little boy who sits in his chair,
Some four years old, and a few months to spare,
With his laughing blue eyes and his long curly hair,
Now sucking his thumb, and now munching his pear.

Again, Sir Guy the silence broke,
'It's hard upon Three! — it's just on the stroke!
Come, serve up the dinner! — A joke is a joke!' —
Little he deems that Stephen de Hoaques,
Who 'his fun', as the Yankees say, everywhere pokes,
And is always a great deal too fond of his jokes,
Has written a circular note to De Nokes,
And De Stiles, and De Roe, and the rest of the folks,
    One and all, Great and small,
Who were ask'd to the Hall
To dine there and sup, and wind up with a ball,
And had told all the party a great bouncing lie, he

Cook'd up, that 'the *fête* was postponed *sine die*,
The dear little curly-wigg'd heir of Le Scroope
Being taken alarmingly ill with the croup!'

When the clock struck Three, And the Page on his knee
Said, 'An't please you, Sir Guy Le Scroope, *On a servi!*'
And the Knight found the banquet-hall empty and clear,
    With nobody near To partake of his cheer,
He stamp'd, and he storm'd — then his language! — Oh dear!
'Twas awful to see, and 'twas awful to hear!
And he cried to the button-deck'd Page at his knee,
Who had told him so civilly, '*On a servi*,'
'Ten thousand fiends seize them, wherever they be!
— The Devil take *them*! and the Devil take *thee*!
And the Devil MAY EAT UP THE DINNER FOR ME!'

    In a terrible fume He bounced out of the room,
He bounced out of the house — and page, footman, and groom,
Bounced after their master; for scarce had they heard
Of this left-handed Grace the last finishing word,
Ere the horn at the gate of the Barbican tower
Was blown with a loud twenty-trumpeter power,
    And in rush'd a troop Of strange guests! — such a group
As had ne'er before darken'd the door of the Scroope!
This looks like De Saye — yet — it is not De Saye —
And this is — no, 'tis not — Sir Reginald Braye —
This has somewhat the favour of Marmaduke Grey —
But stay! — *Where on earth did he get those long nails?*
Why, they're *claws*! — then Good Gracious! — they've all of them
That can't be De Vaux — why, his nose is a bill,   *tails?*
Or, I would say a beak! — and he can't keep it still! —
Is that Poynings? — Oh Gemini! look at his feet!!
Why, they're absolute *hoofs*! — is it gout or his corns
That have crumpled them up so? — by Jingo, he's *horns*!
Run! run! — There's Fitz-Walter, Fitz-Hugh, and Fitz-John,
And the Mandevilles *père et filz* (father and son),
And Fitz-Osbert, and Ufford — *they've all got them on!*

Then their great saucer eyes — It's the Father of lies
And his Imps — run! run! run! — they're all fiends in disguise,
Who've partly assumed, with more sombre complexions,
The forms of Sir Guy Le Scroope's friends and connections,
And He — at the top there — that grim-looking elf —
Run! run! — that's the 'muckle-horn'd Clootie' himself!

And now what a din Without and within!
For the court-yard is full of them. — How they begin
To mop, and to mowe, and make faces, and grin!
    Cock their tails up together, Like cows in hot weather,
And butt at each other, all eating and drinking,
The viands and wine disappearing like winking.
    And then such a lot As together had got!
Master Cabbage, the steward, who'd made a machine
To calculate with, and count noses, — I ween
The cleverest thing of the kind ever seen, —
    Declared, when he'd made, By the said machine's aid,
Up, what's now called, the 'tottle' of those he survey'd,
There were just — how he proved it I cannot divine, —
Nine thousand, nine hundred, and ninety and nine.
    Exclusive of Him, Who, giant in limb,
And black as the crow they denominate *Jim*,
With a tail like a bull, and a head like a bear,
Stands forth at the window, — and what holds he there,
    Which he hugs with such care, And pokes out in the air,
And grasps as its limbs from each other he'd tear?
    Oh! grief and despair! I vow and declare
It's Le Scroope's poor, dear, sweet, little, curly-wigg'd Heir!
Whom the nurse had forgot, and left there in his chair,
Alternately sucking his thumb and his pear.

    What words can express The dismay and distress
Of Sir Guy, when he found what a terrible mess
His cursing and banning had now got him into?
That words, which to use are a shame and a sin too,
Had thus on their speaker recoil'd, and his malison
Placed in the hands of the Devil's own 'pal' his son! —

M

He sobb'd and he sigh'd, And he scream'd, and he cried,
And behaved like a man that is mad or in liquor, — he
Tore his peak'd beard, and he dash'd off his 'Vicary',
   Stamp'd on the jasey As though he were crazy,
And staggering about just as if he were 'hazy',
Exclaim'd, 'Fifty pounds!' (a large sum in those times)
'To the person, whoever he may be, that climbs
To that window above there, *en ogive*, and painted,
And bring down my curly-wi' ' — here Sir Guy fainted!

   With many a moan, And many a groan,
What with tweaks of the nose, and some *eau de Cologne*,
He revived, — Reason once more remounted her throne,
Or rather the instinct of Nature, — 'twere treason
To Her, in the Scroope's case, perhaps, to say Reason, —
But what saw he then? — Oh! my goodness! a sight
Enough to have banish'd his reason outright! —
   In that broad banquet hall The fiends one and all,
Regardless of shriek and of squeak, and of squall,
From one to another were tossing that small
Pretty, curly-wigg'd boy, as if playing at ball:
Yet none of his friends or his vassals might dare
To fly to the rescue, or rush up the stair,
And bring down in safety his curly-wigg'd Heir!

   Well a day! Well a day! All he can say
Is but just so much trouble and time thrown away;
Not a man can be tempted to join the *mêlée*,
E'en those words cabalistic, 'I promise to pay
Fifty pounds on demand', have, for once, lost their sway,
   And there the Knight stands, Wringing his hands
In his agony — when on a sudden, one ray
Of hope darts through his midriff! — His Saint! — Oh, it's funny
   And almost absurd, That it never occurr'd! —
'Ay! the Scroope's Patron Saint! — he's the man for my money!
Saint — who is it? — really I'm sadly to blame, —
On my word I'm afraid, — I confess it with shame, —
That I've almost forgot the good Gentleman's name, —

Cut — let me see — Cutbeard? — no! — CUTHBERT! — egad
St Cuthbert of Bolton! — I'm right — he's the lad!
Oh, holy St Cuthbert, if forbears of mine —
Of myself I say little, — have knelt at your shrine,
And have lash'd their bare backs, and — no matter — with twine,
   Oh! list to the vow Which I make to you now,
Only snatch my poor little boy out of the row
Which that Imp's kicking up with his fiendish bow-wow,
And his head like a bear, and his tail like a cow!
Bring him back here in safety! — perform but this task,
And I'll give! — Oh! — I'll give you whatever you ask! —
   There is not a shrine In the County shall shine
With a brilliancy half so resplendent as thine,
Or have so many candles, or look half so fine! —
Haste, holy St Cuthbert, then, — hasten in pity!' —
   — Conceive his surprise
   When a strange voice replies,
'It's a bargain! — but, mind, Sir, THE BEST SPERMACETI!' —
Say, whose that voice? — whose that form by his side,
That old, old, grey man, with his beard long and wide,
   In his coarse Palmer's weeds,
   And his cockle and beads? —
And, how did he come? — did he walk? — did he ride?
Oh! none could determine, — oh! none could decide, —
The fact is, I don't believe any one tried;
For while ev'ry one stared, with a dignified stride,
   And without a word more, He march'd on before,
Up a flight of stone steps, and so through the front door,
To the banqueting-hall, that was on the first floor,
While the fiendish assembly were making a rare
Little shuttlecock there of the curly-wigg'd Heir. —
— I wish, gentle Reader, that you could have seen
The pause that ensued when he stepp'd in between,
With his resolute air, and his dignified mien,
And said, in a tone most decided, though mild,
'Come! — I'll trouble you just to hand over that child!'

The Demoniac crowd In an instant seem'd cow'd;

Not one of the crew volunteer'd a reply,
All shrunk from the glance of that keen-flashing eye,
Save one horrid Humgruffin, who seem'd by his talk,
And the airs he assumed, to be Cock of the walk,
He quail'd not before it, but saucily met it,
And as saucily said, 'Don't you wish you may get it?'
My goodness! — the look that the old Palmer gave!
And his frown! — 'twas quite dreadful to witness — 'Why, slave!
   You rascal!' quoth he, 'This language to ME!
— At once, Mr Nicholas! down on your knee,
And hand me that curly-wigg'd boy! — I command it —
Come! — none of your nonsense! — you know I won't stand it.'

Old Nicholas trembled, — he shook in his shoes,
And seem'd half inclined, but afraid, to refuse.
   'Well, Cuthbert,' said he, 'If so it must be,
For you've had your own way from the first time I knew ye; —
Take your curly-wigg'd brat, and much good may he do ye!
But I'll have in exchange' — here his eye flash'd with rage —
'That chap with the buttons — he *gave me* the Page!'

'Come, come,' the Saint answer'd, 'you very well know
The young man's no more his than your own to bestow —
Touch one button of his if you dare, Nick — no! no!
Cut your stick, sir — come, mizzle! be off with you! — go!' —
   The Devil grew hot — 'If I do I'll be shot!
An you come to that, Cuthbert, I'll tell you what's what;
He has *ask'd* us to *dine here*, and go we will not!
   Why, you Skinflint, — at least
   You may leave us the feast!
Here we've come all that way from our brimstone abode,
Ten million good leagues, sir, as ever you strode,
And the deuce of a luncheon we've had on the road —
— "Go!" — "Mizzle!" indeed — Mr Saint, who are you,
I should like to know? — "Go!" — I'll be hang'd if I do!
He invited us all — we've a right here — it's known
That a Baron may do what he likes with his own —
Here, Asmodeus — a slice of that beef; — now the mustard! —

What have *you* got? — oh, apple-pie — try it with custard!'
 The Saint made a pause As uncertain, because
He knew Nick is pretty well 'up' in the laws,
And they *might* be on *his* side — and then, he'd such claws!
On the whole, it was better, he thought, to retire
With the curly-wigg'd boy he'd pick'd out of the fire,
And give up the victuals — to retrace his path,
And to compromise — (spite of the Member for Bath).
 So to old Nick's appeal, As he turn'd on his heel,
He replied, 'Well, I'll leave you the mutton and veal,
And the soup *à la Reine*, and the sauce *Bechamel*;
As the Scroope *did* invite you to dinner, I feel
I can't well turn you out — 'twould be hardly genteel -
But be moderate, pray, — and remember thus much,
Since you're treated as Gentlemen, show yourselves such,
 And don't make it late, But mind and go straight
Home to bed when you've finish'd — and don't steal the plate,
Nor wrench off the knocker, or bell from the gate.
Walk away, like respectable Devils, in peace,
And don't "lark" with the watch, or annoy the police!'

 Having thus said his say, That Palmer grey
Took up little Le Scroope, and walk'd coolly away,
While the Demons all set up a 'Hip! hip! hurray!'
Then fell, tooth and claw, on the victuals, as they
Had been guests at Guildhall upon Lord Mayor's day,
All scrambling and scuffling for what was before 'em,
No care for precedence or common decorum.
 Few ate more hearty Than Madame Astarte,
And Hecate, — consider'd the Belles of the party.
Between them was seated Leviathan, eager
To 'do the polite', and take wine with Belphegor;
Here was *Morbleu* (a French devil), supping soup-meagre,
And there, munching leeks, Davy Jones of Tredegar
(A Welsh one), who'd left the domains of Ap Morgan
To 'follow the sea', — and next him Demogorgon, —
Then Pan with his pipes, and Fauns grinding the organ
To Mammon and Belial, and half a score dancers,

Who'd join'd with Medusa to get up 'the Lancers';
— Here's Lucifer lying blind drunk with Scotch ale,
While Beëlzebub's tying huge knots in his tail.
There's Setebos, storming because Mephistopheles
   Gave him the lie, Said he'd 'blacken his eye,'
And dash'd in his face a whole cup of hot coffee-lees; —
   Ramping and roaring, Hiccoughing, snoring,
Never was seen such a riot before in
A gentleman's house, or such profligate revelling
At any *soirée* — where they don't let the Devil in.

   Hark! — as sure as fate The clock's striking Eight!
(An hour which our ancestors call'd getting late,)
When Nick, who by this time was rather elate,
Rose up and address'd them.
                              ''Tis full time,' he said,
'For all elderly Devils to be in their bed;
For my own part I mean to be jogging, because
I don't find myself now quite so young as I was;
But, Gentlemen, ere I depart from my post,
I must call on you all for one bumper — the toast
Which I have to propose is, — OUR EXCELLENT HOST!
— Many thanks for his kind hospitality — may
   We also be able To see at *our* table
Himself, and enjoy, in a family way,
His good company *down-stairs* at no distant day!
   You'd, I'm sure, think me rude If I did not include
In the toast my young friend there, the curly-wigg'd Heir!
He's in very good hands, for you're all well aware
That St Cuthbert has taken him under his care;
   Though I must not say "bless", —
   — Why you'll easily guess, —
May our curly-wigg'd Friend's shadow never be less!'
Nick took off his heel-taps — bow'd — smiled — with an air
Most graciously grim, — and vacated the chair. —

   Of course the *élite* Rose at once on their feet,
And follow'd their leader, and beat a retreat;

When a sky-larking Imp took the President's seat,
And, requesting that each would replenish his cup,
Said, 'Where we have dined, my boys, there let us sup!' —
— It was three in the morning before they broke up ! ! !

    I scarcely need say Sir Guy didn't delay
To fulfil his vow made to St Cuthbert, or pay
For the candles he'd promised, or make light as day
The shrine he assured him he'd render so gay.
In fact, when the votaries came there to pray,
All said there was nought to compare with it — nay,
    For fear that the Abbey Might think he was shabby
Four Brethren thenceforward, two cleric, two lay,
He ordain'd should take charge of a new-founded chantry,
With six marcs apiece, and some claims on the pantry;
    In short, the whole County
    Declared, through his bounty,
The Abbey of Bolton exhibited fresh scenes
From any display'd since Sir William de Meschines ·
And Cecily Roumeli came to this nation
With William the Norman, and laid its foundation.

    For the rest, it is said, And I know I have read
In some Chronicle — whose, has gone out of my head —
That, what with these candles, and other expenses,
Which no man would go to if quite in his senses,
    He reduced, and brought low His property so,
That at last he'd not much of it left to bestow;
And that, many years after that terrible feast,
Sir Guy, in the Abbey, was living a Priest;
And there, in one thousand and — something, — deceased.
    (It's supposed by this trick He bamboozled Old Nick
And slipp'd through his fingers remarkably 'slick'.)
While, as to young Curly-wig, — dear little Soul,
Would you know more of him, you must look at 'The Roll',
    Which records the dispute, And the subsequent suit,
Commenced in 'Thirteen sev'nty-five', — which took root
In Le Grosvenor's assuming the arms Le Scroope swore

That none but *his* ancestors, ever before,
In foray, joust, battle, or tournament wore,
To wit, '*On a Prussian-blue Field, a Bend Or*';
While the Grosvenor averr'd that *his* ancestor bore
The same, and Scroope lied like a — somebody tore
Off the simile, — so I can tell you no more,
Till some A double S shall the fragment restore.

MORAL
This Legend sound maxims exemplifies — e.g.

1mo.   Should anything tease you,
            Annoy, or displease you,
Remember what Lilly says, '*Animum rege!*'
And as for that shocking bad habit of swearing, —
In all good society voted past bearing, —
Eschew it! and leave it to dustmen and mobs,
Nor commit yourself much beyond 'Zooks!' or 'Odsbobs!'

2do.   When ask'd out to dine by a Person of Quality,
Mind, and observe the most strict punctuality!
    For should you come late, And make dinner wait,
And the victuals get cold, you'll incur, sure as fate,
The Master's displeasure, the Mistress's hate.
And — though both may, perhaps, be too well-bred to swear,
They heartily *wish* you — I need not say *Where*.

3tio.   Look well to your Maid-servants! — say you expect them
To see to the children, and not to neglect them!
And if you're a widower, just throw a cursory
Glance in, at times, when you go near the Nursery.
— Perhaps it's as well to keep children from plums,
And from pears in the season, — and sucking their thumbs!

4to.   To sum up the whole with a 'Saw' of much use,
Be *just* and be *generous*, — don't be *profuse*! —
Pay the debts that you owe, — keep your word to your
                                              friends,

But — DON'T SET YOUR CANDLES ALIGHT AT BOTH ENDS!! —
For of this be assured, if you 'go it' too fast,
   You'll be 'dish'd' like Sir Guy
   And like him, perhaps, die
A poor, old, half-starved, Country Parson at last!

Note

I have included this poem partly in tribute to my father's
memory. The Ingoldsby Legends were great favourites of his,
and it was at his instigation that I first read them beginning with
'The Jackdaw of Rheims' and 'Smuggler Bill'. The author,
Barham, was at one time a minor Canon of St Paul's, and his
not wholly canonical wit might have shocked some of his con-
temporaries, but for the charm and uprightness of his character.
His motto seems to have been that of Father O'Flynn: 'Would you
leave gaiety all to the laity?'   *A. P. W.*

THE ROLLING ENGLISH ROAD

G. K. Chesterton

BEFORE the Roman came to Rye or out to Severn strode,
The rolling English drunkard made the rolling English road.
A reeling road, a rolling road, that rambles round the shire,
And after him the parson ran, the sexton and the squire,
A merry road, a mazy road, and such as we did tread
The night we went to Birmingham by way of Beachy Head.

I knew no harm of Bonaparte and plenty of the Squire,
And for to fight the Frenchman I did not much desire;
But I did bash their baggonets because they came arrayed
To straighten out the crooked road an English drunkard made,
Where you and I went down the lane with ale-mugs in our hands,
The night we went to Glastonbury by way of Goodwin Sands.

His sins they were forgiven him; or why do flowers run
Behind him; and the hedges all strengthening in the sun?
The wild thing went from left to right and knew not which
                                was which,

But the wild rose was above him when they found him in the ditch.
God pardon us, nor harden us; we did not see so clear
The night we went to Bannockburn by way of Brighton Pier.

My friends we will not go again or ape an ancient rage,
Or stretch the folly of our youth to be the shame of age,
But walk with clearer eyes and ears this path that wandereth,
And see undrugged in evening light the decent inn of death;
For there is good news yet to hear and fine things to be seen,
Before we go to Paradise by way of Kensal Green.

WHEN 'OMER SMOTE 'IS BLOOMIN' LYRE
Rudyard Kipling

When 'Omer smote 'is bloomin' lyre,
  He'd 'eard men sing by land an' sea,
An' what he thought 'e might require,
  'E went an' took — the same as me!

The market-girls an' fishermen,
  The shepherds an' the sailors too,
They 'eard old songs turn up again,
  But kep' it quiet — same as you!

They knew 'e stole; 'e knowed they knowed.
  They didn't tell, nor make a fuss,
But winked at 'Omer down the road,
  An' 'e winked back — the same as us.

THE JUMBLIES
Edward Lear

I

They went to sea in a Sieve, they did,
  In a Sieve they went to sea:
In spite of all their friends could say,

On a winter's morn, on a stormy day,
　In a Sieve they went to Sea!
And when the Sieve turned round and round,
And every one cried, 'You'll all be drowned!'
They called aloud, 'Our Sieve ain't big,
But we don't care a button! we don't care a fig!
　In a Sieve we'll go to sea!'
　　Far and few, far and few,
　　　Are the lands where the Jumblies live;
　　　Their heads are green, and their hands are blue,
　　　　And they went to sea in a Sieve.

II

They sailed away in a Sieve, they did,
　In a Sieve they sailed so fast,
With only a beautiful pea-green veil
Tied with a riband by way of a sail,
　To a small tobacco-pipe mast;
And every one said, who saw them go,
'O won't they be soon upset, you know!
For the sky is dark, and the voyage is long,
And happen what may, it's extremely wrong
　In a Sieve to sail so fast!'
　　Far and few, far and few,
　　　Are the lands where the Jumblies live;
　　　Their heads are green, and their hands are blue,
　　　　And they went to sea in a Sieve.

III

The water it soon came in, it did,
　The water it soon came in;
So to keep them dry, they wrapped their feet
In a pinky paper all folded neat,
　And they fastened it down with a pin.
And they passed the night in a crockery-jar,
And each of them said, 'How wise we are!
Though the sky be dark, and the voyage be long,

Yet we never can think we were rash or wrong,
  While round in our Sieve we spin!'
    Far and few, far and few,
      Are the lands where the Jumblies live;
    Their heads are green, and their hands are blue,
      And they went to sea in a Sieve.

IV

And all night long they sailed away;
  And when the sun went down,
They whistled and warbled a moony song
To the echoing sound of a coppery gong,
  In the shade of the mountains brown.
'O Timballo! How happy we are,
When we live in a Sieve and a crockery-jar,
And all night long in the moonlight pale,
We sail away with a pea-green sail,
  In the shade of the mountains brown!'
    Far and few, far and few,
      Are the lands where the Jumblies live;
    Their heads are green, and their hands are blue,
      And they went to sea in a Sieve.

V

They sailed to the Western Sea, they did,
  To a land all covered with trees,
And they bought an Owl, and a useful Cart,
And a pound of Rice, and a Cranberry Tart,
  And a hive of silvery Bees.
And they bought a Pig, and some green Jack-daws,
And a lovely Monkey with lollipop paws,
And forty bottles of Ring-Bo-Ree,
  And no end of Stilton Cheese.
    Far and few, far and few,
      Are the lands where the Jumblies live;
    Their heads are green, and their hands are blue,
      And they went to sea in a Sieve.

VI

And in twenty years they all came back,
   In twenty years or more,
And every one said, 'How tall they've grown!
For they've been to the Lakes, and the Terrible Zone,
   And the hills of the Chankly Bore';
And they drank their health, and gave them a feast
Of dumplings made of beautiful yeast;
And every one said, 'If we only live,
We too will go to sea in a Sieve, —
   To the hills of the Chankly Bore!'
     Far and few, far and few,
       Are the lands where the Jumblies live;
       Their heads are green, and their hands are blue,
       And they went to sea in a Sieve.

LOVE, DRINK, AND DEBT

Alexander Brome

I HAVE been in love, and in debt, and in drink,
   This many and many a year,
And those are three plagues enough, any should think,
   For one poor mortal to bear.
'Twas love made me fall into drink,
   And drink made me run into debt,
And though I have struggled, and struggled, and strove,
   I cannot get out of them yet.

There's nothing but money can cure me,
   And rid me of all my pain!
     'Twill pay all my debts,
     And remove all my lets,
And my mistress, that cannot endure me,
   Will love me, and love me again:
Then I'll fall to my loving and drinking amain!

THE BOON COMPANION

OLIVER ST JOHN GOGARTY

IF medals were ordained for drinks,
Or soft communings with a minx,
Or being at your ease belated,
By heavens, you'd be decorated!
And not Alcmena's chesty son
Have room to put more ribbands on!

DRINKING

ABRAHAM COWLEY

THE thirsty earth soaks up the rain,
And drinks and gapes for drink again;
The plants suck in the earth, and are
With constant drinking fresh and fair;
The sea itself (which one would think
Should have but little need of drink)
Drinks twice ten thousand rivers up,
So fill'd that they o'erflow the cup.
The busy Sun (and one would guess
By's drunken fiery face no less)
Drinks up the sea, and when he's done,
The Moon and Stars drink up the Sun:
They drink and dance by their own light,
They drink and revel all the night:
Nothing in Nature's sober found,
But an eternal health goes round.
Fill up the bowl, then, fill it high,
Fill all the glasses there — for why
Should every creature drink but I?
Why, man of morals, tell me why?

BIRDS, BAGS, BEARS, AND BUNS

ANON

THE common cormorant or shag
Lays eggs inside a paper bag.
The reason you will see, no doubt,
It is to keep the lightning out,
But what these unobservant birds
Have never noticed is that herds
Of wandering bears may come with buns
And steal the bags to hold the crumbs.

THE MOTOR BUS

A. D. GODLEY

WHAT is this that roareth thus?
Can it be a Motor Bus?
Yes, the swell and hideous hum
Indicat Motorem Bum!
Implet in the Corn and High
Terror me Motoris Bi:
Bo Motori clamitabo
Ne Motore caeder a Bo —
Dative be or Ablative
So thou only let us live:
Whither shall thy victims flee?
Spare us, spare us, Motor Be!
Thus I sang; and still anigh
Came in hordes Motores Bi,
Et complebat omne forum
Copia Motorum Borum.
How shall wretches live like us
Cincti Bis Motoribus?
Domine, defende nos
Contra nos Motores Bos!

THE KING OF BRENTFORD
William Makepeace Thackeray

There was a King in Brentford, — of whom no legends tell,
But who, without his glory, — could eat and sleep right well.
His Polly's cotton nightcap, — it was his crown of state,
He slept of evenings early, — and rose of mornings late.

All in a fine mud palace, — each day he took four meals,
And for a guard of honour, — a dog ran at his heels.
Sometimes to view his kingdoms, — rode forth this monarch good.
And then a prancing jackass — he royally bestrode.

There were no costly habits — with which this King was curst,
Except (and where's the harm on't?) — a somewhat lively thirst;
But people must pay taxes, — and Kings must have their sport;
So out of every gallon — his Grace he took a quart.

He pleased the ladies round him, — with manners soft and bland
With reason good, they named him — the father of his land.
Each year his mighty armies — marched forth in gallant show;
Their enemies were targets, — their bullets they were tow.

He vexed no quiet neighbour, — no useless conquest made,
But by the laws of pleasure, — his peaceful realm he swayed,
And in the years he reignèd, — through all this country wide,
There was no cause for weeping, — save when the good man died.

The faithful men of Brentford, — do still their King deplore,
His portrait yet is swinging, — beside an alehouse door.
And topers, tender-hearted, — regard his honest phiz,
And envy times departed, — that knew a reign like his.

THE OWL AND THE PUSSY-CAT
Edward Lear

The Owl and the Pussy-Cat went to sea
  In a beautiful pea-green boat.
They took some honey, and plenty of money,
  Wrapped up in a five-pound note.

The Owl looked up to the stars above,
  And sang to a small guitar,
'O lovely Pussy! O Pussy, my love,
  What a beautiful Pussy you are,
       You are,
       You are!
  What a beautiful Pussy you are!'

Pussy said to the Owl, 'You elegant fowl!
  How charmingly sweet you sing!
O let us be married! too long we have tarried:
  But what shall we do for a ring?'
They sailed away, for a year and a day,
  To the land where the Bong-Tree grows,
And there in a wood a Piggy-wig stood,
  With a ring at the end of his nose,
       His nose,
       His nose,
  With a ring at the end of his nose.

'Dear Pig, are you willing to sell for one shilling
  Your ring?' Said the Piggy, 'I will.'
So they took it away, and were married next day
  By the Turkey who lives on the hill.
They dinèd on mince, and slices of quince,
  Which they ate with a runcible spoon;
And hand in hand, on the edge of the sand,
  They danced by the light of the moon,
       The moon,
       The moon,
  They danced by the light of the moon.

THE SONG OF RIGHT AND WRONG
G. K. CHESTERTON

FEAST on wine or fast on water
And your honour shall stand sure,
God Almighty's son and daughter
He the valiant, she the pure;

If an angel out of heaven
Brings you other things to drink,
Thank him for his kind intentions,
Go and pour them down the sink.

Tea is like the East he grows in,
A great yellow Mandarin
With urbanity of manner
And unconsciousness of sin;
All the women, like a harem,
At his pig-tail troop along;
And, like all the East he grows in,
He is Poison when he's strong.

Tea, although an Oriental,
Is a gentleman at least;
Cocoa is a cad and coward,
Cocoa is a vulgar beast,
Cocoa is a dull, disloyal,
Lying, crawling cad and clown,
And may very well be grateful
To the fool that takes him down.

As for all the windy waters,
They were rained like tempests down
When good drink had been dishonoured
By the tipplers of the town;
When red wine had brought red ruin
And the death-dance of our times,
Heaven sent us Soda Water
As a torment for our crimes.

Note

I have always dated some decline in English character from the time when tea replaced beer on the breakfast table. I have lately been glad to find that I have in this been echoing the views of that very sound Englishman William Cobbett, who wrote more than a hundred years ago an impassioned discourse on the vice of tea drinking, which he described as a 'destroyer of health and enfeebler of the frame, an engenderer of effeminacy and laziness, a debaucher of youth, and a maker of misery for old-age.' But in Cobbett's time it was cheaper to brew home-made beer than to buy tea, and that day is far gone. The human digestion has presumably adapted itself to tea, since the soldiers of Australia and New Zealand, the most confirmed tea-drinkers I know, are certainly neither effeminate nor degenerate.   *A. P. W.*

IN PRAISE OF YOUNG GIRLS

RAYMOND ASQUITH

ATTEND, my Muse, and, if you can, approve
While I proclaim the 'speeding up' of Love,
For Love and Commerce hold a common creed,
For scale of business varies with the speed;
For Queen of Beauty and for Sausage King
The customer is always on the wing –
Then praise the nymph who regularly earns
Small profits (if you please) but quick returns;
Our modish Venus is a bustling minx,
But who can spare the time to woo a Sphinx?
When Mona Lisa posed with rustic guile,
The stale enigma of her simple smile,
Her leisured lovers raised a pious cheer,
While the slow mischief crept from ear to ear.
Poor listless Lombard, you would ne'er engage
The busier beaux of our mercurial age,
Whose lively mettle can as easy brook
An epic poem as a lingering look –
Our modern maiden smears the twig with lime
For twice as many hearts in half the time:
Long e'er the circle of that staid grimace
Has wheeled your weary dimples into place
Our little Chloe (mark the nimble fiend)
Has raised a laugh against her bosom friend,
Melted a Marquis, mollified a Jew,
Kissed every member of the Eton crew,

Ogled a Bishop, quizzed an aged peer,
Has danced a tango and has dropped a tear.
Fresh from the schoolroom, pink and plump and pert,
Bedizened, bouncing, artful and alert,
No victim she of vapours or of moods,
Though the sky fall, she's 'ready with the goods',
Will suit each client, tickle every taste,
Polite or gothic, libertine or chaste,
Supply a waspish tongue, a waspish waist,
Astarte's breast or Atalanta's leg,
Love ready made or glamour off a peg.
Do you prefer a thing of dew and air?
Or is your taste Poppaea or Polair?
The crystal casket of a maiden's dreams,
Or the last fancy in cosmetic creams?
The dark and tender or the fierce and bright,
Youth's rosy blush or Passion's pearly bite?
You hardly know perhaps; but Chloe knows
And pours you out the necessary dose,
Meticulously measuring to scale
The cup of Circe or the Holy Grail:
An actress she, at home in every role,
Can flout or flatter, bully or cajole,
And on occasion by a stretch of art
Can even speak the language of the heart,
Can lisp and sigh and make confused replies
With baby lips and complicated eyes,
Indifferently apt to weep or wink,
Primly pursue, provocatively shrink,
Brazen or bashful, as the case require,
Coax the faint baron, curb the bold esquire,
Deride restraint, but deprecate desire,
Unbridled yet unloving, loose but limp,
Voluptuary, virgin, prude and pimp.

Note

I do not think Raymond Asquith's occasional verses have ever
been published. I wish they had been. I know only a few, this

one and a parody of Kipling which began with the striking line:
'The sun like a bishop's bottom, rosy and round and hot.' What
a brilliant and attractive person he was. I was his 'junior' (fag)
for a half (term) at Winchester. He told me I was not a very good
junior, which was true, but he was very kind and tolerant. The
three most brilliant and attractive men I can remember of my
time in College at Winchester all fell in France — Raymond
Asquith, Geoffrey Smith, and my own particular friend Geoffrey
Clarke. No wonder we lacked leadership in the post-war years.

A. P. W.

TO R.K.

J. K. STEPHEN

WILL there never come a season
Which shall rid us from the curse
Of a prose which knows no reason
And an unmelodious verse:
When the world shall cease to wonder
At the genius of an Ass,
And a boy's eccentric blunder
Shall not bring success to pass:

When mankind shall be delivered
From the clash of magazines,
And the inkstand shall be shivered
Into countless smithereens:
When there stands a muzzled stripling,
Mute, beside a muzzled bore:
When the Rudyards cease from kipling
And the Haggards ride no more.

THE MASSACRE OF THE MACPHERSON

W. E. AYTOUN

I

FHAIRSHON swore a feud
  Against the clan M'Tavish;

Marched into their land
  To murder and to rafish;
For he did resolve
  To extirpate the vipers,
With four-and-twenty men
  And five-and-thirty pipers.

II

But when he had gone
  Half-way down Strath Canaan,
Of his fighting tail
  Just three were remainin'.
They were all he had,
  To back him in ta battle;
All the rest had gone
  Off, to drive ta cattle.

III

'Fery coot!' cried Fhairshon,
  'So my clan disgraced is;
Lads, we'll need to fight,
  Pefore we touch the peasties.
Here's Mhic-Mac-Methusaleh
  Coming wi' his fassals,
Gillies seventy-three,
  And sixty Dhuinéwassails!'

IV

'Coot tay to you, sir;
  Are you not ta Fhairshon?
Was you coming here
  To fisit any person?
You are a plackguard, sir!
  It is now six hundred
Coot long years, and more,
  Since my glen was plundered.'

V

'Fat is tat you say?
  Dare you cock your peaver?
I will teach you, sir,
  Fat is coot pehaviour!
You shall not exist
  For another day more;
I will shoot you, sir,
  Or stap you with my claymore!'

VI

'I am fery glad,
  To learn what you mention,
Since I can prevent
  Any such intention.'
So Mhic-Mac-Methusaleh
  Gave some warlike howls,
Trew his skhian-dhu,
  An' stuck it in his powels.

VII

In this fery way,
  Tied ta faliant Fhairshon,
Who was always thought
  A superior person.
Fhairshon had a son,
  Who married Noah's daughter,
And nearly spoiled ta Flood,
  By trinking up ta water.

VIII

Which he would have done,
  I at least pelieve it,
Had ta mixture peen
  Only half Glenlivet.
This is all my tale:
  Sirs, I hope 'tis new t'ye!
Here's your fery good healths,
  And tamn ta whusky duty!

POOR BUT HONEST
Anon

She was poor, but she was honest,
    Victim of the squire's whim:
First he loved her, then he left her,
    And she lost her honest name.

Then she ran away to London,
    For to hide her grief and shame;
There she met another squire,
    And she lost her name again.

See her riding in her carriage,
    In the Park and all so gay:
All the nibs and nobby persons
    Come to pass the time of day.

See the little old-world village
    Where her aged parents live,
Drinking the champagne she sends them
    But they never can forgive.

In the rich man's arms she flutters,
    Like a bird with broken wing:
First he loved her, then he left her,
    And she hasn't got a ring.

See him in the splendid mansion,
    Entertaining with the best,
While the girl that he has ruined,
    Entertains a sordid guest.

See him in the House of Commons,
    Making laws to put down crime,
While the victim of his passions
    Trails her way through mud and slime.

Standing on the bridge at midnight,
    She says: 'Farewell, blighted Love.'
There's a scream, a splash — Good Heavens!
    What is she a-doing of?

Then they drag her from the river,
  Water from her clothes they wrang,
For they thought that she was drownded;
  But the corpse got up and sang:

'It's the same the whole world over;
  It's the poor that gets the blame,
It's the rich that gets the pleasure.
  Isn't it a blooming shame?'

COMMON SENSE

Harry Graham

'There's been an accident!' they said,
'Your servant's cut in half; he's dead!'
'Indeed!' said Mr Jones, 'and please
Send me the half that's got my keys.'

THE MODERN TRAVELLER

Hilaire Belloc

[*Extracts*]

And yet I really must complain
About the Company's Champagne!
  This most expensive kind of wine
In England is a matter
Of pride or habit when we dine
  (Presumably the latter).
Beneath an equatorial sky
You *must* consume it or you die;
And stern indomitable men
Have told me, time and time again,
'The nuisance of the tropics is
The sheer necessity of fizz.'

   .   .   .   .

Blood understood the Native mind.
He said: 'We must be firm but kind.'
  A Mutiny resulted.
I never shall forget the way
That Blood upon this awful day
Preserved us all from death.
He stood upon a little mound,
Cast his lethargic eyes around,
And said beneath his breath:
'Whatever happens we have got
The Maxim Gun, and they have not.'

MUCKLE-MOUTH MEG

ROBERT BROWNING

FROWNED the Laird on the Lord: 'So, red-handed I catch thee?
  Death-doomed by our Law of the Border!
We've a gallows outside and a chiel to dispatch thee:
  Who trespasses — hangs: all's in order.'

He met frown with smile, did the young English gallant:
  Then the Laird's dame: 'Nay, Husband, I beg!
He's comely: be merciful! Grace for the callant
  — If he marries our Muckle-mouth Meg!'

'No mile-wide-mouthed monster of yours do I marry:
  Grant rather the gallows!' laughed he.
'Foul fare kith and kin of you — why do you tarry?'
  'To tame your fierce temper!' quoth she.

'Shove him quick in the Hole, shut him fast for a week:
  Cold, darkness and hunger work wonders:
Who lion-like roars now, mouse-fashion will squeak,
  And "it rains" soon succeed to "it thunders".'

A week did he bide in the cold and the dark
  — Not hunger: for duly at morning

In flitted a lass, and a voice like a lark
    Chirped 'Muckle-mouth Meg still ye're scorning?

'Go hang, but here's parritch to hearten ye first!'
    'Did Meg's muckle-mouth boast within some
Such music as yours, mine should match it or burst:
    No frog-jaws! So tell folk, my Winsome!'

Soon week came to end, and, from Hole's door set wide,
    Out he marched, and there waited the lassie:
'Yon gallows, or Muckle-mouth Meg for a bride!
    Consider! Sky's blue and turf's grassy:

'Life's sweet: shall I say ye wed Muckle-mouth Meg?'
    'Not I,' quoth the stout heart: 'too eerie
The mouth that can swallow a bubblyjock's egg:
    Shall I let it munch mine? Never, Dearie!'

'Not Muckle-mouth Meg? Wow, the obstinate man!
    Perhaps he would rather wed me!'
'Ay, would he — with just for a dowry your can!'
    'I'm Muckle-mouth Meg,' chirruped she.

'Then so — so — so — ' as he kissed her apace —
    'Will I widen thee out till thou turnest
From Margaret Minnikin-mou', by God's grace,
    To Muckle-mouth Meg in good earnest!'

Note

    This rather absurd little poem is probably the first of Browning's which I read, in a book of verse for the young. It is supposed to have had historical warrant in the forays of the Scottish Border. The captured lord was William Scott of Harden, an ancestor of Sir Walter Scott; the laird was Sir John Murray of Elibank. Browning has made a romance of what actually seems to have been a purely business transaction: after seven days of cold and darkness the lord agreed to marry the ill-favoured maiden without seeing her, deciding doubtless, and wisely, that a wide mouth was more tolerable than a narrow grave.   *A. P. W.*

7. HYMNS OF HATE

Dante, who loved well because he hated,
Hated wickedness that hindered loving.

Browning, like Dante, was a good hater as well as a good lover. The Englishman in general is not a good hater, except about cruelty to animals — the subject of the first three poems in this section — and usually mixes humour with his hatred. Indeed two of the poems in this section have appeared in an anthology of Comic Verse and one in an anthology of Light Verse, while Lissauer's *Hymn of Hate* was sung by our soldiers in the trenches to the Germans opposite — to their pardonable bewilderment. Kipling's indictment of the cinema (*Naaman's Song*) has often solaced me when I have been beguiled into seeing some inept production of Hollywood; it has more humour than hate.

A. P. W.

AUGURIES OF INNOCENCE

William Blake

To see a World in a grain of sand
And a Heaven in a wild flower,
Hold Infinity in the palm of your hand
And Eternity in an hour.

A robin redbreast in a cage
Puts all Heaven in a rage.
A dove house filled with doves and pigeons
Shudders Hell through all its regions.
A dog starved at his master's gate
Predicts the ruin of the State.
A horse misused upon the road
Calls to Heaven for human blood.
Each outcry of the hunted hare
A fibre from the brain does tear.
A skylark wounded in the wing,
A cherubim does cease to sing.

The game cock clipped and armed for fight
Does the rising sun affright.
Every wolf's and lion's howl
Raises from Hell a human soul.
The wild deer, wandering here and there,
Keeps the human soul from care.
The lamb misused breeds public strife
And yet forgives the butcher's knife.
The bat that flits at close of eve
Has left the brain that won't believe.
The owl that calls upon the night
Speaks the unbeliever's fright.
He who shall hurt the little wren
Shall never be beloved by men.
He who the ox to wrath has moved
Shall never be by woman loved.
The wanton boy that kills the fly
Shall feel the spider's enmity.
He who torments the chafer's sprite
Weaves a bower in endless night.
The caterpillar on the leaf
Repeats to thee thy mother's grief.
Kill not the moth nor butterfly,
For the Last Judgment draweth nigh.
He who shall train the horse to war
Shall never pass the polar bar.
The beggar's dog and widow's cat,
Feed them, and thou wilt grow fat.
The gnat that sings his summer's song
Poison gets from Slander's tongue.
The poison of the snake and newt
Is the sweat of Envy's foot.
The poison of the honey bee
Is the artist's Jealousy.
The prince's robes and beggar's rags
Are toadstools on the miser's bags.
A truth that's told with bad intent
Beats all the lies you can invent.

It is right it should be so;
Man was made for joy and woe;
And when this we rightly know
Through the world we safely go.
Joy and Woe are woven fine,
A clothing for the soul divine;
Under every grief and pine
Runs a joy with silken twine.
The babe is more than swaddling bands;
Throughout all these human lands
Tools were made, and born were hands,
Every farmer understands.
Every tear from every eye
Becomes a babe in Eternity;
This is caught by females bright
And returned to its own delight.
The bleat, the bark, bellow and roar
Are waves that beat on Heaven's shore.
The babe that weeps the rod beneath
Writes revenge in realms of Death.
The beggar's rags, fluttering in air,
Does to rags the heavens tear.
The soldier, armed with sword and gun,
Palsied strikes the summer's sun.
The poor man's farthing is worth more
Than all the gold on Africa's shore.
One mite wrung from the lab'rour's hands
Shall buy and sell the miser's lands:
Or, if protected from on high,
Does that whole nation sell and buy.
He who mocks the infant's faith
Shall be mocked in Age and Death.
He who shall teach the child to doubt
The rotting grave shall ne'er get out.
He who respects the infant's faith
Triumphs over Hell and Death.
The child's toys and the old man's reasons
Are the fruits of the two seasons.

The questioner who sits so sly
Shall never know how to reply.
He who replies to words of Doubt
Doth put the light of Knowledge out.
The strongest poison ever known
Came from Caesar's laurel crown.
Nought can deform the human race
Like to the armour's iron brace.
When gold and gems adorn the plow
To peaceful arts shall Envy bow.
A riddle or the cricket's cry
Is to Doubt a fit reply.
The emmet's inch or eagle's mile
Make lame Philosophy to smile.
He who doubts from what he sees
Will ne'er believe, do what you please.
If the Sun and Moon should doubt,
They'd immediately go out.
To be in a passion you good may do,
But no good if a passion is in you.
The whore and gambler, by the state
Licenced, build that nation's fate.
The harlot's cry from street to street
Shall weave old England's winding sheet.
The winner's shout, the loser's curse,
Dance before dead England's hearse.
Every night and every morn
Some to misery are born.
Every morn and every night
Some are born to sweet delight.
Some are born to sweet delight,
Some are born to endless night.
We are led to believe a lie
When we see not through the eye
Which was born in a night to perish in a night
When the soul slept in beams of light.
God appears and God is Light
To those poor souls who dwell in Night,

But does a human form display
To those who dwell in realms of Day.

THE BELLS OF HEAVEN

Ralph Hodgson

'Twould ring the bells of Heaven
The wildest peal for years,
If Parson lost his senses
And people came to theirs,
And he and they together
Knelt down with angry prayers
For tamed and shabby tigers,
And dancing dogs and bears,
And wretched, blind pit-ponies,
And little hunted hares.

NEVER GET OUT!

John Galsworthy

I knew a little Serval cat —
    Never get out!
Would pad all day from this to that —
    Never get out!
From bar to bar she'd turn and turn,
And in her eyes a fire would burn —
(From her Zoology we learn!)
    Never get out!

And if by hap a ray of sun –
Came shining in her cage, she'd run
And sit upon her haunches where
In the open she would stare,
And with the free that sunlight share —
    Never get out!

That catling's jungle heart forlorn
Will die as wild as it was born.
If I could cage the human race
Awhile, like her, in prisoned space,
And teach them what it is to face
    Never get out! ...

A HYMN OF HATE AGAINST ENGLAND

ERNST LISSAUER (tr. Barbara Henderson)

[*Extract*]

FRENCH and Russian they matter not,
A blow for a blow, a shot for a shot,
We fight the battle with bronze and steel,
And the time that is coming Peace will seal,
You will we hate with a lasting hate,
We will never forgo our hate,
Hate by water and hate by land,
Hate of the head and hate of the hand,
Hate of the hammer and hate of the crown,
Hate of seventy millions, choking down.
We love as one, we hate as one,
We have one foe and one alone — England!

THE CONFESSIONAL

[SPAIN]

ROBERT BROWNING

IT is a lie — their Priests, their Pope,
Their Saints, their ... all they fear or hope
Are lies, and lies — there! through my door
And ceiling, there! and walls and floor,
There, lies, they lie — shall still be hurled
Till spite of them I reach the world!

N

You think Priests just and holy men!
Before they put me in this den
I was a human creature too,
With flesh and blood like one of you,
A girl that laughed in beauty's pride
Like lilies in your world outside.

I had a lover — shame avaunt!
This poor wrenched body, grim and gaunt,
Was kissed all over till it burned,
By lips the truest love e'er turned
His heart's own tint: one night they kissed
My soul out in a burning mist.

So, next day when the accustomed train
Of things grew round my sense again,
'That is a sin,' I said: and slow
With downcast eyes to church I go,
And pass to the confession-chair,
And tell the old mild father there.

But when I falter Beltran's name,
'Ha?' quoth the father; 'much I blame
The sin; yet wherefore idly grieve?
Despair not, — strenuously retrieve!
Nay, I will turn this love of thine
To lawful love, almost divine.

For he is young, and led astray,
This Beltran, and he schemes, men say,
To change the laws of church and state;
So, thine shall be an angel's fate,
Who, ere the thunder breaks, should roll
Its cloud away and save his soul.

For, when he lies upon thy breast,
Thou may'st demand and be possessed
Of all his plans, and next day steal

To me, and all those plans reveal,
That I and every priest, to purge
His soul, may fast and use the scourge.'

That father's beard was long and white,
With love and truth his brow seemed bright;
I went back, all on fire with joy,
And, that same evening, bade the boy,
Tell me, as lovers should, heart-free,
Something to prove his love of me.

He told me what he would not tell
For hope of Heaven or fear of Hell;
And I lay listening in such pride!
And, soon as he had left my side,
Tripped to the church by morning-light
To save his soul in his despite.

I told the father all his schemes,
Who were his comrades, what their dreams,
'And now make haste,' I said, 'to pray
The one spot from his soul away;
To-night he comes, but not the same
Will look!' At night he never came.

Nor next night: on the after-morn,
I went forth with a strength new-born.
The church was empty; something drew
My steps into the street; I knew
It led me to the market-place:
Where, lo, on high, the father's face!

That horrible black scaffold drest,
That stapled block ... God sink the rest!
That head strapped back, that blinding vest,
Those knotted hands and naked breast,
Till near one busy hangman pressed,
And, on the neck these arms caressed ...

No part in aught they hope or fear!
No Heaven with them, no Hell! — and here,
No Earth, not so much space as pens
My body in their worst of dens
But shall bear God and Man my cry,
Lies — lies, again — and still, they lie!

THE LATEST DECALOGUE

Arthur Hugh Clough

Thou shalt have one God only; who
Would be at the expense of two?

No graven images may be
Worshipped, except the currency:

Swear not at all; for, for thy curse
Thine enemy is none the worse:

At church on Sunday to attend
Will serve to keep the world thy friend:

Honour thy parents; that is, all
From whom advancement may befall:

Thou shalt not kill; but need'st not strive
Officiously to keep alive:

Do not adultery commit;
Advantage rarely comes of it:

Thou shalt not steal; an empty feat,
When it's so lucrative to cheat:

Bear not false witness; let the lie
Have time on its own wings to fly:

Thou shalt not covet, but tradition
Approves all forms of competition.

SOLILOQUY OF THE SPANISH CLOISTER

ROBERT BROWNING

Gr-r-r — there go, my heart's abhorrence!
  Water your damned flower-pots, do!
If hate killed men, Brother Lawrence,
  God's blood, would not mine kill you!
What? your myrtle-bush wants trimming?
  Oh, that rose has prior claims —
Needs its leaden vase filled brimming?
  Hell dry you up with its flames!

At the meal we sit together:
  Salve tibi! I must hear
Wise talk of the kind of weather,
  Sort of season, time of year:
Not a plenteous cork-crop: scarcely
  Dare we hope oak-galls, I doubt:
What's the Latin name for 'parsley'?
  What's the Greek name for Swine's Snout?

Whew! We'll have our platter burnished,
  Laid with care on our own shelf!
With a fire-new spoon we're furnished,
  And a goblet for ourself,
Rinsed like something sacrificial
  Ere 'tis fit to touch our chaps —
Marked with L. for our initial!
  (He-he! There his lily snaps!)

Saint, forsooth! While brown Dolores
  Squats outside the Convent bank,
With Sanchicha, telling stories,
  Steeping tresses in the tank,
Blue-black, lustrous, thick like horse-hairs,
  — Can't I see his dead eye glow,
Bright as 'twere a Barbary corsair's?
  (That is, if he'd let it show!)

When he finishes refection,
  Knife and fork he never lays
Cross-wise, to my recollection,
  As do I, in Jesu's praise.
I, the Trinity illustrate,
  Drinking watered orange-pulp —
In three sips the Arian frustrate;
  While he drains his at one gulp!

Oh, those melons! If he's able
  We're to have a feast; so nice!
One goes to the Abbot's table,
  All of us get each a slice.
How go on your flowers? None double?
  Not one fruit-sort can you spy?
Strange! — And I, too, at such trouble,
  Keep them close-nipped on the sly!

There's a great text in Galatians,
  Once you trip on it, entails
Twenty-nine distinct damnations,
  One sure, if another fails:
If I trip him just a-dying,
  Sure of Heaven as sure can be,
Spin him round and send him flying
  Off to Hell, a Manichee?

Or, my scrofulous French novel
  On grey paper with blunt type!
Simply glance at it, you grovel
  Hand and foot in Belial's gripe:
If I double down its pages
  At the woeful sixteenth print,
When he gathers his greengages,
  Ope a sieve and slip it in't?

Or, there's Satan! — one might venture
  Pledge one's soul to him, yet leave
Such a flaw in the indenture
  As he'd miss till, past retrieve

Blasted lay that rose-acacia
   We're so proud of! *Hy, Zy, Hine ...*
'St, there's Vespers! *Plena gratiâ*
   Ave, Virgo! Gr-r-r — you swine!

A POISON TREE

William Blake

I was angry with my friend:
I told my wrath, my wrath did end.
I was angry with my foe:
I told it not, my wrath did grow.

And I water'd it in fears,
Night and morning with my tears;
And I sunned it with smiles,
And with soft deceitful wiles.

And it grew both day and night,
Till it bore an apple bright;
And my foe beheld it shine,
And he knew that it was mine,

And into my garden stole
When the night had veil'd the pole:
In the morning glad I see
My foe outstretch'd beneath the tree.

THE LOST LEADER

Robert Browning

Just for a handful of silver he left us,
   Just for a riband to stick in his coat —
Found the one gift of which fortune bereft us,
   Lost all the others she lets us devote;
They, with the gold to give, doled him out silver,

So much was theirs who so little allowed;
How all our copper had gone for his service!
  Rags — were they purple, his heart had been proud!
We that had loved him so, followed him, honoured him,
  Lived in his mild and magnificent eye,
Learned his great language, caught his clear accents,
  Made him our pattern to live and to die!
Shakespeare was of us, Milton was for us,
  Burns, Shelley, were with us — they watch from their graves!
He alone breaks from the van and the freemen,
  He alone sinks to the rear and the slaves!

We shall march prospering, — not thro' his presence;
  Songs may inspirit us, — not from his lyre;
Deeds will be done, — while he boasts his quiescence,
  Still bidding crouch whom the rest bade aspire:
Blot out his name, then, record one lost soul more,
  One task more declined, one more footpath untrod,
One more devil's triumph and sorrow for angels,
  One wrong more to man, one more insult to God!
Life's night begins: let him never come back to us!
  There would be doubt, hesitation and pain,
Forced praise on our part — the glimmer of twilight,
  Never glad confident morning again!
Best fight on well, for we taught him, — strike gallantly,
  Menace our heart ere we master his own;
Then let him receive the new knowledge and wait us,
  Pardoned in Heaven, the first by the throne!

Note

This poem is generally supposed to have been prompted by
Wordsworth's abandonment of the Liberal cause. Shelley also
wrote a satire on Wordsworth — Peter Bell the Third, who he
claimed had been bought into the devil's pay for half-a-crown.
It is ill for a poet to fall out with his more robust contemporaries.

                                        A. P. W.

GEHAZI

Rudyard Kipling

Whence comest thou, Gehazi,
  So reverend to behold,
In scarlet and in ermines
  And chain of England's gold?
'From following after Naaman
  To tell him all is well,
Whereby my zeal hath made me
  A Judge in Israel.'

Well done, well done, Gehazi!
  Stretch forth thy ready hand.
Thou barely 'scaped from judgment,
  Take oath to judge the land
Unswayed by gift of money
  Or privy bribe, more base,
Of knowledge which is profit
  In any market-place.

Search out and probe, Gehazi,
  As thou of all canst try,
The truthful, well-weighed answer
  That tells the blacker lie —
The loud, uneasy virtue,
  The answer feigned at will,
To overbear a witness
  And make the Court keep still.

Take order now, Gehazi,
  That no man talk aside
In secret with his judges
  The while his case is tried.
Lest he should show them — reason
  To keep a matter hid,
And subtly lead the questions
  Away from what he did.

Thou mirror of uprightness,
   What ails thee at thy vows?
What means the risen whiteness
   Of the skin between thy brows?
The boils that shine and burrow,
   The sores that slough and bleed —
The leprosy of Naaman
   On thee and all thy seed?

Stand up, stand up, Gehazi,
   Draw close thy robe and go,
Gehazi, Judge in Israel,
   A leper white as snow!

HOLY-CROSS DAY

Robert Browning

Fee, faw, fum! bubble and squeak!
Blessedest Thursday's the fat of the week.
Rumble and tumble, sleek and rough,
Stinking and savoury, smug and gruff,
Take the church-road, for the bell's due chime
Gives us the summons — 'tis sermon-time.

Boh, here's Barnabas! Job, that's you?
Up stumps Solomon — bustling too?
Shame, man! greedy beyond your years
To handsel the bishop's shaving-shears?
Fair play's a jewel! leave friends in the lurch?
Stand on a line ere you start for the church.

Higgledy piggledy, packed we lie,
Rats in a hamper, swine in a sty,
Wasps in a bottle, frogs in a sieve,
Worms in a carcase, fleas in a sleeve.
Hist! square shoulders, settle your thumbs
And buzz for the bishop — here he comes.

Bow, wow, wow — a bone for the dog!
I liken his Grace to an acorned hog.
What, a boy at his side, with the bloom of a lass,
To help and handle my lord's hour-glass!
Didst ever behold so lithe a chine?
His cheek hath laps like a fresh-singed swine.

Aaron's asleep — shove hip to haunch,
Or somebody deal him a dig in the paunch!
Look at the purse with the tassel and knob,
And the gown with the angel and thingumbob.
What's he at, quotha? reading his text!
Now you've his curtsey — and what comes next?

See to our converts — you doomed black dozen —
No stealing away — nor cog nor cozen!
You five that were thieves, deserve it fairly;
You seven that were beggars, will live less sparely;
You took your turn and dipped in the hat,
Got fortune — and fortune gets you; mind that!

Give your first groan — compunction's at work;
And soft! from a Jew you mount to a Turk.
Lo, Micah, — the selfsame beard on chin
He was four times already converted in!
Here's a knife, clip quick — it's a sign of grace —
Or he ruins us all with his hanging-face.

Whom now is the bishop a-leering at?
I know a point where his text falls pat.
I'll tell him to-morrow, a word just now
Went to my heart and made me vow
I meddle no more with the worst of trades —
Let somebody else pay his serenades.

Groan all together now, whee — hee — hee!
It's a-work, it's a-work, ah, woe is me!
It began, when a herd of us, picked and placed,

Were spurred through the Corso, stripped to the waist;
Jew-brutes, with sweat and blood well spent
To usher in worthily Christian Lent.

It grew, when the hangman entered our bounds,
Yelled, pricked us out to his church like hounds.
It got to a pitch, when the hand indeed
Which gutted my purse, would throttle my creed
And it overflows, when, to even the odd,
Men I helped to their sins, help me to their God.

But now, while the scapegoats leave our flock,
And the rest sit silent and count the clock,
Since forced to muse the appointed time
On these precious facts and truths sublime, —
Let us fitly employ it, under our breath,
In saying Ben Ezra's Song of Death.

For Rabbi Ben Ezra, the night he died,
Called sons and sons' sons to his side,
And spoke, 'This world has been harsh and strange;
Something is wrong: there needeth a change.
But what, or where? at the last, or first?
In one point only we sinned, at worst.

'The Lord will have mercy on Jacob yet,
And again in his border see Israel set.
When Judah beholds Jerusalem,
The stranger-seed shall be joined to them:
To Jacob's House shall the Gentiles cleave.
So the Prophet saith and his sons believe.

'Ay, the children of the chosen race
Shall carry and bring them to their place:
In the land of the Lord shall lead the same,
Bondsmen and handmaids. Who shall blame,
When the slaves enslave, the oppressed ones o'er
The oppressor triumph for evermore?

'God spoke, and gave us the word to keep:
Bade never fold the hands nor sleep
'Mid a faithless world, — at watch and ward,
Till Christ at the end relieve our guard.
By His servant Moses the watch was set:
Though near upon cock-crow, we keep it yet.

'Thou! if Thou wast He, who at mid-watch came,
By the starlight, naming a dubious name!
And if, too heavy with sleep — too rash
With fear — O Thou, if that martyr-gash
Fell on Thee coming to take Thine own,
And we gave the Cross, when we owed the Throne —

'Thou art the Judge. We are bruised thus.
But, the judgment over, join sides with us!
Thine too is the cause! and not more Thine
Than ours, is the work of these dogs and swine,
Whose life laughs through and spits at their creed,
Who maintain Thee in word, and defy Thee in deed!

'We withstood Christ then? be mindful how
At least we withstand Barabbas now!
Was our outrage sore? but the worst we spared,
To have called these — Christians, had we dared!
Let defiance to them pay mistrust of Thee,
And Rome make amends for Calvary!

'By the torture, prolonged from age to age,
By the infamy, Israel's heritage,
By the Ghetto's plague, by the garb's disgrace,
By the badge of shame, by the felon's place,
By the branding-tool, the bloody whip,
And the summons to Christian fellowship, —

'We boast our proof that at least the Jew
Would wrest Christ's name from the Devil's crew.
Thy face took never so deep a shade

But we fought them in it, God our aid!
A trophy to bear, as we march, Thy band
South, East, and on to the Pleasant Land!'

LINES TO A DON

Hilaire Belloc

Remote and ineffectual Don
That dared attack my Chesterton,
With that poor weapon, half-impelled,
Unlearnt, unsteady, hardly held,
Unworthy for a tilt with men —
Your quavering and corroded pen;
Don poor at Bed and worse at Table,
Don pinched, Don starved, Don miserable;
Don stuttering, Don with roving eyes,
Don nervous, Don of crudities;
Don clerical, Don ordinary,
Don self-absorbed and solitary;
Don here-and-there, Don epileptic;
Don puffed and empty, Don dyspeptic;
Don middle-class, Don sycophantic,
Don dull, Don brutish, Don pedantic;
Don hypocritical, Don bad,
Don furtive, Don three-quarters mad;
Don (since a man must make an end),
Don that shall never be my friend.

.   .   .   .   .

Don different from those regal Dons!
With hearts of gold and lungs of bronze,
Who shout and bang and roar and bawl
The Absolute across the hall,
Or sail in amply billowing gown
Enormous through the Sacred Town,
Bearing from College to their homes

Deep cargoes of gigantic tomes;
Dons admirable! Dons of Might!
Uprising on my inward sight
Compact of ancient tales, and port
And sleep — and learning of a sort.
Dons English, worthy of the land;
Dons rooted; Dons that understand.
Good Dons perpetual that remain
A landmark, walling in the plain —
The horizon of my memories
Like large and comfortable trees.

.   .   .   .   .

Don very much apart from these,
Thou scapegoat Don, thou Don devoted,
Don to thine own damnation quoted,
Perplexed to find thy trivial name
Reared in my verse to lasting shame.
Don dreadful, rasping Don and wearing,
Repulsive Don — Don past all bearing.
Don of the cold and doubtful breath,
Don despicable, Don of death;
Don nasty, skimpy, silent, level;
Don evil; Don that serves the devil.
Don ugly — that makes fifty lines.
There is a Canon which confines
A Rhymed Octosyllabic Curse
If written in Iambic Verse
To fifty lines. I never cut;
I far prefer to end it — but
Believe me I shall soon return.
My fires are banked, but still they burn
To write some more about the Don
That dared attack my Chesterton.

NAAMAN'S SONG
Rudyard Kipling

'Go, wash thyself in Jordan — go, wash thee and be clean!'
Nay, not for any Prophet will I plunge a toe therein!
For the banks of curious Jordan are parcelled into sites,
Commanded and embellished and patrolled by Israelites.

There rise her timeless capitals of Empires daily born,
Whose plinths are laid at midnight, and whose streets are packed at
morn;
And here come hired youths and maids that feign to love or sin
In tones like rusty razor-blades to tunes like smitten tin.

And here be merry murtherings, and steeds with fiery hooves;
And furious hordes with guns and swords, and clamberings over
rooves;
And horrid tumblings down from Heaven, and flights with wheels
and wings;
And always one weak virgin who is chased through all these things.

And here is mock of faith and truth, for children to behold;
And every door of ancient dirt reopened to the old;
With every word that taints the speech, and show that weakens
thought;
And Israel watcheth over each, and — doth not watch for nought....

But Pharphar — but Abana — which Hermon launcheth down —
They perish fighting desert-sands beyond Damascus-town.
But yet their pulse is of the snows — their strength is from on high,
And, if they cannot cure my woes, a leper will I die!

8. RAGBAG

Ever since I have known her my wife has had a large bag of odd pieces of sober or highly coloured brocade out of which she has meant to construct a patchwork quilt. The bag used always to accompany us on week-ends or on longer travels but the patchwork quilt has never got patched, though the bits of material were often laid out and admired; this and adding to them has obviously given my wife much pleasure.

This section represents a similar ragbag of my poetical memory, pieces of poems that have been put away and are sometimes pulled out to sort over; or little bits are added. I never meant to make a patchwork quilt of them though they are no more oddly assorted than my wife's pieces of brocade. Some of her friends used to enjoy looking through her brocade ragbag, perhaps some of my readers may like to turn over my poetical ragbag.   *A. P. W.*

KILMENY

James Hogg

[Extract]

When many a day had come and fled,
When grief grew calm, and hope was dead,
When mass for Kilmeny's soul had been sung,
When the bedesman had pray'd and the dead bell rung,
Late, late in the gloamin' when all was still,
When the fringe was red on the westlin hill,
The wood was sere, the moon i' the wane,
The reek o' the cot hung over the plain,
Like a little wee cloud in the world its lane;
When the ingle low'd wi' an eiry leme,
Late, late in the gloamin' Kilmeny came hame!

Kilmeny, Kilmeny, where have you been?
Lang hae we sought baith holt and den;
By linn, by ford, and green-wood tree,
Yet you are halesome and fair to see.

Where gat you that joup o' the lily scheen?
That bonnie snood of the birk sae green?
And these roses, the fairest that ever were seen?
Kilmeny, Kilmeny, where have you been?

Kilmeny look'd up with a lovely grace,
But nae smile was seen on Kilmeny's face;
As still was her look, and as still was her e'e,
As the stillness that lay on the emerant lea,
Or the mist that sleeps on a waveless sea.
For Kilmeny had been, she knew not where,
And Kilmeny had seen what she could not declare;
Kilmeny had been where the cock never crew,
Where the rain never fell, and the wind never blew.
But it seem'd as the harp of the sky had rung,
And the airs of heaven play'd round her tongue,
When she spake of the lovely forms she had seen,
And a land where sin had never been;
A land of love and a land of light,
Withouten sun, or moon, or night;
Where the river swa'd a living stream,
And the land a pure celestial beam;
The land of vision, it would seem,
A still, an everlasting dream.

SCOTLAND YET

from THE CANADIAN BOAT SONG

FROM the lone sheiling of the misty island
Mountains divide us, and the waste of seas —
Yet still the blood is strong, the heart is Highland,
And we in dreams behold the Hebrides.

Note

Attributed to D. M. Moir, but the authorship is disputed.
Someone has even troubled to write a whole book on this literary
problem.
                                                    A. P. W.

FAITH

from SACRIFICE *by*

RALPH WALDO EMERSON

THOUGH love repine, and reason chafe,
  There came a voice without reply, —
'Tis man's perdition to be safe,
  When for the truth he ought to die.'

QUESTIONS

C. B. T.

How can she catch the sunlight
And bind it in her hair?
Where is the golden apple
Whose core is not despair?
How shall one cull the honey
And yet not rob the flower?
And how can man, being happy,
Still keep his happy hour?

Note

These lines were written by a friend of mine, the late Lord
Thomson of Cardington who was killed in the disaster to the
R.101. We did the Staff College course together and were good
friends until his death. 'C. B.' was one of the most amusing com-
panions I have had; a genuine socialist in principle, a confirmed
sybarite in practice; a good and witty talker on all subjects, with
much skill in the French tongue, in the choice of wines and
food, in the blandishment of fair ladies. He never wrote other
poetry as far as I know, and I never saw these lines in print. He
quoted them to me one day — I think he said some journal had
given him guineas for them but I forget which — and they have
always stayed in my head, to remind me of a gay and gallant
friend.   *A. P. W.*

ELIZABETH OF BOHEMIA

from ON HIS MISTRESS, THE QUEEN OF BOHEMIA *by*

SIR HENRY WOTTON

You meaner beauties of the night,
That poorly satisfy our eyes
More by your number than your light,
You common people of the skies;
What are you, when the Moon shall rise?

Note

I was once walking down Piccadilly with my friend C. B. of the
poem *Questions*, on the night of a full harvest moon. C. B., warmed
by a good dinner and good wine was speaking in poetical strain
of the moon, when a lady of the night accosted him. He paused,
pointed to the moon, and addressed the lady in the words of Sir
Henry Wotton. With one horrified glance she fled.   *A. P. W.*

STRONG LOVE

from ADDITIONAL POEMS, No. iv, printed in 'A. E. H.' *by*

A. E. HOUSMAN

If death and time are stronger
A love may yet be strong;
The world will last for longer,
But this will last for long.

WISDOM?

from THE TEAK FOREST *by*

LAURENCE HOPE

For this is Wisdom; to love, to live,
To take what Fate, or the Gods, may give,
To ask no question, to make no prayer,
But to kiss the lips and caress the hair,
Speed passion's ebb as you greet its flow, —
To have, — to hold, — and, — in time, — let go!

Note

'I gave my heart to know wisdom, and to know madness and folly: I perceived that this also is vexation of spirit. For in much wisdom is much grief.' (Ecclesiastes i.)

THE CHASE AND THE RACE

from YE WEARIE WAYFARER *by*

ADAM LINDSAY GORDON

YET if once we efface the joys of the chase
　From the land, and outroot the Stud,
Good-bye to the Anglo-Saxon race!
　Farewell to the Norman blood!

MAN'S TESTAMENT

ADAM LINDSAY GORDON

QUESTION not, but live and labour
　Till yon goal be won,
Helping every feeble neighbour,
　Seeking help from none;
Life is mostly froth and bubble,
　Two things stand like stone,
Kindness in another's trouble,
　Courage in your own.

THE LITTLE MEN

from THE FAIRIES *by*

WILLIAM ALLINGHAM

UP the airy mountain,
　Down the rushy glen,
We daren't go a-hunting
　For fear of little men;
Wee folk, good folk,
　Trooping altogether;
Green jacket, red cap,
　And white owl's feather.

THE EAST A-CALLIN'

from AVE IMPERATRIX *by*

OSCAR WILDE

THE almond groves of Samarkand,
   Bokhara, where red lilies blow,
And Oxus, by whose yellow sand
   The grave white-turbaned merchants go.

And on from thence to Ispahan,
   The golden garden of the sun,
Whence the long dusty caravan
   Brings cedar and vermilion....

THE GOLDEN ROAD

from HASSAN *by*

JAMES ELROY FLECKER

WE are the Pilgrims, master; we shall go
   Always a little further: it may be
Beyond that last blue mountain barred with snow
   Across that angry or that glimmering sea.
White on a throne or guarded in a cave
   There lives a prophet who can understand
Why men were born: but surely we are brave
   Who take the Golden Road to Samarkand.

FEY

from THE BATTLE OF OTTERBOURNE

ANON

BUT I hae dream'd a dreary dream
   Beyont the Isle of Skye;
I saw a dead man win a fight,
   And I think that man was I.

CHALLENGE

from MARMION *by*

SIR WALTER SCOTT

MUCH honoured were my humble home
If in its halls King James should come;
But Nottingham has archers good,
And Yorkshire men are stern of mood;
Northumbrian prickers wild and rude,
On Derby hills the paths are steep;
In Ouse and Tyne the fords are deep;
And many a banner will be torn,
And many a knight to earth be borne,
And many a sheaf of arrows spent
Ere Scotland's King should cross the Trent.

MARMION AND DOUGLAS

SIR WALTER SCOTT

'THE hand of Douglas is his own;
And never shall in friendly grasp
The hand of such as Marmion clasp.'
Burned Marmion's swarthy cheek like fire
And shook his very frame for ire,
   And 'This to me!' he said, —
'An 'twere not for thy hoary beard,
Such hand as Marmion's had not spared
   To cleave the Douglas' head!
And, first I tell thee, haughty Peer,
He, who does England's message here,
Although the meanest in her state,
May well, proud Angus, be thy mate:
And, Douglas, more I tell thee here,
   Even in thy pitch of pride,
Here in thy hold, thy vassals near,
(Nay, never look upon your lord
And lay your hands upon your sword,)

I tell thee, thou art defied!
And if thou said'st I am not peer
To any lord in Scotland here,
Highland or Lowland, far or near,
  Lord Angus, thou hast lied!'
On the Earl's cheek the flush of rage
O'ercame the ashen hue of age:
Fierce he broke forth, — 'And darest thou, then
To beard the lion in his den,
  The Douglas in his hall?
And hopest thou thence unscathed to go? —
No, by Saint Bride of Bothwell, no!
Up drawbridge, grooms — what, Warder, ho!
  Let the portcullis fall.'
Lord Marmion turned, — well was his need
And dashed the rowels in his steed,
Like arrow through the archway sprung,
The ponderous gate behind him rung:
To pass there was such scanty room
The bars, descending, razed his plume.

The steed along the drawbridge flies
Just as it trembled on the rise;
Nor lighter does the swallow skim
Along the smooth lake's level brim.
And when Lord Marmion reached his band,
He halts, and turns his clenched hand,
And shout of loud defiance pours,
And shook his gauntlet at the towers.

Note

  Marmion, whatever his faults, was a stout soldier with a gift
for putting it across anyone who challenged him with sword or
tongue, as these two examples show.
  I have seen a tale somewhere that the first of these extracts —
Marmion's reply at the Scottish Court to a threat of invasion —
was quoted by an Englishman before the last war at a German
dinner table, over which some Huns, heated with wine, had

spoken openly and contemptuously of *Der Tag* and the invasion
of England. An apposite quotation if the Hun had the wit to
understand it.

One of my childhood's books had a striking coloured illustra-
tion of Marmion defying Douglas; so this passage is one of the
earliest rags in my bag.   *A. P. W.*

THE EAST

from OBERMANN ONCE MORE *by*

MATTHEW ARNOLD

THE East bow'd low before the blast,
In patient, deep disdain.
She let the legions thunder past,
And plunged in thought again.

Note

If Mr Gandhi knows these lines he probably quotes them in
support of his doctrine of non-violence, which really is traditional
in the Hindu caste system, by which the warrior class was small
and privileged and the mass of the people had no part in war.
                                             A. P. W.

ALEXANDER'S FEAST

JOHN DRYDEN

[*Extract*]

'TWAS at the royal feast for Persia won
  By Philip's warlike son;
Aloft in awful state
The godlike hero sate
  On his imperial throne;
His valiant peers were placed around;
Their brows with roses and with myrtles bound.
  (So should desert in arms be crowned:)
The lovely Thaïs by his side,

Sate like a blooming Eastern bride
In flower of youth and beauty's pride.
Happy, happy, happy pair!
None but the brave,
None but the brave,
None but the brave deserve the fair.

Note

Whatever the deserts are, it is the bold rather than the merely brave who usually get the fair. On the other hand, the shy need never give up hope, some fair will get them one day; a woman out gunning never disdains a sitting shot.   *A. P. W.*

THE BIRKENHEAD

from THE BIRKENHEAD *by*

Sir Henry Yule

The troopship *Birkenhead* was wrecked off Simon's Bay, South Africa, on February 26th, 1852. She had on board close on 700 souls; most of them were soldiers, drafts of the 12th Lancers, 60th Rifles, 2nd, 6th, 43rd, 45th, 73rd, 74th, and 91st Regiments (now the Queen's, Royal Warwickshire, Oxfordshire and Buckinghamshire Light Infantry, Sherwood Foresters, The Black Watch (2nd battalion), Highland Light Infantry, and Argyll and Sutherland Highlanders). The boats would hold only 138, and were used for the women and children. The soldiers were drawn up on deck by their officers and went down with the ship, maintaining perfect discipline to the end.

Not with the cheer of battle in the throat,
Or cannon-glare din to stir their blood,
But, roused from dreams of home to find their boat
Fast sinking, mustered on the deck they stood,
Biding God's pleasure and their chief's command.
Calm was the sea, but not less calm that band
Close ranged upon the poop, with bated breath,
But flinching not though eye to eye with death.

Heroes! Who were those heroes? Veterans steeled
To face the King of Terrors mid the scaith
Of many a hurricane and trenchèd field?
Far other: weavers from the stocking-frame;
Boys from the plough; cornets with beardless chin,
But steeped in honour and in discipline.

Note

Not great poetry, but it commemorates a great feat, the account
of which the King of Prussia ordered to be read on parade to all
units of his army as an example of discipline.   *A. P. W.*

SWAN SONG

from THE GARDEN OF PROSERPINE *by*

ALGERNON CHARLES SWINBURNE

WE are not sure of sorrow;
    And joy was never sure;
To-day will die to-morrow;
    Time stoops to no man's lure;
And love grown faint and fretful,
With lips but half regretful
Sighs, and with eyes forgetful
    Weeps that no loves endure.

From too much love of living,
    From hope and fear set free,
We thank with brief thanksgiving
    Whatever gods may be
That no man lives for ever,
That dead men rise up never;
That even the weariest river
    Winds somewhere safe to sea.

COURAGE
(THE PRAYER)
JOHN GALSWORTHY

IF on a Spring night I went by
And God were standing there,
What is the prayer that I would cry
To Him? This is the prayer:
   O Lord of courage grave,
   O Master of this night of Spring!
   Make firm in me a heart too brave
   To ask Thee anything!

THE WHITE CLIFFS
ALICE DUER MILLER
[*Extract*]

I HAVE seen much to hate here — much to forgive,
   But in a world where England is finished and dead
I do not wish to live.

MY CANDLE
EDNA ST VINCENT MILLAY

MY candle burns at both ends;
   It will not last the night;
But ah, my foes, and oh, my friends —
   It gives a lovely light!

THE TOKENS
from DAISY *by*
FRANCIS THOMPSON

HER beauty smoothed earth's furrowed face.
   She gave me tokens three: —
A look, a word of her winsome mouth,
   And a wild raspberry.

A berry red, a guileless look,
   A still word, — strings of sand!
And yet they made my wild, wild heart
   Fly down to her little hand.

CARPE DIEM

from IN THE EARLY, PEARLY MORNING *by*

LAURENCE HOPE

AND if Fate remember later, and come to claim her due,
What sorrow will be greater than the Joy I had with you?
For to-day, lit by your laughter, between the crushing years,
I will chance, in the hereafter, eternities of tears.

LITANY

from A HYMN *by*

G. K. CHESTERTON

FROM all that terror teaches,
   From lies of tongue and pen,
From all the easy speeches
   That comfort cruel men,
From sale and profanation
   Of honour and the sword,
From sleep and from damnation,
   Deliver us, good Lord!

WHO GOES HOME?

G. K. CHESTERTON

[*Extract*]

MEN that are men again; who goes home?
Tocsin and trumpeter; who goes home?
For there's blood on the field and blood on the foam
And blood on the body when Man goes home.
And a voice valedictory ... Who is for victory?
Who is for Liberty? Who goes home?

ENGLAND

from THE RETURN *by*

RUDYARD KIPLING

IF England were what England seems
An' not the England of our dreams
But only putty, brass an' paint
'Ow quick we'd drop 'er. But she ain't.

GREECE

from CLEON *by*

ROBERT BROWNING

CLEON the poet, (from the sprinkled isles,
Lily on lily, that o'erlace the sea,
And laugh their pride when the light wave lisps 'Greece') —
To Protos in his Tyranny: much health!

THE JUDGMENT OF PARIS

from GODDESSES THREE *in*
WINCHESTER COLLEGE SONGS

ANON

AH! but the third one, ah! but the third,
She only raised her beautiful eyes,
Uttered she not one single word,
Yet she it was that bore off the prize.

THE WIDE, WIDE WORLD

from IN THE NEOLITHIC AGE *by*

RUDYARD KIPLING

STILL the world is wondrous large, — seven seas from marge to
marge —
And it holds a vast of various kinds of man;
And the wildest dreams of Kew are the facts of Khatmandhu
And the crimes of Clapham chaste at Martaban.

GREATNESS

from LLYN-Y-DREIDDIAD-VRAWD, THE POOL OF THE DIVING FRIAR, *in*
CROCHET CASTLE *by*

THOMAS LOVE PEACOCK

HE took castle and towns; he cut short limbs and lives;
He made orphans and widows of children and wives;
This course many years he triumphantly ran,
And did mischief enough to be called a great man.

DODOISM

from THE PARADISE OF BIRDS *by*

W. J. COURTHOPE

By all the Dodos! these are thoughts of weight,
Most venerable, wise, and out of date.

ONE-AND-TWENTY

SAMUEL JOHNSON

[*Extract*]

WEALTH, my lad, was made to wander,
   Let it wander as it will;
Call the jockey, call the pander,
   Bid them come and take their fill.

When the bonny blade carouses,
   Pockets full, and spirits high —
What are acres? What are houses?
   Only dirt, or wet or dry.

JACOBITE TOAST

(TO AN OFFICER IN THE ARMY)

JOHN BYROM

GOD bless the King, I mean the Faith's Defender;
God bless — no harm in blessing — the Pretender;
But who Pretender is, or who is King,
God bless us all — that's quite another thing.

FARMERS

ANON

MAN to the plough,
Wife to the cow,
Girl to the yarn,
. Boy to the barn,
And your rent will be netted;
But
Man tally-ho,
Miss Piano,
Wife silk and satin,
Boy Greek and Latin,
And you'll soon be gazetted.

Note
I learnt this from Lord Allenby with whom it was a favourite.
A. P. W.

MAXIM

from CERTAIN MAXIMS OF HAFIZ *by*

RUDYARD KIPLING

IF He play, being young and unskilful, for shekhels of silver and gold,
Take His money, my son, praising Allah. The kid was ordained to be
sold.

Note

This has stuck in my head simply because a friend with whom I frequently played poker used to say often at the end of a hand: 'Take the money, my son, praising Allah.' One day I found the reference.   *A. P. W.*

EPIGRAMS

I

Sir John Harrington

Treason doth never prosper; what the reason?
For if it prosper, none dare call it treason.

II

Hilaire Belloc

When I am dead, I hope it may be said:
His sins were scarlet, but his books were read.

III

W. N. Ewer

How odd
Of God
To choose
The Jews.

IV

Richard Garnett

'I hardly ever ope my lips,' one cries;
    'Simonides, what think you of my rule?'
'If you're a fool, I think you're very wise;
    If you are wise, I think you are a fool.'

O

THE SICK STOCKRIDER

ADAM LINDSAY GORDON

[Extracts]

I'VE had my share of pastime, and I've done my share of toil,
    And life is short — the longest life a span;
I care not now to tarry for the corn or for the oil,
    Or for the wine that maketh glad the heart of man.
For good undone, and gifts misspent, and resolutions vain,
    'Tis somewhat late to trouble. This I know —
I should live the same life over, if I had to live again;
    And the chances are I go where most men go.

THE TOUCH

from MY DEAR AND ONLY LOVE *by*

JAMES GRAHAM, Marquis of Montrose

HE either fears his fate too much,
    Or his deserts are small,
That puts it not unto the touch
    To win or lose it all.

GRACE

ROBERT HERRICK

HERE a little child I stand
Heaving up my either hand;
Cold as puddocks though they be,
Here I lift them up to Thee,
For a benison to fall
On our meat, and on us all.

WILDNESS

from INVERSNAID *by*
GERARD MANLEY HOPKINS

WHAT would the world be, once bereft
Of wet and of wildness? Let them be left,
O let them be left, wildness and wet,
Long live the weeds and the wilderness yet.

BLONDIE GOES TO HEAVEN

PAUL said and Peter said,
And all the saints alive or dead,
Vowed she had the sweetest head
Of yellow, yellow hair.

Note

This scrap for my Ragbag was given me by a friend, but neither
she nor I know its origin. *A. P. W.*

Note to the Revised Edition

Several friends have sent me the whole of this attractive piece,
which is given below. *A.P.W.*

THE KYE-SONG OF ST BRIDE

FIONA MACLEOD

O sweet St Bride of the
Yellow, yellow hair:
Paul said, and Peter said,
And all the saints alive or dead
Vowed she had the sweetest head,
Bonnie, sweet St Bride of the
Yellow, yellow hair.

White may my milkin' be,
White as thee:
Thy face is white, thy neck is white,
Thy hands are white, thy feet are white,
For thy sweet soul is shinin' bright —
O dear to me,
O dear to see,
St Bridget white!

Yellow may my butter be,
Firm and round:
Thy breasts are sweet,
Firm, round and sweet,
So may my butter be:
So may my butter be O
Bridget sweet!

Safe thy way is, safe, O
Safe, St Bride:
May my kye come home at even,
None be fallin', none be leavin',
Dusky even, breath-sweet even,
Here, as there, where O
St Bride thou

Keepest tryst with God in heav'n,
Seest the angels bow
And souls be shriven —
Here as there, 'tis breath-sweet even
Far and wide —
Singeth thy little maid
Safe in thy shade
Bridget, Bride!

THE BRAVE

G. K. CHESTERTON

Is there not pardon for the brave
And broad release above
Who lost their heads for liberty
Or lost their hearts for love?
Or is the wise man wise indeed
Whom larger thoughts keep whole,
Who sees life equal like a chart,
Made strong to play the saner part
And keep his head and keep his heart
And only lose his soul?

TOO LATE

from THE PRINCE'S PROGRESS *by*

CHRISTINA ROSSETTI

Too late for love, too late for joy,
    Too late, too late!
You loiter'd on the road too long,
    You trifled at the gate:
The enchanted dove upon her branch
    Died without a mate;
The enchanted princess in her tower
    Slept, died, behind the grate;
Her heart was starving all this while
    You made it wait.

SPRING

RALPH WALDO EMERSON

The April winds are magical
And fill our tuneful frames.
The garden walks are passional
To bachelors and dames.

9 · LAST POST

About half of these are military funerals, without benefit of under-taker. All are short and to the point, which is probably why they have stuck in my memory. Long funeral pieces such as *Lycidas*, *In Memoriam*, Gray's *Elegy*, *Adonaïs*, become tedious to me by their length. Heavy mourning, deep black edges, long widowhood, unrestrained grief are out of fashion, as they must be to a generation which has indulged in two world wars. Note, too, with what economy of words most of Shakespeare's characters get their dying done: Hamlet ('The rest is silence'); Romeo and Juliet; Antony and Cleopatra; Arthur ('Heaven take my soul and England keep my bones' — a precocious last line for a young one!); Caesar, Cassius and Brutus: the principal exception is, I regret to say, a Commander-in-Chief, Othello — but he was an Oriental.

A. P. W.

THE SOLDIER'S DEATH

Anne Finch, Countess of Winchilsea

Trail all your pikes, dispirit every drum,
March in a slow procession from afar,
Be silent, ye dejected Men of War!
Be still the hautboys, and the flute be dumb!
Display no more, in vain, the lofty banner;
For see! where on the bier before ye lies
The pale, the fall'n, the untimely Sacrifice
To your mistaken shrine, to your false idol Honour.

THE DEAD

Rupert Brooke

These hearts were woven of human joys and cares,
    Washed marvellously with sorrow, swift to mirth.
The years had given them kindness. Dawn was theirs,
    And sunset, and the colours of the earth.

422

These had seen movement, and heard music; known
   Slumber and waking; loved; gone proudly friended;
Felt the quick stir of wonder; sat alone;
Touched furs and flowers and cheeks. All this is ended.

There are waters blown by changing winds to laughter
And lit by the rich skies, all day. And after,
   Frost, with a gesture, stays the waves that dance
And wandering loveliness. He leaves a white
   Unbroken glory, a gathered radiance,
A width, a shining peace, under the night.

Note

I can well remember Lord Allenby repeating this poem to me
shortly after he had heard the news that his only son, a boy of
great promise, had been killed in action.   *A. P. W.*

THE VOLUNTEER

Herbert Asquith

HERE lies the clerk who half his life had spent
Toiling at ledgers in a city grey,
Thinking that so his days would drift away
With no lance broken in life's tournament:
Yet ever 'twixt the books and his bright eyes
The gleaming eagles of the legions came,
And horsemen, charging under phantom skies,
Went thundering past beneath the oriflamme.

And now those waiting dreams are satisfied;
From twilight to the halls of dawn he went;
His lance is broken; but he lies content
With that high hour, in which he lived and died.
And falling thus, he wants no recompense,
Who found his battle in the last resort;
Nor needs he any hearse to bear him hence,
Who goes to join the men of Agincourt.

HERE DEAD LIE WE

A. E. HOUSMAN

HERE dead lie we because we did not choose
  To live and shame the land from which we sprung.
Life, to be sure, is nothing much to lose;
  But young men think it is, and we were young.

EPITAPH ON AN ARMY OF
MERCENARIES

A. E. HOUSMAN

THESE, in the day when heaven was falling,
  The hour when earth's foundations fled,
Followed their mercenary calling
  And took their wages and are dead.

Their shoulders held the sky suspended;
  They stood, and earth's foundations stay;
What God abandoned, these defended,
  And saved the sum of things for pay.

IN FLANDERS FIELDS

JOHN MCCRAE

IN Flanders fields the poppies blow
Between the crosses, row on row
  That mark our place; and in the sky
  The larks, still bravely singing, fly
Scarce heard amid the guns below.

We are the Dead. Short days ago
We lived, felt dawn, saw sunset glow,
  Loved and were loved, and now we lie
    In Flanders fields.

Take up our quarrel with the foe:
To you from failing hands we throw
   The torch; be yours to hold it high.
   If ye break faith with us who die
We shall not sleep, though poppies grow
     In Flanders fields.

MY BOY JACK

1914-18

RUDYARD KIPLING

'HAVE you news of my boy Jack?'
   Not this tide.
'When d'you think that he'll come back?'
   Not with this wind blowing, and this tide.

'Has any one else had word of him?'
   Not this tide.
For what is sunk will hardly swim,
   Not with this wind blowing, and this tide.

'Oh, dear, what comfort can I find?'
   None this tide,
   Nor any tide,
Except that he did not shame his kind —
   Not even with that wind blowing, and that tide.

Then hold your head up all the more,
   This tide,
   And every tide;
Because he was the son you bore,
   And gave to that wind blowing and that tide!

AN IRISH AIRMAN FORESEES HIS
DEATH
W. B. YEATS

I KNOW that I shall meet my fate
Somewhere among the clouds above;
Those that I fight I do not hate,
Those that I guard I do not love;
My country is Kiltartan Cross,
My countrymen Kiltartan's poor,
No likely end could bring them loss
Or leave them happier than before.
Nor law, nor duty bade me fight,
Nor public men, nor cheering crowds,
A lonely impulse of delight
Drove to this tumult in the clouds;
I balanced all, brought all to mind,
The years to come seemed waste of breath,
A waste of breath the years behind
In balance with this life, this death.

MACPHERSON'S FAREWELL
ROBERT BURNS

FAREWELL, ye dungeons dark and strong,
   The wretch's destiny!
Macpherson's time will not be long
   On yonder gallows-tree.

Sae rantingly, sae wantonly,
   Sae dauntingly gaed he;
He played a spring, and danced it round,
   Below the gallows-tree.

Oh, what is death but parting breath?
   On mony a bloody plain
I've dared his face, and in this place
   I scorn him yet again!

Untie these bands from off my hands,
  And bring to me my sword!
And there's no a man in all Scotland
  But I'll brave him at a word.

I've lived a life of sturt and strife;
  I die by treachery:
It burns my heart I must depart
  And not avengèd be.

Now farewell light — thou sunshine bright
  And all beneath the sky!
May coward shame disdain his name,
  The wretch that dares not die.

DEATH THE LEVELLER

from AJAX AND ULYSSES *by*

JAMES SHIRLEY

THE glories of our blood and state
  Are shadows, not substantial things;
There is no armour against Fate;
  Death lays his icy hand on kings:
    Sceptre and Crown
    Must tumble down,
And in the dust be equal made
With the poor crookèd scythe and spade.

Some men with swords may reap the field,
  And plant fresh laurels where they kill:
But their strong nerves at last must yield;
  They tame but one another still:
    Early or late
    They stoop to fate,
And must give up their murmuring breath
When they, pale captives, creep to death.

The garlands wither on your brow;
  Then boast no more your mighty deeds!

Upon Death's purple altar now
  See where the victor-victim bleeds.
   Your heads must come
   To the cold tomb:
Only the actions of the just
Smell sweet and blossom in their dust.

AN EPITAPH

from THE PASTIME OF PLEASURE *by*
STEPHEN HAWES

O MORTAL folk, you may behold and see
  How I lie here, sometime a mighty knight;
The end of joy and all prosperity
  Is death at last, thorough his course and might:
  After the day there cometh the dark night,
   For though the day be never so long,
   At last the bells ringeth to evensong.

THE CONCLUSION

SIR WALTER RALEIGH

EVEN such is Time, that takes in trust
  Our youth, our joys, and all we have,
And pays us but with age and dust;
  Who in the dark and silent grave,
When we have wandered all our ways,
Shuts up the story of our days:
And from which earth, and grave, and dust,
The Lord shall raise me up, I trust.

A LYKE-WAKE DIRGE

ANON

THIS ae nighte, this ae nighte,
  — *Every nighte and alle,*
Fire and fleet and candle-lighte,
  And Christe receive thy saule.

When thou from hence away art past,
 — Every nighte and alle,
To Whinny-muir thou com'st at last;
 And Christe receive thy saule.

If ever thou gavest hosen and shoon,
 — Every nighte and alle,
Sit thee down and put them on;
 And Christe receive thy saule.

If hosen and shoon thou ne'er gav'st nane,
 — Every nighte and alle,
The whinnes sall prick thee to the bare bane;
 And Christe receive thy saule.

From Whinny-muir when thou may'st pass,
 — Every nighte and alle,
To Brig o' Dread thou com'st at last;
 And Christe receive thy saule.

From Brig o' Dread when thou may'st pass,
 — Every nighte and alle,
To Purgatory fire thou com'st at last;
 And Christe receive thy saule.

If ever thou gavest meat or drink,
 — Every nighte and alle,
The fire sall never make thee shrink;
 And Christe receive thy saule.

If meat or drink thou ne'er gav'st nane,
 — Every nighte and alle,
The fire will burn thee to the bare bane;
 And Christe receive thy saule.

This ae nighte, this ae nighte,
 — Every nighte and alle,
Fire and fleet and candle-lighte,
 And Christe receive thy saule.

IN TIME OF PESTILENCE
1593

THOMAS NASHE

ADIEU, farewell earth's bliss!
This world uncertain is:
Fond are life's lustful joys,
Death proves them all but toys.
None from his darts can fly;
I am sick, I must die —
   Lord, have mercy on us!

Rich men, trust not in wealth,
Gold cannot buy you health;
Physic himself must fade;
All things to end are made;
The plague full swift goes by;
I am sick, I must die —
   Lord, have mercy on us!

Beauty is but a flower
Which wrinkles will devour;
Brightness falls from the air;
Queens have died young and fair;
Dust hath closed Helen's eye;
I am sick, I must die —
   Lord, have mercy on us!

Strength stoops unto the grave,
Worms feed on Hector brave;
Swords may not fight with fate;
Earth still holds ope her gate;
Come, come! the bells do cry;
I am sick, I must die —
   Lord, have mercy on us!

Wit with his wantonness
Tasteth death's bitterness;
Hell's executioner
Hath no ears for to hear
What vain art can reply;
I am sick, I must die —
    Lord, have mercy on us!

Haste therefore each degree
To welcome destiny;
Heaven is our heritage,
Earth but a player's stage.
Mount we unto the sky;
I am sick, I must die —
    Lord, have mercy on us!

MESSAGES

Francis Thompson

What shall I your true-love tell,
    Earth-forsaking maid?
What shall I your true-love tell,
    When life's spectre's laid?

'Tell him that, our side the grave,
    Maid may not conceive
Life should be so sad to have,
    That's so sad to leave!'

What shall I your true-love tell,
    When I come to him?
What shall I your true-love tell —
    Eyes growing dim!

'Tell him this, when you shall part
    From a maiden pined;
That I see him with my heart,
    Now my eyes are blind.'

What shall I your true-love tell?
  Speaking-while is scant.
What shall I your true-love tell,
  Death's white postulant?

'Tell him — love, with speech at strife,
  For last utterance saith:
I, who loved with all my life,
  Love with all my death.'

REQUIEMS
I
CHRISTINA ROSSETTI

WHEN I am dead, my dearest,
  Sing no sad songs for me;
Plant thou no roses at my head,
  Nor shady cypress tree:
Be the green grass above me
  With showers and dewdrops wet;
And if thou wilt, remember,
  And if thou wilt, forget.

I shall not see the shadows,
  I shall not feel the rain;
I shall not hear the nightingale
  Sing on, as if in pain;
And dreaming through the twilight
  That doth not rise nor set,
Haply I may remember,
  And haply may forget.

II
ROBERT LOUIS STEVENSON

Under the wide and starry sky
Dig the grave and let me lie:
Glad did I live and gladly die,
  And I laid me down with a will.

This be the verse you grave for me:
Here he lies where he long'd to be;
Home is the sailor, home from sea,
    And the hunter home from the hill.

GRAVESTONES

I

George Macdonald

Here lie I, Martin Elginbrodde;
Hae mercy o' my soul, Lord God;
As I wad do, were I Lord God,
And ye were Martin Elginbrodde.

II

John Cleveland

Here lies wise and valiant dust,
Huddled up 'twixt fit and just:
Strafford, who was hurried hence
'Twixt treason and convenience.
He spent his life here in a mist:
A Papist, yet a Calvinist;
His Prince's nearest joy and grief:
He had, yet wanted all relief:
The prop and ruin of the State;
The people's violent love and hate.
One in extremes loved and abhorred.
Riddles lie here, or in a word,
Here lies blood, and let it lie
Speechless still, and never cry.

III

Anon (*Camden's Remains*)

Betwixt the stirrop and the ground
Mercy I askt, mercy I found.

TO DEATH

OLIVER ST JOHN GOGARTY

BUT for your Terror
Where would be Valour?
What is Love for
   But to stand in your way?
Taker and Giver,
For all your endeavour
You leave us with more
   Than you touch with decay!

HOW SLEEP THE BRAVE

WILLIAM COLLINS

How sleep the brave, who sink to rest
By all their country's wishes blest!
When Spring, with dewy fingers cold,
Returns to deck their hallowed mould,
She there shall dress a sweeter sod
Than Fancy's feet have ever trod.

By fairy hands their knell is rung;
By forms unseen their dirge is sung;
There Honour comes, a pilgrim grey,
To bless the turf that wraps their clay;
And Freedom shall awhile repair
To dwell, a weeping hermit, there!

FRATRI DILECTISSIMO

W. H. B.

JOHN BUCHAN

WHEN we were little, wandering boys,
   And every hill was blue and high,
On ballad ways and martial joys
   We fed our fancies, you and I.

With Bruce we crouched in bracken shade,
  With Douglas charged the Paynim foes,
And oft in moorland noons I played
  Colkitto to your grave Montrose.

The obliterating seasons flow —
  They cannot kill our boyish game.
Though creeds may change and kings may go,
  Yet burns undimmed the ancient flame.
While young men in their pride make haste
  The wrong to right, the bond to free,
And plant a garden in the waste,
  Still rides our Scottish chivalry.

Another end had held your dream —
  To die fulfilled of hope and might,
To pass in one swift, rapturous gleam
  From mortal to immortal light.
But through long hours of labouring breath
  You watched the world grow small and far,
And met the constant eyes of Death
  And haply knew how kind they are.

One boon the fates relenting gave.
  Not where the scented hill-wind blows
From cedar thickets lies your grave,
  Nor 'mid the steep Himálayan snows.
Night calls the stragglers to the nest,
  And at long last 'tis home indeed
For your far-wandering feet to rest
  For ever by the crooks of Tweed.

In perfect honour, perfect truth,
  And gentleness to all mankind,
You trod the golden paths of youth,
  Then left the world and youth behind
Ah no! 'Tis we who fade and fail —
  And you, from Time's slow torments free,
Shall pass from strength to strength, and scale
  The steeps of immortality.

Dear heart, in that serener air,
  If blessed souls may backward gaze,
Some slender nook of memory spare
  For our old happy moorland days.
I sit alone, and musing fills
  My breast with pain that shall not die,
Till once again o'er greener hills
  We ride together, you and I.

AFTERWARDS

Thomas Hardy

WHEN the Present has latched its postern behind my tremulous stay,
  And the May month flaps its glad green leaves like wings,
Delicate-filmed as new-spun silk, will the neighbours say,
  'He was a man who used to notice such things'?

If it be in the dusk when, like an eyelid's soundless blink,
  The dewfall-hawk comes crossing the shades to alight
Upon the wind-warped upland thorn, a gazer may think,
  'To him this must have been a familiar sight.'

If I pass during some nocturnal blackness, mothy and warm,
  When the hedgehog travels furtively over the lawn,
One may say, 'He strove that such innocent creatures should come to
                                                              no harm,
  But he could do little for them; and now he is gone.'

If, when hearing that I have been stilled at last, they stand at the door,
  Watching the full-starred heavens that winter sees,
Will this thought rise on those who will meet my face no more,
  'He was one who had an eye for such mysteries'?

And will any say when my bell of quittance is heard in the gloom,
  And a crossing breeze cuts a pause in its outrollings,
Till they rise again, as they were a new bell's boom,
  'He hears it not now, but used to notice such things'?

NOTHING FOR TEARS

from SAMSON AGONISTES *by*

JOHN MILTON

NOTHING is here for tears, nothing to wail
Or knock the breast; no weakness, no contempt,
Dispraise or blame; nothing but well and fair
And what may quiet us in a death so noble.

HERACLITUS

WILLIAM CORY

THEY told me, Heraclitus, they told me you were dead,
They brought me bitter news to hear and bitter tears to shed.
I wept as I remember'd how often you and I
Had tired the sun with talking and sent him down the sky.

And now that thou art lying, my dear old Carian guest,
A handful of grey ashes, long, long ago at rest,
Still are thy pleasant voices, thy nightingales, awake;
For Death, he taketh all away, but them he cannot take.

SONNET FOR THE MADONNA OF THE CHERRIES

DEAR Lady of the Cherries, cool, serene,
Untroubled by our follies, strife and fears,
Clad in soft reds and blues and mantle green,
Your memory has been with me all these years.

Long years of battle, bitterness and waste,
Dry years of sun and dust and Eastern skies,
Hard years of ceaseless struggle, endless haste,
Fighting 'gainst greed for power and hate and lies.

Your red-gold hair, your slowly smiling face
For pride in your dear son, your King of Kings,
Fruits of the kindly earth, and truth and grace,
Colour and light, and all warm lovely things —

    For all that loveliness, that warmth, that light,
    Blessed Madonna, I go back to fight.

Northwick Park, *April 29th, 1943*

Note

At the end of my garden of other men's flowers, outside the gate, I have put this little wayside dandelion of my own. It has no business here, even outside the garden, but the owner of the lady for whom it was written is anxious for it to be included. She is a beautiful lady, designed though not actually painted by Leonardo da Vinci, and I have loved her ever since I saw her.

The sonnet was written when I visited her last April after nearly four years of war. I was not allowed, after all, to go back and fight as a soldier against the powers of darkness, as I had hoped and intended. But the Lady of the Cherries smiles not for soldier or for Viceroy, only for her small son playing with the bunch of cherries. A blessing to you, my Lady, and to all beautiful things that help us to forget the dreariness of war.   *A. P. W.*

When the great Flemish Masters visited Italy in the sixteenth century to see what they could learn from the exponents of another splendid branch of art in two dimensions, the Milanese artists showed them a picture, or a cartoon, by Leonardo of this Madonna, and suggested that they should copy, or try to improve on it — doubtless also wishing to see if they too had anything to learn from their Northern colleagues, or rivals. There are twelve such versions of this picture by Flemish artists; and we do not think that this one is inferior in quality to any of them.

The apple often appears in pictures of the Madonna as she is supposed to have undone the harm caused by Eve's persuasion of Adam to eat it.

Joost van Cleves also shows the 'Legend of the Madonna' which tells how, when Herod heard that a family with a baby had fled to Egypt, he sent a posse of soldiers after them to kill the baby. The husbandmen are begging for their lives, and when asked if they had seen such a family pass by, they replied 'Not since we were sowing this corn', and the corn shown in the picture had miraculously grown and ripened in the night.

*

Among other tributes published on my father's death was a poem by an 'ordinary soldier'. Let me here give him our family thanks.

The message of this anthology is that poetry can inspire the lives of us all, and so the fit farewell for the end of the journey when 'the mists of Time no longer confound' is this 'ordinary soldier's' salute.   *A. J. W.*

They say the mirage is the mind's illusion
The dust to the sun's heat, thirst to the parched eye returning:
Well might the mind in Scholarly profusion
Her gifts for a soldier store and reveal, his footsteps turning
Backward again and backward. This is the end
Foretold and dreamed — 'colour and light and all warm lovely things'.
The last, Earth's last horizon eyes transcend
The mirage. Homeward, warrior poet the evening brings —

INDEX OF AUTHORS

INDEX OF TITLES

INDEX OF FIRST LINES